Contesting Land and Custom in Ghana

Law, Governance, and Development

The Leiden University Press series on Law, Governance, and Development brings together an interdisciplinary body of work about the formation and functioning of legal systems in developing countries, and about interventions to strengthen them. The series aims to engage academics, policy makers and practitioners at the national and international level, thus attempting to stimulate legal reform for good governance and development.

Contesting Land and Custom in Ghana

State, Chief and the Citizen

Edited by

Janine M. Ubink
and Kojo S. Amanor

Leiden University Press

This book has been made possible by a grant from the Royal Nether-
lands Embassy in Accra, Ghana.

Cover design: Studio Jan de Boer, Amsterdam
Layout: The DocWorkers, Almere

ISBN   978 90 8728 047 5
e-ISBN   978 90 4850 609 5
NUR   759 / 828

Contents

Abbreviations

ADR	Alternative Dispute Resolution
ARPS	Aborigines Rights Protection Society (Ghana, Gold Coast)
CDR	Committee for the Defence of the Revolution
CLS	Customary Land Secretariat
CPP	Convention People's Party (Ghana)
DA	District Assembly
DCE	District Chief Executive
DFID	UK Department for International Development
DSI	Dispute Settlement Institution
EPA	Environmental Protection Agency
ICOUR	Irrigation Company Of Upper Region Ltd. (Ghana)
GLR	Ghana Law Reports
KND	Kassena-Nankana District (Ghana)
LAP	Land Administration Project
LAPU	Land Administration Project Unit
LC	Lands Commission
LSA	Land Sector Agency
MLFM	Ministry of Lands, Forestry and Mines
MoU	Memorandum of Understanding
NA	Native Authority
NC	Native Court
NLM	National Liberation Movement (Ghana)
NLP	National Land Policy
NPP	New Patriotic Party
NRC	National Redemption Council (Ghana)
NRI	Natural Resources Institute
OASL	Office of the Administrator of Stool Lands
OPEC	Organization of the Petroleum Exporting Countries
PDCI	Democratic Party of Côte d'Ivoire
RDR	Rally of Republicans Party (Côte d'Ivoire)
PAC	Plot Allocation Committee
SNV	A Netherlands based international development organisation
SSNIT	Social Security and National Insurance Trust (Ghana)
TCPD	Town and Country Planning Department

UC	Unit Committee
UST	University of Science and Technology
USAID	United States Agency for International Development
VC	Village Committee

1 Contesting land and custom in Ghana: Introduction

Kojo Amanor and Janine Ubink

Since the 1990s there has been a resurgence of interest in land tenure reform in Africa, which is reflected in a growing academic and policy oriented literature on the subject, and in the implementation of new land tenure reform policies and programmes and new legislation. In policy circles, recent concerns with land tenure are characterised by a distinctive approach, which focusses on building and facilitating the emergence of land markets, on promoting the rule of law and property rights, and on integrating customary and formal land tenures and the 'empowerment' of customary institutions as part of a trend towards decentralised government administration. In contrast to the dominant global approaches to land reform under modernisation during the 1960s, the major focus is now on institutional and administrative reform rather than equitable redistribution of land.

During the 1960s and 1970s land administration in Africa was influenced by the paradigms of modernisation theory, which sought to replace a traditional 'backward' agricultural sector with modern farming based on mechanisation and synthetic inputs. Agricultural modernisation focussed on promoting a cadre of elite or 'progressive' farmers, whose adoption of new technologies would eventually trickle down to the peasantry. Within this modernisation framework customary land tenure was viewed as outdated. It did not provide individual farmers with secure and fungible rights in land. It was argued that this inhibited long-term investment in the productivity of land since users were not sure they would retain ownership over a long period. It also prevented the development of financial and risk markets, in which farmers would be able to use their title to land as collateral for loans and mortgages. Under the influence of modernisation theory, land tenure reform was based on promoting land titling and the creation of state cadastres through which farmers could register their land. However, land registration and titling procedures were cumbersome and expensive and only a tiny minority of rich farmers registered their land. The cost of titling was beyond the means of the majority of smallholders and most of them continued to hold their land under customary or informal arrangements.

With the implementation of structural adjustment programmes and neo-liberal policies in the 1980s, the major emphasis in development policy turned towards opening African economies to the private sector and foreign investment. However, the expansion of foreign investment required an institutional framework which promoted a regulatory framework for transactions in land and which would enable policies promoting free markets to translate into functioning and transparent property and land markets. The requisites for this transformation include easy access to information about transactions, clearly demarcated property rights, the enforcement of property transactions and contracts, and the speedy registration of transactions and ownership changes. Early approaches to land tenure administrative reform under structural adjustment promoted by the World Bank and other donors thus also focussed on promoting land titling and registration (Bruce et al. 1994; Deininger and Binswanger 1999; Feder and Noronha 1987; Feeny 1988; Lipton 1993).

The continued focus on titling and registration was not uncontested. Given that much land lay under customary ownership and that rights in this sector were often contested, the translation of customary land into formal tenure was not easily achieved without establishing procedures for transparency in the recognition of rights in the customary sector. The focus on extending titling was challenged by World Bank sponsored research that looked at the relationship between security of tenure, land markets, and investment in land or agricultural development in various African countries (Bruce and Migot-Adholla 1994). This research argued that there was no direct correlation between titles to land and long-term investment in land, since investment was conditional upon the existence of another set of infrastructures, such as functioning land markets – on which the development of collateral and ability of banks to foreclose on mortgages was dependent – as well as credit and insurance markets. In place of full-titling programmes, the authors recommended 'community-based' solutions that would decentralise land administration to communities.

This approach also resonated with approaches to development policy that had developed from the 1970s in Africa, which were critical of the state and state-community relations. These often focussed on the rationality of local level management strategies and institutional frameworks, and on the adverse effects that state interventions often had on the community level. The inclusion of articles by John Bruce in Reyna and Downs (1988) *Land and Society in Contemporary Africa*, and in Basset and Crummey (1993) *Land in African Agrarian Systems*, and the seminal influence of these articles, marked the convergence of these two approaches and the mainstreaming of community-based development approaches into land policy.

This position led to a polarisation of land reform approaches within the World Bank, between those advocating individual land titling as a way of promoting market development, and those supporting decentralised community-based management in response to rolling back the state (Deininger and Binswanger 1999). Eventually, there was an accommodation between these approaches, which has resulted in the incorporation of a framework supporting the recognition of customary tenures within the evolutionary theory of property rights (Deininger 2003). Within this framework it is now accepted that community-based or customary systems are dynamic and changing, and are evolving towards individual property rights systems in response to economic changes. Thus, by supporting these systems and the institutional process of change within them, secure property rights will eventually emerge in a movement from communal rights to extended family rights, and then to the rights of individuals and atomistic nuclear families. The atomistic family farm is seen as the highest evolutionary form of property (Binswanger and Deininger 1993; Deininger 2003; See Amanor 1999 for discussion on the relationship between the family farm and agribusiness).

The dynamics and negotiability of customary relations

The recognition of the dynamism and adaptability of customary land tenure systems originates within social science research. Berry has argued that African land tenure systems are adaptive arrangements which are negotiated, fluid, open, and ambiguous (Berry 1993). Rather than being fixed and conservative, customary relations are seen as being perpetually negotiated by various actors who use their social networks to redefine and renegotiate customary relations (Berry 1993 and 2001). People invest in social status and networks of community and kin and use their social status to make claims on resources including access to land, demands on labour, and the support of clients. Thus, mobility and fluidity are achieved through social skills in negotiating rules and the definition of what constitutes the customary, which is ever changing in relation to these social networks. The fluidity of the relations mediate markets and the planned interventions of states, which become another potential source of claims on resources. In contrast with policy approaches which seek to establish clearly defined property rights, Berry argues that land rights within the customary sector have been ambiguous over long historical periods and that this has not prevented people from investing in production and in social networks to establish their access and control over property.

Lentz (2006c) has similarly argued that customary rights in land are often deliberately ambiguous to allow room for further re-interpretation or renegotiation. Thus, they accommodate different perspectives and different interests. Juul and Lund (2002) argue that negotiability of rules and relations is one of the fundamental characteristics of African societies. Property rights are institutions in which people's access to, use of, and control over land are regularised and readjusted in the ongoing reconstruction and transformation of social relations. Social identities are contested zones in which people's claims are constantly being disputed and renegotiated. They argue that far from being rooted in ascriptive social relations, customary relations are constantly changing and reaffirmed. Rather than resulting from the static nature of tradition, stable and robust customary relations result from the constant reaffirmation of existing social relations. Thus, customary relations are only as enduring as their on-going re-enactment, negotiation and renegotiation. Juul and Lund argue that this fluidity of the customary not only results from the nature of the customary but also from the interaction between the customary and other institutions, particularly the existence of legal and institutional pluralism and an unwillingness to fix the rules and ensure constancy and compliance. This encourages people to renegotiate identities and social relations to either confirm existing arrangements or to change them. Thus the customary involves a continuous negotiation within and without. It involves a trade off with state institutions in which both sectors attempt to anticipate each other and redefine themselves against the institutional configurations and changes within the other. This results in a state of affairs in which both sectors incorporate elements of the other and in which the formal and informal continually adapt to each other and construct their identities in each other's image. The customary is frequently as modern as the formal sector, and the modern legal framework often bases itself on developments within the informal customary sector.

Harmonising customary and state relations

The emphasis on the flexibility, negotiability and adaptability of customary land tenure, and its social agency or embeddedness in social relations has generated a new policy oriented research which focusses on the institutional relationship between formal and informal land tenure systems. This research sees the customary as largely being inclusive and equitable against a state sector which is exclusive, inequitable, and favours the interests of political elites. While the state sector formulates rules and regulations about land, the majority of land users hold land on customary tenure, in systems that lie beyond the reach of the state and beyond formal legal frameworks. This approach advocates the harmonisation of formal and informal systems through greater recognition of community institutions for land management and through the decentralisation of land administration to community organisations, which enables rural people to negotiate and manage their own solutions for securing access to land (Lavigne Delville 2000; Toulmin and Quan 2000a). It is argued that increasing devolution of land administration to local and customary-based institutions will result in a more equitable management of land, which allows rural people to be involved in the negotiation of rights to lands. Increasing recognition of the customary will also result in its greater accountability and the transparency of land markets at the local level, which will have to conform to criteria negotiated between local institutions and the state.

Social differentiation and power

Several researchers have questioned the conception of the negotiability and equity of customary land tenure systems. They stress the fact that negotiators or contestants in customary land matters seldom operate on level playing fields (Amanor 1999; Cousins 2002; Daley and Hobley 2005; Juul and Lund 2002; Lund 2000; Peters 2002; Shipton 2002; and Woodhouse 2003). Some have more negotiating power and more defining and contesting powers than others, and not everything is negotiable. As Lund (2008:2) puts it, '[t]he openness and contingency of land issues in Africa make absolutely central the questions of how and to whose benefit settlements are reached, who has the capacity to endorse or enforce them, and how and by whom they are challenged'. From a gender perspective Whitehead and Tsikata (2003) argue that customary systems often embody patriarchal values and power, which seeks to exclude women from land. Women are not well positioned within customary political institutional frameworks or within local government frameworks to represent their own interests. Thus, the harmonisation of the customary with the formal, and the turn to the customary, often further marginalise women's rights, and serve to legitimate institutions that undermine women's rights to land. They argue that in many respects, rather than decentralisation to community based structures rooted in customary concerns, a state institutional structure in which gender concerns can be brought to bear can offer better prospects for women's land rights to be addressed.

In a critique of the framework of evolutionary property rights and communitarian perspective on land administration, Amanor (1999) has argued that the qualities which are adduced as the flexibility and negotiability of customary land often emerge from the interests of the

political elites in rural and urban areas who are able to continually redefine customary tenure to meet their interests and to dispossess rural
toilers of their access to land and natural resources. He argues that
since the colonial period governments have recognised and invented
the control of land by chiefs as a strategy for gaining control over land,
natural resources, and agricultural production at the expense of the
poor peasantry. While the customary continually changes in relation to
transformation in policy and the economy, the negotiations over the
customary (or investments in social networks able to carry out processes of redefinition) are limited to those with wealth and power, and
elude the rural poor who increasingly find themselves excluded, dispossessed, and marginalised by the customary. In a similar vein Pauline
Peters (2004) argues that there is mounting evidence of increasing social differentiation within Africa and expropriation of land by local and
non-local elites. Peters (2004:270) urges that:

> More emphasis needs to be placed by researchers on who bene-
> fits and who loses from instances of 'negotiability' in access to
> land, an analysis that, in turn, needs to be situated in broader
> political economic and social changes taking place over the past
> century, particularly during the past thirty or so years. This re-
> quires a theoretical move away from privileging contingency,
> flexibility, and negotiability that, willy-nilly, ends by suggesting
> an open field, to one that is able to identify those situations and
> processes (including commodification, structural adjustment,
> market liberalization and globalization) that limit or end nego-
> tiation and flexibility for certain social groups or categories.

Several studies within Ghana show increasing social differentiation
within rural areas, increasing conflicts over land and rifts between
rural elites, chiefs and producers, which question notions about the negotiability of customary land. Tonah's (2002 and 2006) research in
Northern and Middle Ghana analyses the rising land use conflicts resulting from intense competition between indigenous farmers and migrant Fulani pastoralists for the most fertile land. In these areas chiefs
prefer to give land to migrants, especially the pastoralists who are rich
in cattle and can afford to make substantial payments as settlement
fees. Allocating land to migrant pastoralists has become a 'gateway to
prosperity' for many chiefs. As a result, farmers do not see traditional
authorities as impartial dispute settlers, but believe them to take sides
with stockowners and pastoralists because they benefit directly from
their presence and activities in the area. In the Sefwi area of Western
Ghana Boni (2005; 2006) has shown that chiefs have consistently
changed and revised the conditions on which land has been given out

to migrants, and how recently redefined customary norms apply retrospectively to previous contractual agreements. Thus, transactions which
were understood as the alienation of land have been re-interpreted as
the payment of tribute for land leases, and amounts paid as tribute
have been constantly inflated. Attempts to redefine customary tenure
have often been resisted by migrants, and chiefs have mobilised dis-
gruntled youth within the area to engage in violent confrontations with
migrants as a way to force them to accept the new impositions or to
dispossess them of the land. When land was first given out to migrants, it had little scarcity value and was given on favourable terms,
since the migrants, unlike locals, had the capital to invest in cocoa
farming. The early migrants thus opened up the area for development
initiatives, with the state investing in areas which became important
cocoa growing centres. The opening up of these areas brought an influx of new migrants and new demands for land, which raised the
value of land. As land values increased, chiefs found new ways to aug-
ment their revenues from older lands transacted on more favourable
terms to the farmers, particularly when the already allocated land began to exceed remaining unclaimed forests. In this context, the ever-
changeability of customary land does not create security for cocoa
farmers but creates increasing insecurity as chiefs are increasingly empowered over customary land. Similar experiences have been documented for Côte d'Ivoire (Chauveau 2005).

Ubink (2008a) has described how, in peri-urban areas around Kumasi with a growing demand for real estate, chiefs are attempting to redefine customary tenure as a way of dispossessing farmers on the peri-
meters of towns, to give out the land to wealthy urban dwellers willing
to pay large amounts for residential land. Ubink documents differing
relations and outcomes in different settlements depending on the 'en-
lightenment' of the chief, which serves to highlight the lack of accountability of chiefly authority and the ability of chiefs to redefine customary relations to meet their interests. Ubink argues that the failure of
the state to hold chiefs accountable results in a complicity in failing to
establish accountability in customary land tenure.

Current land administration initiatives

National laws and government policies constitute a structure of opportunities for the negotiation of rights and redistribution of resources,
although the result is neither coherent policy implementation nor a
complete disregard of law and policy (Lund 2008:4). Several policy initiatives have been launched in African countries during the 1990s to
create new institutional land management frameworks that give greater

Yew

Taxus spp.
Yew Family

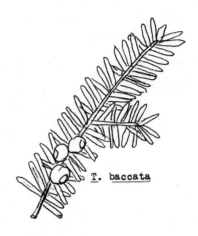

T. baccata

GROWTH HABIT: Evergreen shrubs (or trees)
LEAVES: Linear, flat, more or less 2-ranked and usually alternate, mostly not over 1″ long
FLOWERS: Male as small globose heads at branch tips; female axillary
FRUITS: Fleshy cup-shaped scarlet structure largely surrounding a bony seed
SEEDS: 1 per fruit
LIGHT: Full or partial sun
SOIL: Clay loam
MOISTURE: Moist
SEASONAL ASPECT: None
ZONE: 3
USES: Interest, informal shrub border, foundation
CARE: None
PROPAGATION BY: Seedings
NATIVE OF: See below
OTHER: *T. baccata*, English Yew; Europe, n. Africa and w. Asia.
T. cuspidata, Japanese Yew; n.e. Asia; leaves abruptly pointed. Many horticultural varieties of each.
T. floridana, small tree of the Apalachicola River basin of northwest Florida and south Georgia.

seen as parties with particular interests in land who may use the opportunity to extract revenues from the litigants or dispossess them of the
land, and often prefer to appeal to state institutions, if the disputes cannot be settled within extended family and village institutions (Crook et
al. 2007). Paradoxically, while the communitarian perspective aims to
create more negotiability in land and voice for the rural poor, its attempt to harmonise the customary with tree formal often closes down
the multiple institutional choices available within the situation of institutional and legal pluralism and forces rural land users to deal with
customary authorities who are not democratically elected or accountable. This carries the danger of further marginalising and disempower-
ing marginalised groups, including the rural poor and the poorer sections of women, youth, and toiling migrants.

The scope of this work

The various contributions to this book critically examine notions of
customary land tenure. They examine the relations between the customary and statutory tenure and the institutional interactions between
the state and traditional authorities in land administration, addressing
issues of power, economic interests, transparency, accountability, conflicts and notions of social justice, equity, and negotiation. They examine both past and contemporary policy issues, and present a number of
case studies with implications for the integration of customary institutions into the framework of state land administration. The first four papers by Berry, Amanor, Boni, and Tonah are concerned with the nature
of customary institutions, historical changes in the customary, and the
ways in which notions of the customary are manipulated by local elites
and the state and are subject to political reinterpretation, redefinition,
and invention. The next two papers by Crook and Ubink are concerned
with local perceptions of customary and state institutions involved in
land management, the ways in which the plurality of institutions are
negotiated and utilised, issues of accountability, and the role of the
state in enforcing accountability and transparency in customary settings. The final chapter by Quan, Ubink, and Antwi examines problems of implementing contemporary land policy reform in the Land
Administration Project (LAP).
    In the first contribution to this volume, Sara Berry analyses the sal-
ience of history in local struggles over property and power through a
comparative study of socio-economic and political change in the former
cocoa frontiers of southwestern Ghana and Côte d'Ivoire. In both countries, the process of forest clearance and tree crop cultivation was carried out by migrant farmers. While the first migrants in both countries

encountered little difficulty in getting access to land, the terms on which they did so and their subsequent relations with host communities differed significantly. In Ghana immigrants obtained cultivation rights from local chiefs, for which they paid substantial annual payments. In Côte d'Ivoire farmers obtained land from village elders or family heads, and relations between hosts and migrants were discussed in terms of the *tutorat*, a form of guardianship which perpetuates a patronage relationship between autochthones and strangers, serving as an institution for transacting land with migrants and incorporating them into the local community based on a moral economy of obligation and reciprocity, including presentation of gifts and mutual assistance at times of funerals and other social events.

Within Ghana the state did not interfere in local tenure arrangements between hosts and migrants, while in Côte d'Ivoire the state intervened to ensure migrants gained access to land, while assuring the host communities that their claims on the land remained intact. This was done ambiguously, without abolishing or reforming customary tenure or customary laws and conventions. The Ivorian president Houphouet-Boigny merely announced in 1963 that 'land belongs to the one who develops it'. On the ground, party cadres and local officials followed his lead, reassuring local villagers of the moral force of the *tutorat*, while settling individual disputes in favour of the migrants who produced the greater part of the cocoa that fed the state's coffers. The claims of the migrants were dependent upon the patronage of the state. This generated social conflicts and tensions based on notions of entitlement, ancestry, origins, and interpretations of history, as well as the renegotiation of the *tutorat*. Local communities maintained their claims to land on the basis of custom while migrants made claims on the basis of their relationship with the state. With increasing shortage of land in Côte d'Ivoire, the intensification of rural struggles provided fertile ground for political mobilisation with the return of multi-party elections at the end of the 1980s. This coincided with ethno-regional antagonisms over national power and political exclusion, which brought 'ethnic' conflicts into electoral politics with disastrous effects. This was further exacerbated by the crisis in the cocoa-growing areas and neo-liberal insistence on the promotion of a single model of 'open' markets and multi-party elections, and by political opportunism on the part of the main competing political factions. While many of these conflicts over 'ancestral' belonging and 'traditional' prerogatives also occurred in Ghana, they were fought along more localised lines. By placing contemporary land issues in historical and comparative perspective, Berry underscores the connections between land, politics and citizenship, and the directions in which they change under different policy and political initiatives.

In the second chapter Kojo Amanor also deals with processes of transformation and contestation of customary law. He argues that the characterisation of customary land relations is a product of the dominant interests of political alliances rather than a historical fact. He shows how the depiction of customary relations as based on communal forms of tenure – in which the chief holds the land in trust for the community – is a political invention. This invention was created in the colonial period firstly to constrain the development of land markets, which were viewed by the colonial authority as a threat to the peasant-based export crop economy which they sought to promote, and secondly to empower chiefs on whom the system of rural administration by Native Authorities depended. During the nineteenth century, there was marked social differentiation within the Gold Coast, and considerable transactions in land took place. Under colonial rule the colonial administration sought to protect customary land tenure systems from the market by vesting lands in paramount chiefs and by preventing the rise of a class of indigenous land speculators. Since indigenous community members had an inherent right to use land for free, chiefs who wanted to gain revenue alienated land to outsiders. This resulted in the rapid alienation of land to migrant farmers, hungry for land to invest in cocoa farming and foreign concessionaires. This has often resulted in land scarcity for local poor farmers, youth, and women, as unused land is alienated to migrants and appropriated for sale. It often creates insecure access to land for migrants, who find that as land becomes more valuable, chiefs attempt to renegotiate the terms of ownership.

Amanor argues that present policy initiatives, which attempt to make land distribution more equitable and transparent by strengthening customary forms, are misplaced, since the customary forms are reinvented traditions which express the interests of elite factions. He illustrates this by showing a multiplicity of customary forms, which are marginalised and do not enter into policy frameworks. Contemporary notions of customary tenure assume that notions of ownership or rights over particular plots of land are based on entitlements to fixed plots of land, mapped out by customary rulers and family heads. However, in many farming systems based on shifting cultivation, rights to land arise out of the changing dynamics of the rotation of land, which requires constant movements over changing plots of land and negotiations between neighbouring farmers. Farming plots expand and retract according to the farmers' access to labour, soil fertility, the concentration of farmers, conflicts over resources, and other factors. Under these types of farming systems land plots are not easily mapped and digitised, since they are constantly changing. However, within these areas, contemporary notions of customary land ownership open up the alienation of land and dispossession of shifting cultivators to a class of wealthy local and

migrant tree planters. Amanor argues that notions of customary privilege are often used by an alliance of local elites, aspiring investors, and
agents of the state to justify accumulation and the dispossession of the
poor and marginalised of their land.

Amanor's contribution shows that the customary realm is not independent of the state. On the contrary, the shaping and reconstruction of
custom by local elites often take place through a close alliance with the
state. Economic and administrative considerations have led the state to
side with the powerful elite, accepting claims of chiefly control over
smallholders' claims for livelihood rights, and the demands of paramount chiefs over local chiefs, ignoring historical evidence pointing in
other directions. The state institutions justify their actions with the discourse of egalitarian communities and traditional leadership in the best
interest of the entire community and nation. In reality, however, chiefs
often use their power to expropriate and profit from community land.
Thus, state policy that strengthens chieftaincy and chiefly control over
land, and ignores contested definitions of the customary presented by
other interest groups, will tend to promote highly unequal development
in rural areas and ignite considerable social turmoil and upheaval.

Stefano Boni's contribution continues with the topic of struggles
around chiefly prerogatives. The chapter is based on field study in the
Sefwi Wiawso and Juabeso-Bia districts of the Western Region. He describes disputes in four different realms: conflicts among chiefs, disputes concerning the rights of immigrant farmers, age-related confrontations, and conflicts concerning the determination of appropriate compensation for wives' marital toil. In all these realms Boni shows that
the customary tenure system is ambiguous and constantly shifting,
and that this ambiguity and indeterminacy are being defended and pre-
served by the chiefs, the people with interpreting powers. This allows
for differentiation of norms according to people's ethnicity, ancestry,
gender, and age. The customary elite who control the administration of
land consists of the same people who have interpreting powers. They
are therefore able to preserve and exploit the unequal conditions and
profit from new values in land. This becomes especially evident in the
cases concerning immigrants; when chiefs try to unilaterally change
the conditions of land 'contracts' with immigrants, disputes arising
from these redefinitions are mainly dealt with in the 'courts' of the very
same chiefs. This shows the near impossibility to circumvent chiefly arbitration, as well as the lack of alternative and more impartial channels
for redress for the immigrant farmers.

The disputes within these four realms again clearly show the impact
of the state on customary land tenure – sometimes through certain direct actions, but often also through decisions *not* to intervene in local
struggles. Boni argues that the state's actions should be seen within

the existent 'land tenure orthodoxy'; a discourse of egalitarian communities, traditional leadership administering land on the basis of a clear set of unchanging criteria of land allocation in the best interest of the entire community, in which conflicts are considered as misunderstandings of the interpretation of tradition. The dominant idiom and interpretation of traditions are constantly questioned by the marginalised groups, but they often do not find accessible platforms through which they can address their grievances and complaints to state agencies.

Steve Tonah presents a case study of the village of Biu and its neighbouring communities in the Kassena-Nankana District of northeastern Ghana. Tonah traces the transformation of land tenure arrangements in that area, in the context of, first, colonial rule and then the development of a large-scale state-sponsored irrigation project from the 1970s. Both periods witnessed continuing struggles between earth priests, chiefs, and state agencies for control, allocation and management of lands. Prior to colonial rule, settlements in the area were under the political and religious headship of earth priests (*Tengnyono*), the traditional leaders of the first-comer clans, who would also function as the custodians and administrators of the land. Each clan within a settlement was autonomous and governed by its own clan head, who would consult the earth priest in cases of disputes and for general directions on the administration of the clan. During the colonial period, the various clan heads were transformed into headman, and later chiefs, whom the colonial government regarded as the political representatives of the people. This sidelined the earth priests and altered the balance of power. The various hitherto independent and autonomous chiefs were later grouped into a hierarchy with the creation of village, divisional, and paramount chiefs, which led to a great number of conflicts among them. The declaration of all lands in Northern Ghana as 'public lands', under the management and control of the Governor in 1927, further curtailed the powers of the earth priests and chiefs, as their powers with respect to land management were made subordinate to that of the colonial government. However, the control of land by the government was only effective in the major towns. In the rural areas, land continued to be administered according to 'customary law'. Since 1979, when the lands were de-vested and returned to the ownership and control of the 'traditional owners', there has been an intense competition between the earth priests and chiefs over who has allodial title to the land.

In 1974 the government decided to construct an irrigation project in the research area. Land used for the construction of the irrigation facility was expropriated by the government without consulting the landowners, and the payment of compensation to the landowners, through the chiefs, was far from adequate. In all matters concerning land the government dealt exclusively with the chiefs, bypassing the earth priests, which enabled the local chiefs to gradually legitimise their hold on land in their traditional areas with the connivance and active support of the state. For instance, the Land Allocation Committee, responsible for the allocation of zones and plots of land on the project, included chiefs, not earth priests. In 1987, management was transferred from Land Allocation Committees to Village Committees, which generally include earth priests. With the increasing participation of the communities in the project, the earth priests seem to be regaining part of the authority over land that they had lost to the state. This again increases the contestations between chiefs and earth priests, as membership of the Village Committee offers opportunities for economic gain and for ensuring political support and patronage within the community through the allocation of irrigation plots. Tonah's paper highlights the heavy interference of governments since the colonial period in local power structures and customary land management in Northern Ghana and the ways in which chiefs and earth priests have struggled to capitalise on new opportunities to gain control over land and access to power.

Richard Crook examines the plurality of dispute settlement institutions (DSIs) in Ghana and the DSIs to which customary landholders turn if their land rights are threatened by the state, local government, or the chief, or if they come into conflict with other parties. There is a wide range of possible dispute settlement institutions to which they can turn, ranging from state courts and administrative agencies through superior chiefs' customary courts to village level arbitrations by village chiefs, family heads, elders, and community leaders. Given the reality that most landholders in practice use mainly local and customary forms of dispute resolution, and given the congestion and huge backlogs in the state courts, state policy in Ghana now favours an emphasis on encouraging these local and customary DSIs. Crook examines the legitimacy, effectiveness, and inclusiveness of these customary and informal local level systems of land dispute settlement based on case studies in peri-urban Kumasi (Ashanti Region), Asunafo District (Brong-Ahafo Region), and Nadowli South District (Upper West Region). He examines their viability as alternative dispute resolution (ADR) institutions, and their ability to reduce the backlog of land cases facing the state courts.

In his contribution, Crook clearly shows the influence of the colonial government on the courts of superior chiefs. Ranger's 'invention of tradition' thus also applies to the functioning of customary courts (Ranger 1983). The bad reputation of these courts, often accused of corruption, oppressive procedures, high fees, and lack of accountability for funds, shows the ambiguity of this legacy. Crook furthermore shows how the

ADR orthodoxy ignores differences in status and power (cf. Nader 2001), the paramount importance of which is also demonstrated in the contributions of Amanor and Boni. He argues that superior chiefs' courts do not in fact seem very suitable as ADR solutions, since those with land disputes in peri-urban Kumasi and Asunafo District tended to resort to local state courts in preference to superior chiefs' courts, especially if they were non-locals.

Janine Ubink examines claims and conflicts between chiefs and smallholders over the ownership of land in peri-urban Kumasi. The chiefs play a central and often negative role in the conversion of farmland to residential land, causing loss of land, jobs, and income for local citizens. A discussion of local contestations over land rights in peri-urban Kumasi reveals how chiefs abuse their position as guardians of stool land and authorities in the field of customary law to claim changes in the unwritten, ambiguous customary law. Resistance of local citizens against the chiefs' land conversions takes various forms, but hardly goes through DSIs: chiefs' courts are avoided since the chiefs are themselves a main party in these disputes; family elders cannot hear cases involving chiefs; and state courts are unsuited because of their long delays in delivering judgements. In general, popular actions of resistance are often not very effective due to a combination of eroded traditional checks and balances and the 'policy of non-interference' of the current government. Ubink shows in her contribution that the current government is not willing to place any checks and balances on the customary realm and to a large extent leaves the interpretation of local tenure arrangements to the local elite, for political and economic reasons, and as a result of close connections between state elite and chiefs. Again, we see the government justifying its non-interference with an appeal to local checks and balances.

In the second part of her paper, Ubink examines the relationship between the negative role of chiefs in land administration and people's views on the institution of chieftaincy and the other tasks and activities of chiefs – including involvement in local development, sustaining law and order, and the performance of traditional religious practices. Her data reveal a clear correlation between chiefs' style of land management and overall popular assessments. These overall assessments of chiefs, however, show no correlation with the assessments of the institution of chieftaincy, a fact that leads Ubink to conclude that people's opinion about chieftaincy hardly depends on the performance of current village chiefs, or – to put it differently – the way a chief governs barely reflects on the institution.

The last contribution to this book, a joint paper by Julian Quan, Janine Ubink, and Adarkwah Antwi focusses on the policy response to these problems. It describes the Land Administration Project (LAP)

Ghana, a long-term program with multi-donor support, started in 2003, that intends to reform land institutions and develop land policy so as to provide greater certainty of land rights for ordinary land users and enable greater discipline and efficiency in the land market. The reform seeks to divest government of responsibility for the management of stool lands and to transfer this to Customary Land Secretariats (CLSs). In initial project documents, these CLSs were characterised as local secretariats with appropriate governance structures to assure institutionalised community-level participation and accountability in the use of stool land and the revenue it generates. During the pilot implementation phase, however, government made the political choice that CLSs should fall under the aegis of traditional authorities rather than opting for more community based approaches to the management of customary land.

Quan et al. discuss a number of difficulties encountered in the implementation phase of the LAP that lie both in the customary realm and in the state sphere. Considering the far from undisputed position of the chiefs in Ghana and their continuous renegotiation of chiefly prerogatives, the unwillingness of chiefs to enhance transparency and accountability of the new CLSs – the first obstacle described by Quan et al. – does not come as a surprise, as chiefs are profiting from these attributes of customary land management. The implementation of LAP is furthermore hampered by the resistance of staff of land sector agencies who are supposed to implement the LAP in such a way that it will decrease their own importance and revenue – both officially in the forms of stipulated fees and unofficially in the form of bribes. The implementation of donor-supported programs as an integral aspect of an existing ministry's business – mainstreaming – furthermore risks the subjection of the project to motives of politicians and officials who aim to utilise and allocate project resources in such a way as to legitimate their authority, entrench bureaucratic self interest, resist institutional change, and maximise votes, without necessarily having regard to objectives of equity and/or efficiency. A last obstacle in implementation links up with earlier papers: the unwillingness of the government to impose checks and balances on chiefs and to command their accountability. Quan et al. conclude that the approach taken in the first years of LAP amounts to the further empowerment of chiefs through the resourcing of CLSs without progressing appropriate checks and balances. This brings significant risks that powerful customary leaders may utilise CLSs to consolidate their political control over land, which will have the perverse effect that people are disenfranchised rather than empowered.

The various contributions to this book are characterised by two concerns: a focus on processes of transformation and contestation of cus-

tomary land tenure; and the relationship and interaction between customary institutions and state institutions. They examine political di-
mensions of customary tenure and point to the complexity of social,
economic, and power relations involved in the harmonisation or articulation of customary and state sectors. They argue that customary institutions have always involved power struggles to define the control of
land, as well as alliances and interactions between state and local-level
actors to legitimise and redefine the customary. The papers examine
the contestation over rights to land between competing traditional
authorities, between chiefs and cultivators, between chiefs, local
youths, women, and migrants, as well as the various ways in which
concepts of belonging, ancestry, history, and family relations are used
and reinterpreted to validate claims.

Tonah describes the considerable impact of the colonial and post-
colonial state on customary land management in Northern Ghana
through its policy of placing land in the north under the colonial
authority, while implementing a policy of rural administration based
on chieftaincy. This marginalised the control that earth priests exercised over land and has led to struggles between earth priests and
chiefs to redefine and clarify customary ownership of land. The flow of
these local power struggles is influenced by the changing framework of
development policy and projects and the various political alliances built
by government to initiate development activities. Decisions by the state
not to intervene in customary tenure may also influence the nature of
customary tenure, allowing chiefs to redefine customary land in their
own interests as long as these do not contradict state policies. Both
kinds of state influence – direct local interventions as well as decisions
not to intervene in local struggles – can be found in the case described
by Boni. Amanor similarly argues that the existing definitions and
transformations of customary tenure result from an alliance between
state and traditional rulers that represents elite interests and justifies a
process of dispossession and land appropriation by elites in the 'national interest'. This is echoed by what Ubink calls the 'policy of non-
interference' and Quan et al.'s description of the current government's
approach to land tenure reform in the Land Administration Project.

The papers by Crook, Ubink and Quan et al. also focus on institutional accountability and popular perceptions of accountability. While
Crook focusses on the legitimacy and accountability of dispute settlement by chiefs, Ubink analyses a wide panoply of chiefly functions.
Both Crook and Ubink point to the need to place administration by traditional authorities within a broader framework of plural institutions
involved in administration and local government. This leads Ubink to
conclude that policymakers who wish to build on customary systems
should critically assess chiefly rule – and popular perceptions of it – in

various fields, taking into account the performance of other actors in these fields, including local government representatives. Based on such assessments, governments should determine the desirability to recognise, formalise, and enhance or curtail the various functions of the chiefs. Quan et al.'s paper demonstrates, however, that this has not been the approach taken in the implementation of the current Land Administration Project, which has tended to empower traditional authorities to evade downward accountability. Berry, on the other hand, cautions that state interference in customary arrangements and attempts to establish a national framework for regularising customary relations can exacerbate local level tensions, drawing them into wider political conflicts which mobilise ethnic and xenophobic emotions to achieve political ends. These types of conflicts can ultimately result in civil war and considerable loss of life.

Note

1   Drafts of papers can be found on line at: http://www.isser.org/index.php?option=-com_content&task=view&id=24&Itemid=11.

2 Ancestral property: Land, politics and 'the deeds of the ancestors' in Ghana and Côte d'Ivoire

Sara Berry

Introduction

For the last 25 years, western governments and international donor institutions have waged a concerted campaign to liberalise African political economies – deregulating markets; privatising assets, enterprises, and services; replacing authoritarian with elected governments; and urging African states to conduct their affairs in an open, 'transparent', manner according to 'the rule of law'. Presented as a forward-looking agenda of economic, political, and institutional reform, neo-liberal interventions promise peace and prosperity through closer integration into the global economy. Ironically, given its resolutely modernising thrust, implementation of the neo-liberal agenda has coincided with renewed emphasis on the past as a source of entitlement and legitimacy in the present. From demands for reparations from descendants of oppressed peoples, to 'indigenous peoples' claims to territory and resources, contemporary struggles over wealth and power are filled with appeals to the past. Far from heralding 'the end of history' (Fukuyama 1992), recent neo-liberal efforts to remake Africa in America's self-image have gone hand-in-hand with vigorous debates over questions of origin and precedent and the salience of these questions in ordering the affairs of the present.

Struggles over land have figured prominently in neo-liberal policy agendas and in West Africans' experiences with them, in part because land is both property – an economic resource valued as a means of production and a store of wealth – and territory – governed space that gives those who control it leverage over other people. In many West African contexts, neo-liberal efforts to 'clarify' patterns of land ownership and bring transparency to land transactions (through land registration, legislation, and administrative reorganisation) have added to already intense pressures on access to and control of land, intensifying contestation not only over land *per se*, but also over questions of who is eligible to make claims and who has the authority to decide. Such struggles challenge neo-liberal assumptions about the separability of market transactions from political processes. They also give rise to intense debates over historical precedents, raising questions about widely

held assumptions that 'customary' rights and institutions provide a
stable or even knowable social base on which to build adjusted political
economies that are equitable as well as efficient.

The present paper addresses these questions through a comparative
case study of socio-economic and political change in the former cocoa
frontiers of southwestern Ghana and Côte d'Ivoire. After briefly de-
scribing the two rural localities and their respective national economic
and political contexts, the paper examines the changes in land and labour relations that accompanied the process of frontier settlement and
agricultural expansion in each, discusses the role of the state in shaping processes of economic growth and local governance in the cocoa
frontier regions, and describes the way struggles over land and labour
both invoked and informed debates over the relevance of the past for
questions of citizenship and belonging in the present. By placing contemporary land issues in perspective, historically and comparatively,
the paper underscores the connections between land, politics, and citizenship, and outlines the directions in which these connections are
changing in the era of structural adjustment.[1]

Setting

Beginning in the late 1940s, the rich semi-humid forests of southwestern Ghana and Côte d'Ivoire became target destinations for migrant
farmers and workers seeking access to land for growing cocoa, coffee,
and other marketable tree crops, as well as food crops for home consumption and sale. Cocoa in particular served as a leading export commodity, fuelling the growth of national income, imports, and state revenue during the early years of independence, and increasing both
economies' vulnerability to global market fluctuations. Within the
cocoa-growing regions, the process of frontier expansion created lines
of social division and interdependence between migrants and hosts
that intensified from the 1970s onward, as virgin forest lands were
used up, farms aged, and world cocoa prices fell. In the aftermath of
frontier expansion, tensions over land and income within the forest
zone intersected with political struggles that often reverberated well beyond their immediate local contexts.

On the national level, the political and economic histories of post-
colonial Ghana and Côte d'Ivoire present a striking combination of par-
allels and contrasts. While the post-war boom in cocoa production
ended earlier in Ghana than in Côte d'Ivoire, both followed similar trajectories of frontier expansion and closure in the southwestern forests,
and both experienced rising levels of social tension and conflict over
land, authority, and access, as opportunities for expansion shut down.[2]

Given the primary importance of cocoa as a source of export earnings and state revenue in both economies, one might expect that developments in the main cocoa-producing regions would have had similar repercussions at the national level, but this was not the case. Once the euphoria of independence and cocoa prosperity wore off in the mid-1960s, patterns of national economic growth, decline, and political (in)stability moved in opposite directions. Beset by falling income and a series of short-lived military and civilian governments after the overthrow of President Nkrumah in 1966, Ghana's economic and political situation only began to stabilise in the mid-1980s. Economic recovery was modest, at best, for the last fifteen years of the century, with many Ghanaians struggling to make ends meet in the face of stagnant levels of income and employment and persistent erosion of the value of the currency. Politically, however, the country regained a measure of stability under the leadership of J.J. Rawlings who, after a decade of military rule in the 1980s, succeeded himself (as duly elected President of the Fourth Republic) when civilian rule was restored in 1992. Eight years later, in one of sub-Saharan Africa's first peaceful changes of electoral regime, the opposition party was voted into power. In contrast, Côte d'Ivoire – which was hailed throughout the 1960s and 70s as an international icon of export-led economic growth and political stability – slid into a deepening economic crisis in the 1980s, which undermined the ruling party's hold on power and paved the way for increasing conflict following the death of President Houphouet-Boigny, after 33 years in office, in 1993.

Read against the parallel histories of frontier expansion and closure in the main export-crop producing regions of Ghana and Côte d'Ivoire, these divergent trajectories of national transformation and turmoil raise questions about the interrelations between state power and local society in both countries, and the extent to which they challenge or bear out key assumptions of the neo-liberal agenda. Framed from the outset as a critique of the state, neo-liberal policy interventions have worked diligently to curtail state regulation of economic activity, to transfer assets and enterprises to private owners, and to privatise public services and many functions of government. Confident that, once 'liberated,' African political economies would emulate those of Europe and North America, the architects of neo-liberalism moved in the 1990s to add political to economic restructuring – replacing authoritarian regimes with governments chosen through multi-party elections, decentralising governing institutions and practices, and clarifying rights of ownership and lines of authority in both public and private spheres. Predicated on a hidden hand of frictionless regulatory capacity, sometimes referred to euphemistically as 'the rule of law,' neo-liberal reforms take for granted the feasibility of removing special interests from

markets and governing institutions, and of resolving conflicts before
they get out of hand. The utopian and paradoxical qualities of these assumptions are well known and do not need reiteration. Rather than another critique of neo-liberal principles, this study views them through a
lens of recent West African history, asking how local struggles over
land and authority have shaped or collided with governing practices,
political competition, and resource use at the level of the state, and
how the multi-layered dynamics of resource mobilisation, regulation,
and conflict in West Africa have absorbed or deflected international efforts to reorder them in the name of neo-liberal reform.

In a recent study, Catherine Boone compares the governing strategies of post-colonial national regimes in three West African countries –
Senegal, Côte d'Ivoire and Ghana – in the 1960s and 70s (Boone
2003). Fiscally dependent on their ability to tax peasant agriculture,
Boone argues, all three governments calibrated their strategies for consolidating and exercising state power to the structural realities of rural
society. '[B]road political trajectories, state forms, and perhaps even the
viability of the center' were shaped by the 'dynamics of indigenous rural societies,' (Boone 2003:318) as well as the character of colonial rule
and the nationalist leadership[3] Confronting strong politically mobilised
rural elites in the cocoa growing regions of Ghana, Nkrumah 'usurped'
their power by building direct institutional links between the state and
the peasants. By contrast, Houphouet-Boigny left rural society in the
western forests as he found it – decentralised, relatively egalitarian and
politically weak. Under Houphouet, Boone argues, 'authority was cen-
tralized, and state institutions remained "suspended above" rural society' (ibid:143).

Boone's contrast – between an Ivorian state that consolidated its
power by keeping aloof from rural society, leaving decentralised and divided communities to hold one another at bay, with a Ghanaian regime
that extended state power directly to the rural masses in order to
strengthen its own position by sidelining rural elites – views rural society's influence from the perspective of the state. Viewed from below,
I would argue, state policies appear both less single-minded and more
intrusive, especially in Côte d'Ivoire, than Boone's analysis suggests.
Both regimes sought to gain political as well as economic leverage over
rural electorates as well as incomes – Nkrumah and the Convention
People's Party (CPP) through extensive formal institution-building, and
Houphouet-Boigny and the *Parti Démocratique de Côte d'Ivoire* (PDCI)
through equally extensive but largely informal influence over rural land
rights and local administrative practices. In both cases, state policies
helped to shape conditions under which farmers gained access to land
and labour. Neither government was entirely consistent in policy or
practice, however, nor were they effectively in control of the resources

or the sympathies of rural inhabitants. In the following pages, I discuss the repercussions of state strategy and local practice in both countries, focussing in particular on the way negotiations and struggles over agricultural land intersected with the politics of entitlement and belonging both locally in the cocoa frontier zones, and nationally in struggles over control of the state and its economy. The multi-layered dynamics of resource access, governance, and social control in these two cases illustrate the complex economic and political fields in which neo-liberal 'reformers' are seeking the ownership society.

Dynamics of frontier expansion

In both Ghana and Côte d'Ivoire, the process of forest clearance and tree crop cultivation was carried out by thousands of migrant farmers, who either acquired land on arrival or worked on others' farms until they had the means to start farms of their own. In Ghana, many of the migrants came from older cocoa-growing areas in Asante and the Eastern Region, where yields from aging trees were declining, and many farms had been destroyed by swollen shoot disease. In some cases, they or their forebears had already established more than one farm during the earlier phase of cocoa expansion, leaving each farm in the hands of a relative or a hired caretaker, and travelling between them to supervise their work (Hill 1963:179ff). As world prices rose and wartime shipping restrictions were lifted after 1945, farmers seized the opportunity to offset 'the exhaustion of cocoa land in their homes of origin' (Arhin 1986:14) by moving into untapped forest zones in the west [Figure 2.1] (See also Adomako-Sarfoh 1974:134; Berry 2001:106,116; Dunn and Robertson 1973:11; Konings 1986:62-64;). There they were joined by migrants from the savanna regions of Northern Ghana and neighbouring countries, who worked as labourers on the farms of older residents and 'pioneers' and, in a few cases, went on to establish farms of their own (Arhin 1986:2; Hear 1998:ch. 5. See also Allman and Parker 2005:91ff and *passim*).

In Côte d'Ivoire, cocoa and coffee growing developed much more slowly in the early decades of colonial rule – hampered by state policies of forced labour, heavy taxation, and discrimination against African planters in favour of Europeans. In 1928, for example, cocoa exports from Ghana reached 229,000 mt, compared to 16,000 mt from Côte d'Ivoire (Crook 1991b:219). Following the abolition of forced labour in 1946, however, migrants flocked to the forests of west Central Côte d'Ivoire, clearing plots of land and planting cocoa and coffee on rich forest soil [Figure 2.2]. Many of the 'pioneer' farmers were Baule and Dyula from savanna areas on the eastern and northern borders of the

Figure 2.1   *The cocoa frontier*

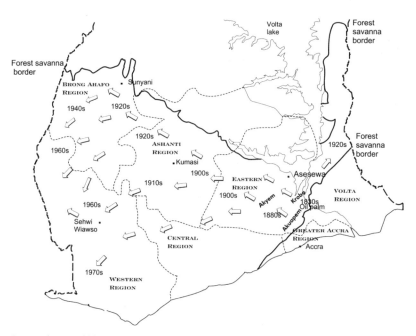

Source: Amanor 1994

forest zone, including some who had worked on French or African-
owned plantations in the southeast before the war. Clearing and planting a few hectares at a time, they soon filled up their first plots of land
and moved on to establish additional farms further west. Their efforts
attracted a growing number of migrants from further north, including
many from Burkina Faso and Mali, who worked as labourers on the
growing expanse of tree crop farms. By the 1970s, migrants outnumbered host populations in many villages in the west Central Region,
with Burkinabes, Malians, and late arrivals from Northern Côte d'Ivoire
making up the bulk of the farm labour force.

Acquiring land

While the first migrants encountered little difficulty in getting access
to land in the sparsely populated southwestern forest zones, the terms
on which they did so, and their subsequent relations with host communities, differed significantly within Ghana and Côte d'Ivoire. In the decentralised communities of west central and southwestern Côte
d'Ivoire, migrants obtained land from village elders or family heads,
whose authority did not extend beyond their immediate circle of kin or

Figure 2.2 *Moving cocoa frontiers: Côte d'Ivoire, 1920-1993*

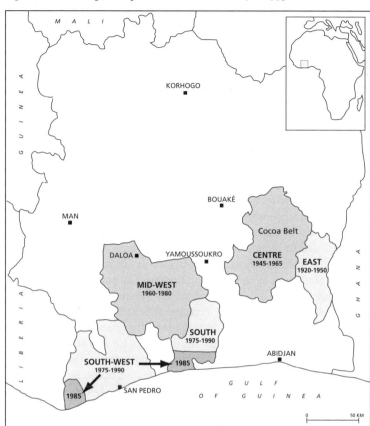

Source: Léonard and Oswald 1995:126. © Hans Gordijn.

Table 2.1 *Social demography of migrants in southwestern Côte d'Ivoire*

	Autochthones	Immigrants	
		Allochthones[4]	Étrangers
Bodiba village			
1953	100		
1975	35	65	
1998	22.4	45.9	31.7
Districts			
Divo Dept, 1980	33	67	
Southwest, 1988	7.5	35.7	34.4
Oume Dept, 1998	22	46	32

Sources: Bodiba-Chauveau and Léonard 1996:114, Chauveau and Bobo 2003:13-14; Divo-Hecht 1985:37; Southwest Region-Chauveau and Léonard 1996:185; Oume Dept-Chauveau and Bobo 2003:13.

local community. Apart from a token gift – sometimes supplied by the
land giver – to ratify the initial agreement between migrant and host,
the former did not pay for the land in advance, nor did they agree to
rent it for a prearranged annual payment of cash or share of the crop.
Instead, it was generally understood that immigrants were free to plant
both permanent and annual crops, sell the resulting produce, and pass
their farms to their descendants. In exchange, migrant farmers were
expected to show their appreciation with annual gifts of farm produce;
contributions to marriage and funeral ceremonies in the host's family;
and assistance, in times of need, in the form of loans or occasional labour on the host's farm. Relations between hosts and migrants were
discussed, in local parlance, in terms of guardianship (*tutorat*) rather
than tenancy. Following an outbreak of violence in Gagnoa in 1970,
after Bete villagers tried to stop Baule migrants from obtaining more
land, local officials promoted the 'fiction' that relations between hosts
and migrants were mutually supportive rather than openly commercial.[5] In addition to providing land, *tuteurs* were expected to protect
their immigrant clients in case of difficulty or dispute, and clients to
show their gratitude by assisting their *tuteurs* in times of need. In practice, according to one life-long student of the region, these arrangements 'verge on, or hide, largely commercial transfers of land – however, the commercial aspect does not erase the social relation stem-
ming from the "gratefulness" that the migrant (or his heirs) owes to
his *tuteur* (or the latter's heirs)' (Chauveau 2005:215).

The moral and emotional overtones of the *tutorat* both facilitated the
spread of cocoa cultivation and complicated relations between migrants
and hosts. As immigrant farmers prospered, many *tuteurs* came to depend on their 'assistance' – relying on clients to lend them money or
help with farm work while, at the same time, reaffirming their claim
to social precedence by asserting their right to request and receive their
clients' help. As land became scarce and cocoa prices fell, *tuteurs* tried
to renegotiate the terms of their original agreements, restricting clients'
rights and demanding higher payments (Chauveau 2005:226ff). Un-
derstandably, stranger farmers resisted these demands, arguing that
their farms were theirs to use, sell, or pass on to their heirs. The resulting tensions highlighted the paradoxical implications of the *tutorat*. *Tuteurs* demanded increased payments in cash both for new allocations of
farming rights, and in the form of loans and gifts from their existing
tenants. In turn, these payments tended to reaffirm both the *tuteurs'*
continued authority over the land, and 'the migrants' claims of having
been engaged in a purchase-sale transaction' (Chauveau 2005:234).

In Ghana, immigrants who arrived in Ahafo or the Central or Western Region in the 1940s and 50s obtained cultivation rights, directly
or indirectly, from local chiefs. In some cases, an immigrant might

conduct negotiations with the head of a local family rather than directly with the chief, although chiefs expected to be informed of such arrangements, in recognition of their ultimate authority over stool land.[6] Whether strangers applied directly to the chief, or indirectly via the head of a local family, they made an initial payment in exchange for permission to farm and, once their cocoa trees began to bear, turned over a portion of each year's harvest, in cash or in kind, to the 'owner(s)' of the land which, in most cases, meant the chiefs. These annual payments were substantial: demands for a third or half of the crop were not uncommon, and the chiefs might additionally levy an annual tax (Boni 2006:176). In some cases, chiefs refused to specify annual rents or crop shares in advance, 'waiting until the cocoa farm came into fruition when the landowner, after making a thorough inspection of the farm and the yield-potential, released his terms like a bomb, which the farmer could (...) reject (...) only (...) at the risk of being dispossessed of the land and the fruits of his labour' (Arhin 1986:30). Farmers rarely sought redress in the courts, Arhin adds, not only because many could not afford the expense, but also 'because he (the landowner), who was also the chief, was bound to be the judge' (idem. See also Arhin 1986:18; Berry 2001:15ff; Boni 2006:176; Dunn and Robertson 1973:53ff; Rathbone 1993:ch.13; Simensen 1975a).

Chiefs also used their political leverage to renegotiate agreements with stranger farmers – raising rents, and reclaiming (or expanding the scope of their control over) land by reducing the duration of contracts or curtailing tenants' rights of usage or land transfer. Some engaged in outright fraud, selling the same plot of land more than once or allocating land to strangers which had previously been acquired by the state (such as forest reserve lands) or included in concessions to timber companies (Arhin 1986:32; Boni 2006:178). Indeed, by continuing to re-enact their authority over land and the terms of land access, recurring demands for increased tax payments, reductions in tenants' rights or outright repossession of defaulters' farms served to reinforce chiefs' authority in general, as well as reaffirming their ultimate, or 'allodial,' title to the land.[7]

The demands chiefs placed on 'stranger' farmers have been a subject of recurring dispute since the early years of cocoa cultivation and colonial rule.[8] Repeated efforts by state officials to limit chiefs' control over cocoa income have rarely succeeded in effecting lasting reductions in rates of chiefly appropriation. In 1962, the CPP regime passed a Rents Stabilisation Act (109), limiting stools' tax on stranger farmers to 5s/ acre, but the law was repealed after Nkrumah was overthrown in 1966, and subsequent regimes have been disinclined to reinstate it. By law, chiefs are required to deposit rental income from stool lands in a special account managed by the state, which oversees the mandatory trans-

Table 2.2 *Average areas acquired by immigrants, west Central Region (ha)*

Gbehiri village, Divo Department	
1940-9	34.2
1950-9	20.1
1960-9	9.1
1970-9	2.9

Villages south of Gagnoa	
Before 1970	23.8
1970	10.7
After 1970	8.8

Sources: Gbehiri village–Hecht 1985:35; Gagnoa Region–Ruf 1991:111.

fer of a portion of these moneys to local government, to be used for public purposes. The laws are rarely enforced, however, and chiefs continue to exercise *de facto* control over the terms under which 'strangers' acquire and use rural land. Twenty-five years after Nkrumah's downfall, Boni found that chiefs still held the upper hand in Sefwi. He reports that land transactions between chiefs and strangers are negotiated with reference to written 'memoranda of agreement,' drawn up by the chiefs, which specify tax rates, tenants' rights of use and transfer, and chiefs' rights to oversee them. Revised from time to time as circumstances change, the memoranda represent a form of *de facto* local legislation which has worked, since the 1940s, to reduce tenants' rights, while increasing rates of taxation, and expanding chiefly prerogatives (Boni 2006:176-178).

In Côte d'Ivoire, the state also played an ambivalent role in regulating land relations on the cocoa frontier. When Houphouet-Boigny and the PDCI took control of the state in 1960, the agricultural export boom was in full swing and the newly independent regime did not want to interrupt it. Rather than invite organised opposition by formally abolishing customary rights, President Houphouet-Boigny simply announced, in 1963, that 'land belongs to the one who develops it' ('la terre appartient a celui qui la met en valeur'). At the time, his pronouncement contravened Ivorian law, under which the 'national domain' was vested in the state, and private contractual arrangements with respect to any part of it were prohibited (Chauveau 2000:10). Thanks to Houphouet's prestige, and the power of his 'patronage machine', however, the President's word carried as much force as the law. On the ground, party cadres and local officials followed his lead, reassuring local villagers of the moral force of the *tutorat*, while settling individual disputes in favour of the migrants who produced the greater part of the cocoa that fed the state's coffers. The effect was to create a space of ambiguity in which local villagers could claim that even though they had granted cultivation rights to strangers in perpetuity, the land belonged to them, while migrants could invoke the President's dictum to argue that they owned the land on which they had established their farms.

Mobilising labour

In both Côte d'Ivoire and Ghana, migrants often hired themselves out when they first arrived in the forest zone, but did so only until they had saved enough money to acquire land and start their own farms (Arhin 1986:16; Boni 2006:175; Chauveau and Richard 1977:491). Labour arrangements were predicated on upward mobility: aspiring to become independent farmers, migrant labourers sought out potential employers who could help them negotiate access to land. Writing of west central Côte d'Ivoire in the 1970s, Chauveau & Richard argued that the growth of cocoa and coffee production turned on a contradiction: 'to get more labour, it is necessary to have land; land attracts a rural "proletariat" at the same time that it allows them to "deproletarianise"' (Chauveau and Richard 1977:513, my translation). Predicated on mobility, relations between hosts and migrants worked to accelerate the pace of forest clearance and the growth of agricultural output and exports.

Expectations of upward mobility also figured in family labour arrangements. Young people who worked for their fathers or elder kinsmen were rarely paid for their services, but they too anticipated moving on to start their own farms, with assistance from the relatives whom they had helped in the past. Young men who had worked on their fathers' farms might ask for land when they were ready to marry and start households of their own, or for money either to start businesses or pay school or apprenticeship fees, the latter enabling them to move out of farming and into salaried employment in the cities. Wives might receive gifts of cash or cloth after the cocoa harvest, and husbands, in recognition of their wives' contributions to the family farm, sometimes contributed trading capital or money to purchase equipment.[9] In Ghana, a number of women acquired cocoa farms of their own, either through inheritance or with money saved from trade. In Brong-Ahafo, the number of women farmers increased in the 1920s and 30s then declined again, as men reasserted control over family property and women diversified into trade and other non-agricultural occupations (Mikell 1984 and 1985. Compare Allman and Tashjian 2000:74). In the mid-1940s, Meyer Fortes reported that 18 per cent of the adult women in Asokore (a village in eastern Asante) owned cocoa farms, compared to only 15 per cent of the men (Fortes 1948:163). In another Asante village, Okali found that 76 per cent of the adult men and 43 per cent of adult women owned cocoa farms in the early 1970s – up from about

36 per cent and 24 per cent, estimated from a survey carried out in
1933 (Okali 1983:49).

Partly because of the high degree of mobility in the frontier economy, late arrivals in a given locality were often at a disadvantage in
terms of access to both land and labour. In areas where local farmers
had already ceded much of the available land to earlier arrivals, migrants who came later received smaller allotments than their predecessors, as illustrated in table 2.2.

Between 1981 and 1991, the price of forest land in the Nekeide district, west central Côte d'Ivoire, rose 40 per cent, and rental rates on
fallow land tripled (Ruf 1995:39. See also Chauveau, 1995:114; Colin
2005; Léonard and Ibo 1994). In the far southwest, Burkinabes and
other northerners who arrived late had to contribute labour on their *tuteurs'* farms, in addition to giving annual payments of money or produce (Chauveau 2005:221ff). In addition, farmers with larger holdings,
who could reallocate part of their land to aspiring workers, were also
able to employ labourers on more favourable terms and earned higher
rates of profit than those with smaller amounts of land (Chauveau and
Richard 1977:512-513; Hecht 1985:47). Differences between early and
late arrivals were at least partly offset, however, by the expansionary
process itself. Farmers who reached the limit of their allotments, or
who could not get as much land as they wanted in well-settled localities, moved on to establish new farms in uncultivated forest areas
further south and/or west. As long as land was available, the expansionary process continued, generating rising export earnings and revenue for the state, and permanently altering the social demography of
the forest zone.

'Cocoa cycles': Ecology, mobility and markets

Based on forest clearance and continuing frontier expansion, the extensive process of cocoa cultivation described above could not continue in-
definitely. As Francois Ruf has argued in a number of publications, cocoa production tends to move in cycles. Output increases rapidly as forest land is cleared and planted, then evens out and eventually declines
as trees age and the supply of uncultivated land is exhausted. High
yields obtained from previously uncultivated forest land represent a
kind of forest rent which diminishes as the forest is cleared, trees age,
and accumulated nutrients are extracted from the soil. Old trees may
be uprooted and replaced, but the next generation of trees will require
increased inputs to restore soil fertility, control pests and plant disease,
and clear invasive species such as *chromolaena odorata*, popularly
known as Sekou Toure – 'revolutionary' and out of control (Ruf
1991:113). In both Côte d'Ivoire and Ghana, farmers preferred to aban-

don old farms rather than rehabilitate them. As one explained, graphically, to Francois Ruf, 'an old plantation is like an old wife who is dying. Medicines to keep her alive would cost too much. It's better to keep them for the young wife.'[10]

As long as uncut forest land remained, 'shifting cycles' of expansion into the southwestern forests sustained the growth of total cocoa output and exports, masking the process of forest depletion and declining yields in the older frontier areas. By the late 1970s, however, the growth of Ivorian exports, combined with fresh supplies from new cycles of cocoa cultivation in southeast Asia, had begun to saturate the global market. World prices fell after 1978, putting downward pressure on Ivorian export earnings just as supplies of uncultivated forest land began to run out. Coming on the heels of OPEC's second major oil price increase in the late 1970s, the convergence of cocoa cycles and closure of the southwestern frontier helped to push the Ivorian economy into a prolonged crisis that has yet to be resolved (Crook 1990; IMF et al. 2005; Ruf 1991, 1995).

In Ghana, the rate of frontier expansion began to slow in the late 1960s, a decade earlier than in Côte d'Ivoire. After twenty years of more or less steady growth, cocoa output peaked in 1965, then fell steadily, bottoming out in 1984 at 28 per cent of the level it had reached in 1965 (Oduro 2000:173). Already in debt from the overextended spending of Nkrumah's later years in power, the economy floundered after 1966, under a succession of short-lived military and civilian regimes, each apparently too caught up in internal rivalries and personal ambitions to give serious attention to the economy. Entirely dependent on imports for supplies of gasoline and other petroleum-based products, Ghana suffered badly from the OPEC oil price increase in 1973, and the next ten years were 'nothing short of an unmitigated economic disaster. Real GDP per capita, real export earnings, cocoa exports, import volumes and domestic savings and investment all declined dramatically...' (Aryeetey et al. 2000:11). The worsening economic situation culminated in a crisis in 1983/1984, when the 'worst drought in living memory' (Tabatabai 1988:720) coincided with a refugee crisis caused by Nigeria's sudden decision to expel all undocumented aliens then living within its borders. Ghanaians who had escaped economic decline by emigrating to Nigeria's oil-rich markets in the 1970s and early 80s now found themselves summarily ejected, forced to leave their possessions behind in the rush to meet the Nigerian government's deadline for departure. Over a million Ghanaians (9 per cent of Ghana's population at the time) flooded back into the country in a period of three to four weeks, most to homes in the southern regions where they were met by internal migrants fleeing hunger in the drought-stricken north (Van Hear 1998 and others).[11] In the ensuing crisis, imported goods

disappeared from the domestic market and the output of food crops, already reduced by the exodus of migrants in the 1970s, was decimated
by the drought.[12] '[M]aize, millet and sorghum were lost over much of
the country,' and the 'unprecedented fall in the level of the Volta river
and hence of the Volta Lake dam' reduced the supply of electricity to 5
per cent of its normal level (Derrick 1984:286). Abandoning his earlier
commitment to socialist transformation, J.J Rawlings turned to the
IMF and World Bank for help.

Plural governance? State power and rural society in the era of frontier expansion

By the early 1980s, the cocoa cycles of the post-war era had come to an
end, leaving densely populated rural communities to face land
shortages, forest depletion, and dwindling opportunities for income
and employment, not only in the rural areas but throughout the nation
and the regional economy beyond. Ghanaians returned from Nigeria
and Côte d'Ivoire to find their own economy in worse shape than they
had left it. In Côte d'Ivoire, the economic crisis sent thousands of urban youth – many of them children of cocoa farmers, whose parents
had paid for them to attend school and relocate to the cities – back to
the land, only to discover that their place had been taken by upwardly
mobile immigrants, and that their elders had no land left to give them.
In both countries, declines in income and employment, as well as deep
uncertainty about the future, converged with land scarcity and forest
depletion to generate intense competition and conflict over land, particularly in the former frontier areas of export crop expansion. In Côte
d'Ivoire, as we've seen, these tensions fed directly into emerging struggles over national political restructuring and control of the state, contributing to an escalation of political conflict that derailed state efforts to
restart the economy and paved the way for civil war. In Ghana, on the
other hand, the economy began a faltering recovery after the debacle of
1983/1984 and regained enough political stability in the 1980s to effect
a peaceful transition to civilian rule that remains in place today. Before
turning to a more detailed discussion of these events, I need to say a
bit more about the parts played by the Ghanaian and Ivorian states in
the earlier process of forest clearance and agricultural growth.

   Like the layered and unsettled claims on land that accumulated in
the process of frontier expansion, relations between migrants and hosts
were affected by government strategies for consolidating state power,
as well as policies of economic and rural development. Both governments had a direct interest in promoting the growth of cocoa output
and income, from which they appropriated much of the revenue that

sustained the ruling party as well as the state, and both worked with and around rural authorities to extend their political control over rural society. In Ghana, Nkrumah built an elaborate apparatus of state institutions designed to control as well as 'transform' the rural economy (Boone 2003:142ff). Under the banner of rooting out the vestiges of colonial oppression, the CPP regime punished chiefs who had supported the Asante-based opposition party (NLM) in elections leading up to independence, stripping them of administrative and judicial authority, confiscating their stool lands, and putting some of their most outspoken opponents in prison.[13] Rather than the single-minded campaign to abolish chieftaincy which some contemporary observers perceived, however, Nkrumah followed a more complicated strategy – courting chiefs who supported him as well as punishing his opponents, and playing rivals off against each other (Arhin 2001; Dunn and Robertson 1973:198-199, 204ff; Rathbone 2000).[14] On the issue of land, the CPP regime placed legal restrictions on chiefly rents and expanded the state's power to acquire stool land for public purposes (Kotey 2002:204-205), but stopped short of outright expropriation of the chiefs.[15] Weakened by internal rivalries, Nkrumah's successors were more inclined to court chiefly support than to curb their prerogatives. The military regime that overthrew Nkrumah in 1966 released his jailed opponents and restored their confiscated lands, and their successors varied in their reactions from tacit acceptance to open support of chieftaincy as a time-honoured institution (Arhin 2001:46, ch. 4 passim).

In Côte d'Ivoire, Houphouet-Boigny and the PDCI sought to extend and consolidate state power over rural society and income in varied, sometimes contradictory, ways. Assured of ready access to export crop income through the Caisse de Stabilisation,[16] the state sought to maximise the rate of growth of cocoa and coffee production in the forest zone. In addition to Houphouet's famous dictum that anyone who developed a piece of land owned it – customary (and statutory) prescriptions notwithstanding – the Ivorian state enthusiastically promoted the migration of aspiring farmers into the rich uncultivated forests of the southwestern quadrant of the country. In addition to encouraging the movement of Baule, Dioula, and others from savanna to forest zones within Côte d'Ivoire, Houphouet's regime welcomed foreign investors and immigrants alike. Envisioning Côte d'Ivoire as 'a sub-regional economic pole that attracted ... labour, capital, and all kinds of expertise' to the Ivorian centre (Akindès 2004:8-9), Houphouet opened the borders not only to French companies and highly placed bureaucrats, but also to merchants, artisans, farmers, and unskilled labourers from neighbouring countries in the region. With abundant supplies of untilled land, and cities fed by the proceeds of the expanding agricultural econ-

omy, Côte d'Ivoire's expanding economy acted as a magnet for capital
and labour from across West Africa and beyond, far outdoing the efforts of its erstwhile colonial rulers to draw labour from across the region into the colonial centres of Côte d'Ivoire.

At the time of independence, non-Ivorians dominated the civil service and occupied whole neighbourhoods in Abidjan and other cities,
working in trade, artisanal and clerical jobs, as well as in manual labour, and the pace of immigration accelerated in the following years.[17]
Throughout the 1960s and 70s, migrants poured into Côte d'Ivoire,
especially from landlocked neighbouring countries of the Sahel. Mostly
illiterate men and some women from rural areas in their home countries, Burkinabes, Malians, and others provided a steady stream of
cheap labour for the expanding agricultural economy of the western
forest zone. The number of Burkinabes, in particular, who were living
and working in Côte d'Ivoire rose from ca. 250,000 in the late 1950s,
to 726,000 in 1975, and 1,564,000 in 1988 (Blion and Bredeloup
1997:723).

The ruling regime reaped political as well as economic gains from
the swelling immigrant population. Seeking to place Côte d'Ivoire at
the forefront of enlightened African development, Houphouet-Boigny
propounded an ethos of 'pan-Africanism in one country' (quoted in
Dozon 2000:15), premised on a 'logic of maximizing the sub-regional
labor force as a basis for a solid Ivorian economy...rather than [Nkru-
mah's] idea of an Africa that would be strengthened by the unity of its
components....' (Akindès 2004:8-9). In implementing Houphouet's
policy of 'land to the developer,' officials made no distinction between
Ivorians and foreigners: Burkinabe labourers who could save enough
to plant their own farms were treated on the same basis as migrant
farmers from inside the country. However, far from leaving rural residents to keep each other at bay, allowing the state to drain off most of
the cocoa surplus at the point of sale, Ivorian officials intervened regularly in local affairs. Rather than being managed through an elaborate
apparatus of state-run courts and explicit legal rules, disputes over land
and labour relations were handled on an ad hoc basis by local officials
– the ubiquitous *prefets* and *sous-prefets* left behind by the colonial state
– under the watchful eye of PDCI cadres, who controlled appointments
and promotions throughout the civil service, and who used their influence to insure that local officials fostered export growth by deciding
these cases in the migrants' favour. Ad hoc interventions were characteristic of the President's extra-legal style of governance. In addition to
his policy of land-to-the-developer, which effectively guaranteed rights
of private ownership in contravention of the law, Houphouet extended
de facto privileges of citizenship to all residents on Ivorian soil, regardless of nationality. Foreign immigrants were not only encouraged to

work and invest in all sectors of the Ivorian economy – they were also allowed to vote. Needless to say, they voted en masse for the President and the ruling party that had welcomed them so warmly (Akindès 2004:16; Blion and Bredeloup 1997:728; Boone 2003).

As state policies and politics converged with emerging land shortages in the former frontier regions, hosts and migrants sought to protect their livelihoods and options for the future by invoking histories of past rights and wrongs, re-imagined through the lens of current anxieties. Citing their long-term presence in the region and history of marginalisation under colonial rule, villagers whose ancestors were present in the forests when the migrant farmers arrived pictured themselves as 'indigenous' people, historically entitled to claim precedence in access to and control over land. In both Ghana and Côte d'Ivoire, claims to 'indigeneity' invoked ethnic identities that owed as much to colonial administrative and judicial practice as to older cultural practices and boundaries. In each case, tensions between 'indigenes' and 'strangers' reflected the specific history of forest expansion and closure in the country in question. Local residents of forest villages in western Côte d'Ivoire felt exploited by the migrants – who not only outnumbered local residents in many parts of the cocoa zone but controlled the greater part of the land – and felt angry at the PDCI regime that had welcomed the migrants so liberally. In Ghana, on the other hand, migrants felt exploited by local *authorities* – chiefs who appropriated substantial shares of their farm proceeds and threatened to dispossess tenants who resisted their demands. In both cases, rival claims to land and income were articulated in terms of historical precedent, giving participants a potentially inexhaustible repertoire of antecedents, and giving rise to intense debates over competing interpretations of the past.

Ancestral property: History and the politics of belonging

As migrants moved into the forests of southwestern Ghana and Côte d'Ivoire, their acquisition of land and increasingly important role in cocoa production inscribed differences between 'locals' and 'strangers' into the social and economic fabric of everyday life. In a recent essay, entitled 'Indigenous blood and foreign labour: the ancestralization of land rights in Sefwi, Ghana,' Stefano Boni charts the complex constructions of social identity and difference that developed in the process of frontier expansion and converged into a pattern of increasing inequality and exclusion, as virgin forest land was exhausted, cocoa yields declined, and economic conditions worsened from the 1970s onwards (Boni 2006). As chiefs increased their demands for rent (or 'taxes') and curtailed the land rights of strangers, questions rose over who

could be considered a 'stranger' and how far the scope of chiefly
authority might extend. Framed in terms of 'ancestry,' these debates
turned on 'the deeds and privileges of the ancestors' as well as on lines
of uterine descent. 'Ancestry' is a historical construct rather than a geneaological fact – 'the social representation of descent, strategically redefined within the limits of what is thought to be collectively credible'
(ibid:170). As supplies of allocable land diminished, chiefs in Sefwi
sought to reclassify local residents as taxable 'strangers,' challenging
people's claims to belonging by invoking histories of settlement and
migration that traced their ancestors' origins to other places. Protesting
a chief's demand that he surrender a third of his crop, one farmer asserted his 'birthright and privilege as a pure Sefwi born,' denouncing
the chief's claim as 'a drastic innovation of custom never practiced in
the history of Sefwi Wiaso state' (quoted in Boni 2006:173). Another
refused the chiefs' demand for a share of his grandfather's estate, de-
claring that his grandparents had settled in Sefwi over a hundred years
ago, and asking how he 'who was born in [Sefwi] (...) resided [there] for
over 85 years (...), and left behind 15 children in the same district could
be termed as a stranger?' (ibid:174).[18]

The ancestralisation of land rights that Boni describes in Sefwi has
been repeated, with variations, in communities across Ghana since colonial times. Framed around narratives of settlement and migration,
'the deeds of the ancestors' link claims to land, authority, and origin in
a discourse of belonging that speaks to issues of political entitlement
as well as to property claims. People who claim membership in a local
community call themselves 'citizens' – as distinct from 'strangers' –
suggesting that local belonging conveys rights of participation and entitlement analogous, if not equivalent, to those of citizenship in the nation. Unlike national citizenship, which is defined, at least jurally, in
the Constitution, criteria for distinguishing citizens of one community
from those of another are matters of local understanding, subject to no
formal legal code and open to multiple interpretations. In my own
fieldwork in Asante, I found not only that claims to land and local citizenship were based on historical narratives, but that these narratives
were invariably framed as histories of migration, which usually included a list of places where their ancestors had stayed, and the length
of their sojourn in each, en route from a point of origin to the narra-
tor's present location. In other words, 'citizens' of a given community
usually claim that their ancestors came there from someplace else.
Thus, while I agree with Boni that 'ancestralisation' has entailed a
'hardening of boundaries of belonging' (Boni 2006:183) akin to those
of 'ethnicity' and 'tribe,' and that these boundaries gained much of
their contemporary resonance under the aegis of colonial rule, I think
it is also useful to distinguish between local 'citizenship' as it is under-

stood and practiced in post-colonial Ghana, and constructions of 'ethnicity' in other contexts. Côte d'Ivoire is a case in point.

In Côte d'Ivoire, popular understandings of who had gained and lost in the process of frontier expansion drew on perceptions of social identity and difference that owed as much to state practices during and after colonial rule, as to local histories of social engagement and conflict. Interpreting 'the results of their own actions as demonstrating a differing potential for "civilisation" among ethnic groups,' colonial authorities in Côte d'Ivoire geared strategies of development to an imagined 'racial psychology,' encouraging 'peoples of the south-east to develop their "wealth-producing aptitudes by growing export crops,"' "hardworking northerners" [to supply] foodstuffs and labor,' and relegating Baule and peoples of the southwest to manual labour (Chauveau and Léonard 1996:179). Within the bottom tier, ethnographers and colonial officials grouped small, decentralised communities into ethnic categories noted more for their descriptive and administrative convenience than their relation to social realities. 'Bete' ethnicity was one such category. Used as a collective designation for peoples of the western forests, the 'Bete' were relegated to the bottom of an imagined ethnic hierarchy, destined in the minds of their colonial rulers for manual labour and submission to the authority of more developed cultures and civilisations (Chauveau and Dozon 1987: 238, 249, 260-261; Dozon 1985).

Following independence, colonial ethnic hierarchies were reworked rather than repudiated in the social imaginaries of Ivorians seeking to understand and rationalise their claims to power and to representation in the post-colonial order. In an illuminating study, Ivorian scholar Francis Akindès suggests that Houphouet's celebrated strategies of economic openness and export-led development also worked to reproduce the ethnic imaginaries of colonial rule. President Houphouet-Boigny's celebrated liberality towards immigrants was not inspired, he argues, by any idealistic notion that all West Africans were created equal. Part nationalism, part personality cult, the President's ideology of 'houphouetisme' ranked Ivorians in an ethnic hierarchy, with Akan (or, more specifically, Houphouet's own Baule subgroup) figured as 'natural rulers' destined to preside over a middle tier of 'Dioulas' (another catchall term referring not only to Mande-speaking Muslims known for their skill as merchants and entrepreneurs, but also to Senufo and other people from the northern regions), with acephalous 'Bete,' Bakwe, and other Kru-language peoples of the western forest zone at the bottom.[19] In effect, Houphouet's 'liberal' vision of residential citizenship as a product of pan-regional participation in the Ivorian national project went hand-in-hand with a myth of ethnically differentiated capacities to contribute to that project, which paralleled and to some extent reproduced the ethnographic imaginaries of colonial rule.

Colonial officials in Ghana also referred to Africans as 'tribes' but governed through localised polities based on imagined boundaries of 'native authority' and jurisdiction. In the 1950s, the NLM's failure to gain popular support outside of Asante allowed Nkrumah and the CPP to portray the party as a throwback to 'tribal' politics that had no place in a modern state, and to insist that Ghana become independent as a unitary state, rather than a federation of semi-autonomous regions, as demanded by the NLM. Despite the authoritarian excesses of Nkrumah's later years in power, by taking federalism off the table as a viable constitutional option, his regime may have spared Ghana the kind of violent ethno-regional power struggles that pulled Nigeria into civil war in the late 1960s, and exploded in Côte d'Ivoire at the end of the century. Unlike Côte d'Ivoire, where intensifying struggles over land and economic opportunity coincided, in the 1980s and 90s, with ethno-regional antagonisms over national power and political exclusion, in Ghana struggles over land, and over at least some forms of power, have been fought along more localised lines of 'ancestral' belonging and 'traditional' prerogative.

In short, by the 1980s, tensions over land and livelihood on Ghana's and Côte d'Ivoire's declining agricultural frontiers had hardened into 'ethnic' antagonisms that both reflected and reproduced differential patterns of wealth and influence in the nation as a whole. In Ghana, however, 'ethnic' differences were constructed along multiple lines, many of them corresponding to chiefly jurisdictions created, in part, under colonial rule. In Côte d'Ivoire, by contrast, ethnic tensions in the forest zone mapped onto both the population and the 'national domain' in large ethno-regional blocs that, along with the return to multi-party elections at the end of the decade, provided fertile ground for political mobilisation. As rising levels of debt forced states across the region to renegotiate outstanding obligations and seek additional loans from the IMF, the World Bank, and major donor governments, on-going struggles over power, resources, and belonging intersected with neo-liberal agendas of policy and political reform in ways that complicated rather than clarified contested claims to economic and political entitlement and belonging.

Political and economic change in the neo-liberal era

After thirty years of steady growth fed by rising agricultural exports and inflows of foreign capital, by 1980 the Ivorian economy had begun to falter. With ready access to foreign credit, the government weathered the oil price crises of the 1970s by running up a large external debt (Crook 1990:649). Eager to maintain its credit rating by keeping up with its debt service obligations, the state was ill-prepared to cope with the drop in world cocoa prices that began in the late 1970s, just as the supply of uncultivated forest land began to run out. Hoping to avoid a recession and sustain state revenues, Côte d'Ivoire was one of the first West African countries to apply for a Structural Adjustment Loan. Cuts in state spending mandated under IMF 'conditionality' led to declines in income and employment, especially in the urban areas (Sogodogo 1997:143).

A dozen years and four Structural Adjustment Programs later, the Ivorian economy was in worse shape than it had been in 1980 (Diomande 1997:121). Cocoa production continued to rise, levelling off near 800,000 tons per annum in the early 1980s, but falling world prices reduced export earnings, cutting into state revenue, forcing layoffs and reductions in government spending, and threatening the stability of the ruling regime. Struggling to reverse the downward slide in state revenue, the Caisse de Stabilisation cut the producer price of cocoa from FCAF 200/kg in 1988 to FCAF 50/kg three years later, helping to spread economic decline from the cities to the countryside. In some villages, average farm revenue fell by as much as 60-80 per cent (Ruf 1991:115; 1995:5). Devaluation of the CFA franc, mandated by the IMF and the World Bank in 1994, added to the misery, putting further downward pressure on purchasing power and standards of living. By 2000, 12 per cent of the population was living in extreme poverty (as measured by the World Bank's standard of less than $1 per day) and half subsisted on $2 or less (Akindès 2004:23-24). Despite the cutbacks, government spending continued to rise (Sogodogo 1997:143), and the country's dependence on cocoa increased.[20]

Unlike Côte d'Ivoire, where structural adjustment coincided with and accelerated falling income and employment, in Ghana the first Structural Adjustment Loan brought a measure of relief after the collapse of imports and basic food supplies in 1983/1984. With the help of good weather and a rise in the world price of cocoa in 1985/1986-1986/1987, staple food crops and other basic commodities reappeared in the markets, and income stabilised, especially in the rural areas. Recovery was modest, however. Under structural adjustment, price controls were removed, state employees were laid off, and the modest gains in rural income were offset by sharp declines in average real earnings in the urban areas (World Bank 1986:19). World cocoa prices fell continuously from 1987 through 1992, undercutting the effects of cocoa rehabilitation projects financed with structural adjustment loans. Gold mining showed the biggest gains from market deregulation, leaving the country dependent on a few resource-based exports (gold, cocoa, and timber) for access to foreign exchange. Persistent trade deficits weakened the cedi, limiting gains in real income for the majority of the people. A decade after structural adjustment was introduced, half the population was living in poverty.

Memories of the crisis remained fresh, however, and Rawlings gained popularity, despite unease with the continuation of military rule, in part by investing money from structural adjustment loans in road repair and rural electrification. When civilian rule was restored in 1992, his party gained control of the National Assembly, and Rawlings was elected President with strong support from the rural areas. During the rest of the decade, political openness gained momentum. Press censorship was lifted, local government reorganised, with elected District Assemblies in charge of service provision in their respective jurisdictions, and an increasingly vocal population engaged in vigorous debate over the performance of state officials and politicians. Driven in part by increasing evidence of corruption in the ruling regime, voters rejected the President's hand-picked successor in elections at the end of 2000, bringing the leading opposition party to power in one of sub-Saharan Africa's first peaceful electoral changes of regime in the post-colonial era.

In Côte d'Ivoire, political stability unravelled in the 1990s despite – or because of – the introduction of multi-party elections in 1990. Although Houphouet-Boigny and the PDCI held on to power in 1990, and again in 1995 under Houphouet's successor, Henri Bedie, the continued deterioration of the economy generated widespread discontent, much of it directed at the ruling party and its leaders. When Prime Minister Alassane Ouattara broke with the regime after 1995 to emerge as a leading contender for national power, popular frustration crystallised along ethno-regional lines. Drawing his main support from the northern regions, Ouattara became a symbolic target for southerners' fears of permanent displacement at the hands of foreign immigrants and migrant northerners long favoured under PDCI rule (Dembélé 2003:36). These anxieties were especially acute in the former cocoa frontier areas of the southwest, where 'autochthonous' communities felt themselves doubly disadvantaged, not only by immigrant 'Burkinabes,' but also by members of the President's own Baule ethnic group and 'Dioulas' from the savanna regions, who had led the first wave of 'cocoa pioneers' into the southwestern forests in the 1950s and 60s (Chauveau and Léonard 1996, and many others).

Bedie's efforts to recoup his party's fortunes did nothing to calm political tempers. Reacting to popular criticism, he repudiated his predecessors' liberal treatment of immigrants, replacing '*houphouetisme*' with an ethno-nationalist rhetoric of '*ivoirite*,' effectively transforming the basis of citizenship from residence ('*droit du sol*') to descent ('*droit du sang*') (Dozon 2000:17). Having barred Ouattara from the presidential elections in 1995 because he did not meet legal residence requirements,[21] Bedie then moved to disqualify him permanently on the grounds that his grandfather had been born outside the country and that Ouattara was therefore not really '*ivoirien*'.[22]

Bedie's manoeuvres served to heighten ethno-regional tension throughout the country. Suspicions about Ouattara's national origin spread to northerners in general: those who could not prove that their parents were born in Côte d'Ivoire found themselves relegated to 'legal second class citizenship' (ibid:18). Fearful and angry, northerners rallied behind Ouattara and the RDR, raising the likelihood of an RDR victory in the next round of elections scheduled for 2000, and feeding xenophobia in the south (Dembélé 2003:38).

If Bedie anticipated that southerners would unite behind the PDCI to stop the threat of a northern takeover, however, he failed to reckon with the PDCI's own unpopularity, especially in the southwest. Rather than vote for the party that, in their view, had sent northern migrants and foreigners to take over their land, Bete and other southwestern-based peoples threw their support to one of their own, a professor named Laurent Gbagbo, known for his socialist sympathies, who already commanded a significant following among university students and urban youth. By the late 1990s, the next electoral contest appeared to be shaping up as a three-way struggle between the RDR, the PDCI and Gbagbo's FPI, none of which appeared able to muster much support outside of the leader's home region (Crook 1997:238-239 and passim). When the National Assembly finally enacted a new rural code in 1998, replacing the 'legal anarchy' of land tenure arrangements under Houphouet-Boigny with a statutory system of private ownership in fulfilment of a long-standing demand from the IMF and the World Bank, the effects were explosive.[23] Limiting rights of land ownership to '*ivoiriens*,' the law played directly into the hostilities between *autochtones* and *etrangers* in the southwest, reinforcing ethno-regional party loyalties and driving another nail into the coffin of political stability, not only in the former frontier areas, but throughout the country as a whole.

Concluding thoughts: Land conflict, politics and citizenship in the time of structural adjustment

The conflicts over land and economic opportunity that developed in the wake of frontier expansion in the cocoa-growing regions of southwestern Ghana and Côte d'Ivoire, reflected the histories of migration and settlement that had brought thousands of migrant farmers and labourers into the forests in the 1950s and after, fuelling a process of agricultural expansion based on extensive cultivation and the non-renewable riches of newly cleared forest soil.[24] In Ghana, conflicts over land turned on issues of chiefly prerogative and 'ancestral' claims to property and belonging that assigned rights to land according to people's status as 'citizens' or 'strangers'. Determining a person's ancestry is an exercise in historical interpretation, in which people draw on 'geneaological memory,' historical narratives of ancestral deeds, and both formal and informal sources of documentation to assert and challenge one another's claims to community membership, traditional authority, and associated rights over land. Far from rigid or stable, historical precedents and their implications for authority and entitlement in the present have been debated and reworked as people confront new opportunities and pressures. Reaffirmed, in various ways, under both colonial and post-colonial rule, chiefs' authority over land has drawn on and reinforced their leverage in debates over ancestry, ensuring them a level of influence in contemporary economic and political affairs that goes well beyond their constitutional prerogatives, which are limited to jurisdiction over 'chieftaincy affairs' (see chapter 22 of the Constitution of the Republic of Ghana, 1992).

As Arhin, Boni, and many others have argued, Ghanaian chiefs have used their leverage to garner disproportionate returns from cocoa farming and other land-based enterprises, particularly at the expense of producers who are (or who have come to be) considered 'strangers' in areas under chiefly jurisdiction. Local 'citizens' have been similarly displaced in peri-urban areas (Berry 2001:123-124; Ubink 2008a). Chieftaincy has served, accordingly, as a magnet for social contestation. Some of the most violent conflicts in recent Ghanaian history have erupted in disputes over chiefly succession, jurisdiction and/or related claims to land. Chiefs also wield considerable influence, not only within their respective jurisdictions, but at the highest levels of the state, drawing politicians, judges, bureaucrats and others into efforts to influence and capitalise on chieftaincy politics, as well as resolving disputes. Unlike Côte d'Ivoire, however, where conflicts over land and belonging played directly into state politics, connections between chieftaincy, state and local governance in Ghana are multi-faceted, operating in overlapping but parallel spaces of political engagement and contestation. Chiefs wield power, but they don't stand for election[25] – a situation that many have condemned, with reason, as placing them beyond meaningful public accountability, but one that also leaves room for explosive conflicts over land and authority to occur in recent years without bringing down the government.

In Côte d'Ivoire, on the other hand, where conflicts over land and entitlement also converged with debates over ancestry and origin, especially in the frontier areas of expanding cocoa production, rural tensions converged with national political contests in the 1990s, contributing to an escalation of xenophobic rhetoric that brought 'ethnic' hatreds

into electoral politics with disastrous consequences. Political opportunism certainly contributed to this process, as Ivorian scholars have
been some of the first to point out. 'Contrary to situations in which
hotbeds of nationalism emerge and the state is forced to take measures
to offset its effects,' writes Akindès, 'in Côte d'Ivoire, ...the state itself
is responsible for the retribalisation' of political discourse and participation (Akindès 2004:26). At the same time, one might argue that the
force of popular response to the ugly rhetoric of '*ivoirite*' owed as much
to the convergence of state politics with the crisis in the cocoa-growing
areas and the neo-liberal insistence that all economic and political 'reforms' in Africa conform to a single model of 'open' markets and multi-party elections, as is owed to the power of opportunistic politicians to
manipulate the popular mind. Most of these processes were also at
work in Ghana, but they came together differently, allowing neo-liberal
advocates to claim that country as something of a 'success' – as long as
they focus attention on the right areas of economic and political engagement.

Notes

1   The present essay is part of a larger study that seeks to explore the salience of 'history' in local struggles over property and power in different parts of Ghana and some
of its francophone neighbours. Using case studies from my own and others' research, I compare local histories of resource access, use, and control in Ghana and
neighbouring francophone countries – asking how understandings of the past figure
in contemporary economic and political affairs, and how local histories of economic
and political change have shaped West Africans' experiences with neo-liberalism. In
doing so, I am interested both in how global hegemony of neo-liberalism has influenced people's lives in West Africa, but also in how the neo-liberal project itself has
been reworked through encounters with West African political economies.

2   Reaching a peak in the mid-1960s, cocoa production in Ghana declined for the next
twenty years, and remained well below previous levels for the rest of the twentieth
century. In Côte d'Ivoire, cocoa output continued to expand into the early 1980s, generating increases in export earnings despite steep declines in world market prices.

3   Much of her argument rests, empirically, on demonstrating that each regime employed different strategies in different regions of their country, depending on the
structure of rural society and the strength or weakness of rural elites.

4   The term 'allochthones' refers to Ivorian nationals who do not come from the local
area and are therefore not considered to be autochtones.

5   Estimates of people killed in these riots run from several hundred to as many as
4,000 (Boone 2003:207, 220; Stryker 1970:134).

6   The stool is the symbol of chiefly office in Akan-speaking areas in Ghana and south-
eastern Côte d'Ivoire. When the British established colonial rule in Asante, they incorporated 'loyal' chiefs into the colonial administration, endorsing chiefs' authority
over their 'subjects' as well as the lands attached to their stools. Invoking their traditional right to a share of anything of value (game, timber, nuggets of gold) found on
stool land, chiefs argued that a farmer who 'found' value by growing cocoa outside

the jurisdiction of his/her own stool, should give part of the proceeds to the stool
whose land s/he cultivated. These claims were accepted by colonial officials as legitimate under 'native customary law' and incorporated into colonial policy on land. For
further information and examples, see Berry 2001.

7   A similar point is made by Lund 2002:32 and passim.

8   Boni 2006; Arhin 1986; compare Nugent 2002 and Mensah 1996 on Volta Region.
     Similar disputes had been common in the early decades of the twentieth century, in
     the older cocoa growing areas of Asante and Eastern Regions (Berry 2001:42-43;
     Rathbone 1993:ch. 13; Simensen 1975a:201ff).

9   Such contributions were by no means automatic, however. For studies of conjugal la-
     bour and household economies in cocoa growing areas, see, inter alia, Allman and
     Tashjian 2000; Clark 1999; Mikell 1985; Okali 1983.

10   '(...) une vielle plantation est comme une vielle femme qui meurt. Les medicaments
     couteraient trop pour la maintenir en vie. Il vaut mieux garder les medicaments pour
     la jeune femme' (Ruf 1991:107).

11   For more on transnational migration in the region, and the 1983 refugee crisis in
     Ghana, see text following footnote below.

12   One study estimated that reductions in Ghana's agricultural labour force resulting
     from emigration to Nigeria, contributed significantly to declining food output from
     1975 on (Tabatabai 1988:720ff).

13   On the history of the NLM, see Allman 1993. Nkrumah's relationships with Gha-
     naian chiefs are discussed in Arhin 1993 and 2001, Boone 2003, and Rathbone
     2000. See also Dunn and Robertson 1973.

14   Never fully abrogated during the First Republic despite the state's energetic appro-
     priation of substantial tracts of both urban and forest land 'in the public interest,' the
     principle that 'stool and skin lands shall vest in their respective stools' has been reaf-
     firmed in every subsequent constitution, and interpreted more broadly by successive
     regimes. For a useful discussion of the legal and practical implications of the differ-
     ence between land appropriated 'for public purposes' and 'in the public interest,' see
     Kotey 2002. The widening of the effective scope of chiefly authority through subtle
     changes in the wording of later constitutions is discussed in Arhin 2001. On the
     spread of the Akan chieftaincy model to other regions of Ghana, and its implications
     for the distribution of power and practices of governance in recent years, see Arhin
     2001:ch. 5.

15   Stools' authority over land, described in legal parlance as allodial (ultimate) title, has
     been reaffirmed in each of Ghana's last three constitutions. Under colonial laws, the
     state could acquire land needed 'for public purposes,' powers that were reaffirmed
     and elaborated in the State Lands Act (125) and the Administration of Lands Act (123)
     of 1962. Act 125 transfers allodial title to the state. Under Act 123, 'the administration
     and management of "stool land" is vested in the state in trust for the stool,' to be
     used in the public interest (Kotey 2002:205). State use of such lands has been a sub-
     ject of much controversy in recent years (Kasanga and Kotey 2001; Kotey 2002).

16   Like the Cocoa Marketing Board in Ghana, the Caisse de Stabilisation held a mono-
     poly over sales of cocoa and coffee to foreign buyers, and used its control to appropri-
     ate the major part of export crop revenues for the ruling party and the state. For de-
     tails and analysis, see Crook 1990:650.

17   Houphouet and the PDCI worked closely with French officials and investors, main-
     taining an open door to foreign investment as well as immigrant labour, working
     with its francophone neighbours to maintain a common currency pegged to the
     French franc, negotiating protected quotas for Ivorian exports to France, and appoint-
     ing French officials to some of the most senior positions in the Ivorian administra-
     tion. The open door was not limited to senior government positions, but applied at

all levels of the Ivorian economy. In 1976, 'foreign Africans accounted for 57% of all jobs in the urban "informal and artisan" sector, ...42% in the..."unskilled modern sector"' and 'a staggering 72.7% of all paid jobs' in the primary sector in 1971 (Blion and Bredeloup 1997; Crook 1991b:225).

18 The practice of paying an estate tax to the stool derives from pre-colonial Asante, and was a subject of intense debate during the colonial era. See, e.g. Arhin 1974; Berry 2001:24, 40.

19 Akindès 2004:12-16; Losch 2000; and others; Memel-Foté 1997, 1999.

20 Cocoa income rose from 25 per cent of total export earnings in 1990 to 50 per cent in 2000 (IMF, World Economic Outlook data base, http://www.imf.org/external/ns/cs.aspx?id=28).

21 A former senior official of the IMF, Ouattara had lived abroad for many years, returning to Côte d'Ivoire in the early 1990s, at the behest of his employers, to deal with the worsening economic and financial situation.

22 In responding to these claims, Ouattara himself has given different accounts of his family's history (Akindès 2004:36-39).

23 Passed at the end of December 1998, Loi no. 98-750 sur le Domaine foncier rural has been credited with helping bring about Côte d'Ivoire's first military coup in 1999, and the escalation of violent political struggle in the early years of the new millennium. In addition to restricting ownership to Ivorian nationals, the law mandates a process for recognising and registering individuals' 'customary' rights of ownership which is so complex and cumbersome that very few rural dwellers are likely to be able to complete it. All land which has not been so registered within ten years (by the end of 2008) will revert to the national domain, effectively nullifying the legalisation of customary rights as private property (Chauveau 2002).

24 Francois Ruf's term 'forest rent,' coined to describe the gains from cocoa and other crops grown on newly cleared forest soil, has been taken up by others (Austin 2005; Chauveau and Léonard 1996; Ruf 1995).

25 Chiefs are not chosen to succeed to stools on the basis of open popular elections nor, under the current Constitution, are they allowed to stand for election to public offices. They may hold positions in the civil service, if their qualifications meet those required of other public employees.

3 The changing face of customary land tenure

Kojo Amanor

In recent years there has been growing interest in promoting custom-ary institutions and arrangements in land tenure administrative reform within Africa. This forms part of a policy approach concerned with pro-moting democratic participation in governance by decentralising ad-ministration from national state agencies to community-based institu-tions. In Ghana, this strengthening of community-based institutions revolves around chieftaincy, and in recent years chieftaincy is re-emer-ging as an institution of governance, with increasing responsibility for local development, to the extent that donors and the World Bank have been funding foundations established by chiefs. Chiefs are represented by national and regional houses of chiefs, and their customary rights and rights to revenues and royalties are recognised in the Constitution. In the land sector, reform programmes are underway to strengthen chiefly administration of land and establish Customary Land Secretar-iats under their aegis in all the regions.

In policy circles, it is often assumed that the customary represents traditional or indigenous institutions that preceded modernisation, and which are widely accepted within rural areas. The customary is often defined in terms of an idyllic Arcadian past, which was characterised by communal and egalitarian values, based on group solidarity and rooted in spiritual and moral values. This results in the association of customary tenure with equitable access to land. Kasanga reflects this perspective, when he writes:

> Ghanaian customary tenurial systems are therefore a source of social security and continuity. The full enjoyment of the fruits of one's labour and efforts are guaranteed, and in regard to land, no man is 'big' or 'small' in his own village or town (Kasanga 1996:89).

In this communitarian approach, the morality of customary systems is seen to be disrupted by the state, which has usurped management over land and placed it in the hands of a bureaucracy. This state bureaucracy is accused of appropriating land for state enterprises and for the wealthy clients of government, and of engaging in corrupt practices.

roles to customary institutions and authorities and create institutional
linkages between state and customary systems (Benjaminsen and Lund
2003; Toulmin et al. 2002; Toulmin and Quan 2000a).

Within Ghana the main vehicle for attaining land administration reform has been the Land Administration Project (LAP). The stated aim
of the LAP is to lay the foundation for an accountable, harmonious,
and transparent customary land administration system from the bottom up which will then form the bedrock for an enhanced formal land
administration in Ghana. This is done with the intention of both en-
hancing the tenure security of smallholder farmers and facilitating
speedy transactions and registration of land to enable investors to purchase land in Ghana with confidence. To achieve an effective registration of land in Ghana, administration is being decentralised to Customary Land Secretariats (CLSs), which are associated with traditional
rulers. At present a number of pilot secretariats have been established
in different parts of the country. By placing the CLSs under the authority of chiefs the LAP ignores the fact that chiefs often exercise customary privileges and use their powers to redefine land relations in their
interest and to dispossess the powerless. The LAP has chosen to work
within the existing power structures of chieftaincy rather than to attempt to create a more democratic framework for land management.
This enables the traditional elites to further their interests in land.
There is evidence that chiefs are resisting attempts to introduce more
transparent and accountable procedures for recording their incomes
from land transactions and are using the CLSs to gain further control
over land (Ubink and Quan 2008).

LAP implementation began without the promotion of systematic dialogue in Ghana about the form and content of land reform, although a
series of ten regional land policy consultation fora and one national
forum took place in late 2007. The LAP has largely been implanted
through recommendations of foreign consultants and the national land
sector bureaucracy. It fails to take into account the considerable recent
research on customary land within Ghana and the critique of neo-liberal land policies. It is only following the adoption of the LAP that a major research project has been funded in Ghana to examine land policies, the ISSER Land Tenure and Land Reform Project, which is producing a large number of case studies and generating a debate through a
number of workshops.[1] Within rural areas the incorporation of the
CLS under the authority of traditional authorities has inhibited debate
about land, since farmers who can be dispossessed by chiefs may fear
being critical which might result in the wrath of chiefly power. In contrast to the communitarian perspective which presents the customary
as the site of open and equal negotiation, rural producers are often
wary to carry their land cases to traditional authorities, since they are

Communitarians argue that strengthening the management of land by customary authorities will result in a more equitable and transparent system of land management.

A second more sophisticated variant of communitarian land reform focusses on the nature of articulation between customary and statutory tenure. It argues that the present problems in land administration emerge from the poor harmonisation between the two spheres. Most people gain access to land under the customary system, but there are few institutional arrangements, that enable customary arrangements to be formally recognised within the state system of land administration. This lack of recognition of customary or informal arrangements results in land relations being largely unregulated and subject to a large number of abuses by both chiefs and bureaucrats, since there are few avenues through which people can gain access to justice and retribution. This enables customary authorities to engage in the multiple selling of land plots, since their transactions are largely unrecorded within the state system, and allows bureaucrats to demand excessive payments for those seeking to register their lands, since there is no transparent documentation of existing landholdings. Thus, it is argued that by strengthening the position of customary land authorities and building their capacities to manage land and document transactions, customary transactions will be increasingly documented and made transparent. This will prevent corruption in both customary and bureaucratic sectors (Antwi and Adams 2003; Toulmin and Quan 2000b).

This approach assumes that the major problem lies in the nature of transactions and the documentation of these transactions. The claims of chiefs to own and to be able to transact land are not seen as problematic. However, this may result in the dispossession of land users by chiefs before land reaches the market. For instance, Ubink (2006) shows that in peri-urban areas of Kumasi, chiefs use their claims as custodians of tradition and owners of the allodial title to land to appropriate the lands of farmers and sell them to purchasers of real estate, since they can make considerable profit from this.

In contrast to the assumptions in policy circles that customary land relations are widely accepted and recognised in rural communities, this chapter draws upon a number of historical and contemporary cases to show that customary land relations have always been contested. These case studies also show that the customary is not autonomous and independent of the state. It does not arise out of the solidarity of local interests in opposition to the state. On the contrary, customary relations are frequently constructed around an alliance between local power elites and the state, which comes to redefine what constitutes custom in a situation of change. Thus, the definition and redefinition of the customary frequently occurs in periods of rapid social and economic change and is associated with an adaptation to changing conditions rather than resistance to change. This chapter examines the role of the chiefs in the transformation of land tenure and their relationship with the national state. It also draws attention to the multiple constructions that exist in customary land practices, and the ways in which different groups, including marginal groups, frequently develop their own rival and often 'subversive' versions of the customary, which frequently challenge the dominant discourse of local elites but which are not accepted into the official canonical and elite versions of customary tenure.

The construction of customary land relations

Within the state sector, customary land relations in Ghana are based on a formulation that differentiates allodial and user (usufructuary) rights. Allodial rights are vested in chiefs who through their political hegemony are granted ultimate control over the land. This concept is ultimately derived from some notion of communal land tenure in which the land is vested in chiefs to manage on behalf of the community, or in which, as founders of the polity and the political order, chiefs acquired rights to the political allegiance of subjects on their land. This is essentially a political definition of land rights, which empowers chiefs as the trustees of communities to control land. Their 'subjects' (the peasantry) only hold user rights in land, which confer on them rights to use the land to make a livelihood, but not rights to sell land. Only the products emerging from the use of land and from their labour belong to the subjects of the chief, such as the farm plot, but the actual land belongs to the chief. This framework ultimately denies the peasantry secure rights in land by enabling them to be 'extinguished by the action of a paramount power which assumes possession of the entire control of the land' (Lord Haldane in *Sobluza II* v. *Miller and others 1926 A.C., 518 at 525*, quoted in Chanock 1991:67[1]). As Chanock (1991) points out, customary rights do not reside in the peasantry but derive from a political authority.

The origins of customary and state control over land

The origins of the formulation of customary tenure date back to the early colonial period, to the failed attempts of the British colonial administration to control land and vest it in the colonial state, and to the ultimate creation of a system of Indirect Rule based on Native Authorities and chiefly rule. During the 1880s, the Gold Coast became the scene of a gold rush. Fearing that Asante would sign a trade treaty with France, Britain rushed to conquer the hinterland of the Gold Coast and

to occupy Kumasi in 1893-1894. In 1895, following the occupation of
Kumasi, the status of the Gold Coast was transformed from a protecto-
rate to a colony. This declaration overturned the Bond of 1844 in which
a free trade colony in the southern Gold Coast had been negotiated between African and European sovereigns of equal power. The Gold
Coast was transformed into an imperial colony without consultation
with the chiefs or people of the Gold Coast and without military defeat.
This resulted in considerable concern among the people of the Gold
Coast, which manifested itself in the organisation of opposition in the
Aborigines Rights Protection Society (ARPS), an alliance of chiefs and
business and intellectual elites on the Gold Coast. This transformation
of the status of the Gold Coast had great significance for the land question. Fox Bourne (1901:41), a noted philanthropist of this period, commented on the British campaign against Asante:

> One of the main motives of the expedition of 1895, not admitted
> till after its conclusion was, of course, command of the minerals
> in which the interior of the Gold Coast is supposed to abound.
> Before the troops had returned from Kumasi, in fact, several
> speculators had begun arrangements with local chiefs and
> others, with the objective of obtaining valuable concessions at
> low prices.

In the 1890s more than 400 mining companies were established on
the Gold Coast and vast tracts of land were given out as concessions
(Howard 1978; Kimble 1963). The largest concession in this period
was an area of 100 sq miles, which became the site for Ashanti Gold-
fields. Land was often acquired by Gold Coast property speculators
who then sold it on to gold mining companies. In this period land
transactions with foreign concessionaires were not the monopoly preserve of chiefs. The rapid pace of land sales were of concern to the colonial government, particularly since it had little control over the process. In 1894 the colonial government of the Gold Coast attempted to
enact a Crown Lands Ordinance which would place 'waste land, forest
land and minerals' under the British Crown and enable the colonial
government to gain control over the granting of concessions. However,
this was met with considerable opposition from the Gold Coast elite
and the ARPS. The ARPS argued that the Crown Lands Ordinance was
unconstitutional since the Gold Coast had not been established by con-
quest, but by a treaty. They sent a deputation to London to appeal to
the Privy Council. This resulted in the early development of a literature
on customary land relations, written by the Gold Coast intelligentsia.
The most important of these works included *Fanti Customary Law* by
John Mensah Sarbah, which appeared in 1897, and two works by

Casely Hayford, *The Truth about the West African Land Question* which appeared in 1898 and *Gold Coast Native Institutions: With Thoughts upon a Healthy Imperial Policy on the Gold Coast,* which appeared in 1903. These works attempted to explain and codify local practices and address policy concerns arising from the British imperial presence. They suggested that customary practice was vital and that it should form the basis on which colonial rule built a modern African state. However, these writings largely represented propertied interests, and the growth of a stratum of concession lawyers and property speculators who had made considerable wealth from transacting land. The Gold Coast elite was legitimately concerned that the Crown Lands Ordinance and the vesting of land in the British crown would prevent them from engaging in land transactions and undermine their commercial interests. However, they couched their positions in terms of the customary rights of Africans to land and the violation of customary land by colonial interventions, rather than in addressing the concerns of modernising land relations and creating reforms to promote economic growth (Howard 1978).

The Crown Lands Ordinance was also opposed by British mercantile interests in West Africa, organised through the Liverpool, Manchester, and London Chambers of Commerce. They opposed increasing state intervention and argued that this would hinder private investment in West Africa. With increasing popular agitation against the Crown Lands Ordinance, the legislation was rescinded on technical grounds and replaced by the Lands Bill of 1897. The Lands Bill declared all waste land within the colony to be Crown Land. This formulation was again opposed by the ARPS, which following Mensah Sarbah (1897) argued that all land on the Gold Coast had an owner, and that the declaration of Crown Lands was a violation of the rights of the people of the Gold Coast. The Forest Bill of 1910 was also met by popular opposition within the Gold Coast. The clauses to place all unused forest land under government for management for posterity were regarded as an attempt to re-introduce the Lands Bill through the back door (Kimble 1963).

During this period colonial policy circles for West Africa were polarised by debates between those who supported constructivist imperialism and a more *laissez-faire* policy based on liberalism. Constructivist imperialism, as advocated by Chamberlain, advocated direct intervention of the colonial government in promoting industrial investment in Africa to transform the economy. The liberals, on the other hand, whose position was vociferously advocated by E.D. Morel, supported the development of West Africa as a region of peasant agriculture production, producing agricultural resources for European markets with minimal interventions from the state (Cowen and Shenton 1994; Phillips 1989). Those advocating constructivist imperialism supported control of the land by the colonial state, while the liberals supported a more indirect arrangement involving alliances with the tribal nations of West Africa. The liberal position gained the ascendancy, and colonial administration was established through a policy of Indirect Rule, in which colonial rule was effected through an alliance with traditional rulers organised into Native Authorities, overseen by District Commissioners. From this period, the management of land came under the authority of chiefs, and the British colonial administration supported the privileges of chiefs and their control over land and natural resources. Chiefs were recognised as the only social group who could transact land. A theory of African communal tenure was developed, in which land was vested in chiefs to manage on behalf of the communities. This effectively constrained the development of free land markets and speculation in land, since land could now only be transacted by chiefs with concessionaires.

This theory of African communal tenure was largely worked out in southern Nigeria, through the precedence set in the case of Amadu Tijani, which was brought before the Privy Council in London in 1928. During the nineteenth century, land sales were prevalent in the Lagos Colony, with many migrants including the Saro, recently returned Brazilian freed slaves, purchasing significant tracts of land. In the nineteenth century, land in Lagos lay under the control of the *Idejo* chiefs, who had the power to allocate unoccupied land under their jurisdiction to family heads and migrants (Cowen and Shenton 1994). The *Idejo* shared temporal and spiritual power with the *Akarigberes* (the royal chiefs), the *Ogalades* (spiritual chiefs), the *Agagbons* (war chiefs) and the *Oba*, the political head of Lagos society. Cowen and Shenton (1994:232) stress that this complex of power:

> (...) never had the time to become 'traditional'. Rather, it was an accretion of the political culture of those who had made Lagos their home, further modified in an accelerating fashion from the beginning of the nineteenth century onwards as a result of economic growth and the dramatic increase in immigration into the Lagos area, which followed the economic expansion of Lagos.

By virtue of their control over land, the power and economic wealth of the *Idejo* chiefs had grown during the nineteenth century. By 1910, over half of Lagos land had been sold to migrants. In 1913, the government of Southern Nigeria expropriated 250 acres under the Public Lands Ordinance of 1903. The *Idejo* chief of this land, the *Oluwa*, Amadu Tijani applied for compensation, claiming that the land constituted a portion of his personal estate. The claim was rejected by the Supreme Court of the colony on the basis that it had no validity in customary law. The *Oluwa* appealed to the Privy Council in London. In their appeal to the Privy Council, the council for the *Oluwa* changed the original petition, arguing that the land in question constituted the land of the community, of which the *Oluwa* was the elected head and trustee. Compensation was demanded upon the basis of trusteeship over customary land. The case revolved around what constituted authentic Yoruba customary law, and this was established through readings of missionary and government official reports. The final decision found that individual ownership was foreign to native ideas, and that land was vested in communities or families, but not individuals. While community members held rights to use the land, the land was vested in the chief as its trustee. The Privy Council rejected the nineteenth century history of Lagos as an aberration. Quoting from Chief Justice Rayner's *Report on Land Tenure in West Africa,* Lord Haldane declared: 'There is a pure native custom along the whole length of the coast, and wherever we find, as in Lagos, individual owners, this is again due to the introduction of English ideas' (quoted in Cowen and Shenton 1994:242). The *Oluwa* won his claim to compensation, but only by acceding to British colonial notions of what constituted communal or customary tenure. The ruling on this case now set a precedent for the whole British Empire on what constituted communal land tenure. Cowen and Shenton (1994) argue that this conception of communal land tenure was rooted in European philosophical notions rather than in an empirical analysis of land relations in African societies.

In the Gold Coast, this theory of communal land tenure was used to constrain and control land sales. Land was vested in the hands of paramount chiefs who possessed allodial rights over land, and who were the only social group able to sell land. Through control over paramount chiefs, the colonial government was able to control land. The construct of customary land that developed in the 1920s sits uneasily with history. It did not reflect the social relations and transactions in lands that had existed in the nineteenth century. In Asante, for instance, wealthy lords and chiefs could sell and pledge settlements under their control, including both land and inhabitants. Wilks (1975) writes that in the nineteenth century the *Mamponhene* sold the three villages of Safo, Nantan, and Asoromaso, in the vicinity of Ntonso to the *Asantehene* Opoku Ware for 100 peredwan (225 ounces) of gold. Wilks (1975:107-108) comments:

> Although sales prices have not been systematically recorded and analysed the market in towns and villages was clearly a lively one. One *Asokorehene* (...) sold to Kumase the town of Asokore

and all of its villages (...). When Nunu *Akyeremadehene* of Kumase, incurred a debt of 30 peredwans, he decided to put his
land and people up for sale; the *Asantehene* Osei Kwadwo purchased them, and granted them to the new Hiawu Stool.

Early land sales on the Gold Coast

In the southeast of the Gold Coast, land sales had developed during
the early nineteenth century, as Krobo and Akwapem farmers expanded their territories beyond their boundaries into land under the
Akyem. These lands were not purchased from paramount chiefs, but
often from town chiefs. Originally, the Krobo entered into oil palm production by seizing lands from their neighbours. As they began to develop a prosperous economy, they sued for peace with their neighbours,
offering to pay them compensation for lands they had seized and
money for any other lands they were willing to sell (Amanor 1994). In
the period between 1830 and 1850 land sales began to develop in this
area. The main vendors of land were the chiefs of Akyem Abuakwa,
and the main purchasers of land were the Krobo and the Akuapem.
Among the Krobo, the military companies that were involved in seizing
land were transformed into land purchasing companies, and the various sections of Krobo methodically purchased land from their neighbours, gradually extending their territory through the purchase of con-
tiguous blocks of land. The Krobo political structure of sectional chiefs
(*wetsongwatsemei*) and generals (*asafotsemei*) of the various sections and
subsections negotiated the purchase of land from Akyem town chiefs
on behalf of their subjects (Amanor 1994).

The early land sales were transacted with a particular ceremony
known as the *guaha,* which represented a contract. The ceremony began with the potential buyers presenting the sellers with drink, which
in the early days was rum. The buyers notified the sellers of their interest in purchasing land. The sellers identified suitable land, and the two
parties to the contract negotiated the price. After the conclusion of the
contract, the sellers then performed a libation in which they reiterated
that the land had been sold outright to the buyers. The sellers then
called on the ancestral spirits of the land to vacate the land and settle
elsewhere. The ceremony was concluded with the buyers and sellers
each putting forward a child who squatted on the ground facing each
other. A leaf from a plant known as *Kesenekesene,* or from a palm tree,
was given to the children. The children pulled the leaf tight until it tore
and each party retained the portion of the leaf as evidence of the transaction. In the case of a dispute, the witnesses to the transaction would
come forward and the two halves of the leaf would be pieced together

to see if they fit. Children were used since they were likely to live long-er as witnesses to the transaction than elders (Opoku 1963).

From the mid-nineteenth to early twentieth century large areas of Akyem territory were alienated to migrants. In the case of the Krobo, much of this territory was incorporated into the Manya and Yilo Krobo states. From the late nineteenth to early twentieth century, many of the land sales were drawn up in written documents. An instance of this is the sale of the land of Odometa by the town chiefs of Begoro in Akyem Abuakwa to the Krobo:

> Know all men by these present that in consideration of the sum one hundred and seventy four pounds and three sheep paid to us and our Chief Gyamarah of Begoro we agreed and approved and sold Odumetta land to Konor E. Mate Kole of Odumase Eastern Krobo (...).
> Therefore at a meeting at Sontreso plantation on 25th October 1907 it was unanimously agreed by ourselves being the Chief and elders of Begoro, to confirm that the abovementioned land is henceforth for ever to be recognised as the property of Kono Mate Kole and his sons and heirs.
> And we further promised to help, defend, and assist the said Ko-nor Mate Kole, his sons and heirs against any attempt to dispute their rights to or to disturb them in occupation, and use the said land which is their bona fide property.
> We therefore in the Year of Our Lord 1907 and on the 28th day of October at Sontriso plantation do make this paper in the pre-sence of the witnesses whose signatures and marks are here at-tached given in good faith to the said Konor Emmanuel Mate Kole of Eastern Krobo a substantial title to the abovementioned land.[2]

Early land sales, before the advent of Indirect Rule, took place within an institutional context that recognised the rights of town chiefs to sell land and the perpetual alienation of the land in these transactions.

The hegemony of the paramount chief in land matters

Under the Native Authority system, land was placed under the jurisdic-tion of the paramount chief. Land relations were determined by what was considered customary practice and by the proclamations of bye-laws by paramount chiefs defining these relations. These Native Authority bye-laws were vetted by the colonial authority.[3] However, through much of the nineteenth century the states of the Gold Coast were characterised by social turmoil, rapid transformation, a series of long interminable wars between polities, and internal conflicts. This hardly provided the stable foundations for reaching a consensual determination of what constituted customary land arrangements. The definitions of customary land relations were essentially inventions of tradition. This was no more the case than in Akyem Abuakwa, which was in many respects the model Native Authority. The paramount chief (*Okyenhene*) Ofori Atta I, an educated Christian with a clerical background, enthusiastically embraced the Native Authority system and became a major architect in the formulation of the Native Administration Ordinance of 1928. Ofori Atta sought to modernise Akyem Abuakwa and centralise control over its vast wealth in natural resources. Rathbone (1993:56) writes that Afori Atta:

> (...) sought to create a command economy in which the centre would control not only taxation but also resource allocation. He tried to control land sales and entrepreneurial activity. In this too he made enemies; and because of this the potential support of the colonial state was an important element in his arsenal.

To establish new economic controls the *Okyenhene* sought to redefine land relations. In the *Akim Abuakwa Handbook*, J.B. Danquah (the nephew and aide to Ofori Atta) wrote:

> Land in Akim Abuakwa belongs to no particular person. All the stool lands in the state are held as communal property by the stools in trust and to the use of the people of Akim Abuakwa. Any member of the Akim Abuakwa tribe can cultivate any forest land in the State without the necessity of having the same sold or leased to him. Proprietary rights in land only begin from the time of occupation, and such occupied area is held by the occupier as and because he is a member of the Akim Abuakwa tribe and a subject of the Paramount Stool. A member of the stool so holding a piece of land can use it for raising any kind of economic activity, for building a residential house, or a mercantile factory. He pays neither rent nor tribute. Only he cannot alienate the communal interest in the land to any person who is not a member of the tribe. The ultimate right of disposal is reserved for and by the state stool in the interest of the public or for the general welfare of the State (Danquah 1928a:43).

This depiction of customary land rights in Akyem was far from what had occurred in Akyem in the not-too-distant past. During the nineteenth century the control of land did not lie under the Paramount

Stool, but with the various town stools. The Akyem Abuakwa state had arisen out of the collapse of the Akwamu Empire in the eighteenth century, in the context of a long civil war, in which various groups that came to constitute the Akyem Abuakwa moved into the area and eventually established political control in 1730. While the Abuakwa dynasty claimed overlordship of this area, it had never been able to consolidate its rule, since it was soon defeated by Asante in 1745. Much of the history of the late eighteenth and early nineteenth century in Abuakwa is made up of wars of resistance to Asante overlordship, and conflicts between different factions and towns allying with and against the Asante. Abuakwa control of the former Akwamu territories was achieved by an alliance with some of the town chiefs of Akwamu towns, who continued to maintain considerable autonomy. Much of the southern area of Abuakwa was never successfully brought under Abuakwa jurisdiction (Wilks 1958). During the nineteenth and in the early twentieth century, land was largely transacted by town chiefs and a considerable area of Akyem land was alienated by these town chiefs to migrant cocoa farmers, before the creation of a system of Native Administration. Without access to the control of significant areas of land, the paramount authority in Abuakwa attempted to redefine land relations to enable it to extract rents from migrant cocoa farmers and to control concessions. With the development of Indirect Rule, Ofori Atta used his new powers to displace the rights of town chiefs to alienate land to immigrants. He declared transactions in land a violation of Akyem custom and attempted to gain access to parts of the proceeds of land rents and royalties (Rathbone 1993). He was instrumental in alienating considerable tracts of land and signing mining concessions. In this, he was backed by the colonial authority, which supported the idea that the Akyem Paramount Stool was entitled 'by native custom' to one-third of all rents and profits of alienated land. He extracted considerable revenues from migrant cocoa farmers within his domain. Since Ofori Atta was frequently consulted by the colonial authority in drafting native administration legislation he was able to 'use the law skilfully within the Indirect Rule structure (...) to ordain what was and was not "customary" law' (Rathbone 1993:62)

The attempts by the *Okyenhene* to refashion customary rights stirred up considerable opposition in Akyem Abuakwa. Other social interest groups began to contest this particular interpretation of the customary and to articulate their own interests within the framework of customary rights, pointing out how those in authority violated customary norms, and presenting their actions and opposition as based on the real precedent of custom. The town chiefs in Akyem began to insist upon their customary rights to transact land. When diamonds were found in the Akwatia and Asamankese area, the chiefs of these towns

insisted on their historical rights to claim control over these resources
and to negotiate the concessions. When this failed, they then insisted
on their historical rights to secession from the Abuakwa state, leading
to a protracted court case (Addo-Fening 1997; Rathbone 1993).

Similarly, the selling of land and attempts to impose forced labour,
fines and fees, and other exactions on commoners led to a resurgence
of popular organisation. The commoners began to revive the *asafo* companies and transform them into political organisations. Historically,
the *asafo* were paramilitary organisations, which mobilised commoners
for military service in wartime and social infrastructure development
in peacetime. They also played important roles in representing the interests of commoners and in destooling (dethroning) unpopular chiefs.
This role was consolidated and built upon in the colonial period. In colonial Akyem and neighbouring Kwahu, commoners reshaped the *asafo*
to defend their interests and to develop checks on the newfound
powers of chiefs under Indirect Rule, through mass demonstrations
(Simensen 1975b). Commenting on the *asafo* movement in Kwahu,
Asiamah (2000: 73) writes:

> Notably, the Asafo severely criticized the astronomical court
> fines imposed upon the commoners accused of breaking the
> chiefs' oath, laws and taboos. Other more serious charges were
> bribery and misappropriation of stool land revenues. For in-
> stance, money that accrued from land sales, tolls, special levies,
> timber concessions, mineral concessions, cocoa revenues, and
> others, were freely squandered, as if they were the personal in-
> comes of the chiefs while the commoner who toiled to bring in
> the revenue did not benefit from his labour.

In Akyem Abuakwa, commoner perceptions of wide scale abuses of
privilege by chiefs under Indirect Rule led to a movement to destool
unpopular chiefs. Between 1904 and 1944 thirty-five chiefs were destooled in Abuakwa. During the 1930s, the *Okyenhene* became the focus of attempts at destoolment from both the *asafo* and town chiefs. In
1932 the *Okyenhene* was saved from destoolment by the intervention of
a colonial force sent to defend him. In neighbouring Kwahu, two paramount chiefs were destooled in 1915 and 1927 (Asiamah 2000).

By the 1950s, the *asafo* movement had become integrated into the
anti-colonial struggle, and a major support base for the radical wing of
the Convention People's Party, as a wave of destoolments developed.
Amamoo (1958:99) comments:

> (...) many people were beginning by the end of 1950 to associate
> the chiefs with British rule. The situation was worsened by the

rather too close friendship between some of the chiefs and the
British officers, by a statement from Nkrumah to the effect that
reactionary and other chiefs who refused to move with the people would be destooled, and by the spasmodic waves of 'destoolment' of chiefs which swept the country between the period
1949 to 1952. The chiefs, therefore, felt their position was at
stake; and their institutions in danger of being abolished.

By the late 1940s, the Native Administration system lay in tatters. It
was now clear that the system of chieftaincy did not reflect the social
heterogeneity of many of the areas over which they presided and had
alienated much of the population. As Macmillan (1946:90-91) commented:

> The Akim country, in particular has not only scattered aliens as
> individual owners but whole village communities of 'alien' occu-
> pants. In many market towns, of which Suhum is an often
> quoted type, the aliens are definitely in the majority (...). and yet
> the only local tribunals are those of the home tribe, with appeal
> to the local tribal Paramount. The worst feature of all this is that
> anything up to 20 per cent of the population of such towns are
> Northern Territories labourers (....). But the labourers must look
> for redress of grievances in the first instances to a tribal court,
> which is certainly not their own, and may very often be com-
> posed if not of their actual employers then of their employers'
> friends and relatives (...). In some of the cocoa country, and cer-
> tainly in the towns, one-tribe courts are therefore an anachron-
> ism. It is a fair inference that successful government in the Gold
> Coast demands a revision by the Colonial Office of its exclusive
> devotion to a doctrine of Indirect Rule based on tribal institu-
> tion. The confusion, finally, as it concerns both land-ownership
> and those questions of tribal jurisdiction, is constantly spreading
> to any area newly brought under cocoa, especially in the Wes-
> tern Province, but also in Ashanti and Togoland.

During 1948, riots and looting spread through the major urban centres
in the Gold Coast. A Commission of Enquiry was set up under Aitken
Watson to examine the underlying causes of the disturbances. Many of
the commoners or young men consulted by the Commission complained of the system of Native Administration, the autocratic impositions made by chiefs and elders on the population at large, and the lack
of any democratic representation of the commoners. These representations called for the establishment of a system of local democracy and
the reduction of the role of the chief to an ornamental figure. The re-

commendations of the Watson Commission were taken up by the Coussey Committee, which was charged with making practical recommendations for constitutional reform based on the findings of the Watson Commission, and the creation of a system of democratically elected local government. However, the Coussey Committee was sympathetic to the institution of chieftaincy and made some provision for chiefs to be represented in local government and to preside over its functioning. While democratic election of local authorities marked the transition years to independence, chiefs had rights to appoint one-third of local representatives and continued to enjoy rights of control over land. Since independence, one-third of local government representatives continue to be appointed by configurations of government, chiefs, and alliances between chiefs and central government. This has effectively blocked downward accountability and popular reform in local government (Aryee 1992; Crook and Manor 1998).

Since independence, no deep-seated reform of land tenure has been carried out. While chiefly revenues now officially come under government scrutiny and administration, there has been no attempt to reform the rights of cultivators and provide them with security of tenure. The allodial rights of chiefs have often been upheld and used by government, which frequently works through the chiefs to expropriate peasant cultivators. Governments continue to maintain the claims of chiefs on allodial rights in land, since it often serves the interests of the political elite. These claims enable rural farmers to be easily expropriated in the national interest or in the interest of development. Compensation for the land is only paid to the chief as the owner, while farmers only receive compensation for the crop on the land. Thus the chiefs gain direct economic benefit from the expropriation of their subjects. However, the provision of land titling options within land management institutions protects the investments of commercial investors in land, since those with title can claim compensation for land. Through the existence of complicated and expensive titling procedures, an exclusive system of land titling is maintained which prevents peasant farmers from protecting their rights in land and thus maintains their vulnerability to expropriation, while creating different rights for the rich and privileged.

Family land, accumulation, and frontiers

Since the late nineteenth century, cocoa developed as a frontier crop in which large groups of migrant farmers accumulated capital, investing capital in the purchase of new land in forest areas and the conversion of land into cocoa plantations (Hill 1963). The cocoa farmers depended

upon family labour and migrant hired labour for production. They attracted members of their extended family lineages to work with them.
In return for helping them establish their cocoa plantations the relatives were provided with gifts of land and the inheritance of cocoa plantations they had helped to create. Profits acquired in cocoa were rapidly
reinvested in new land and plantations. This led to the rapid development of the cocoa frontier throughout the forest region of Ghana.
From its beginning in the Eastern Region in the nineteenth century,
the cocoa frontier rapidly expanded into Ashanti, the Central Region,
Brong Ahafo, and the Western Region. The opening up of the frontier
resulted in a diverse ethnic population within the forest region in Ghana, as farmers from all previous frontiers migrated to the new frontier.
Today the frontier has exhausted itself: there are no new frontier areas
in Ghana in which new lands can be opened up and new purchases of
empty forestland made.

Figure 3.1   *The cocoa frontier*

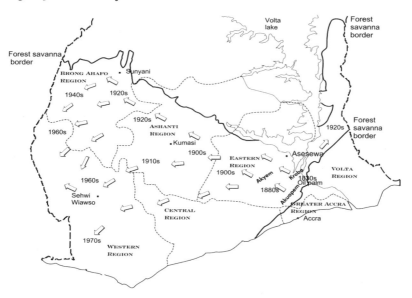

Source: Amanor 1994

The cocoa frontier has led to the rapid alienation of land and has often
created shortages of land for the youth and subsequent generations.
This affects both the autochthonous population in the new frontier
areas and the migrants. With the development of land sales to cocoa
farmers, chiefs began to define their alienable stool lands (that is the
areas which they could transact with non-locals) as the areas within

their domain, which were not occupied by the existing or autochthonous farming population. They began selling these lands to migrants
to gain revenues from them. Since the local farming population had
rights as citizens to farm freely, chiefs could only gain revenues by selling land to migrants or finding other ways of expropriating land from
locals. Chiefs were also under pressure to carry out rapid alienation of
the land, since the expansion of local farmers into cocoa production
would result in a decline in the area of land chiefs could sell or transact
with migrants. The development of cocoa, thus, created new interests
in land for chiefs that had not existed before. This essentially led to a
redefinition of stool lands as lands that could be transacted by the stool
under conditions of expanded commodity production, export agriculture, and integration into world commodity markets.

Family relations and commodification: Migrants, youth, elders and chiefs

Until the 1920s, the dominant form of transaction between chiefs and
migrants was the direct sale and alienation of land for cash. However,
land purchasers often paid in instalments, and maximised accumulation of land for plantation development by making multiple payments
of instalments on different plots of land, and by delaying the final payments of instalments (Hill 1963). By the 1920s, there was a large influx of labour into the cocoa belt, largely from Northern Ghana and
neighbouring Sahelian countries. These migrants came from regions
that had been integrated into the colonial economy as labour reserves,
where imposition of taxation forced men to migrate to the colonial en-
claves to gain money with which tax obligations could be met. The cocoa belt in the Gold Coast was one of the most popular and favoured
destinations for migrant labourers. This influx enabled migrant farmers to hire labour and expand farm operations. It also enabled chiefs to
develop new arrangements in which they released land to labourers or
tenants rather than sell land outright to purchasers.

Sharecropping arrangements began to predominate from the 1920s
(Austin 1987; Hill 1956). Chiefs would release mature forestland to migrant farmers (with some capital) who were responsible for converting
it into cocoa plantation. In some arrangements the cocoa plantation
was then divided between the chiefly stool and the sharecrop tenant,
and the portion worked by the tenant was recognised as their own
land. In other arrangements, the tenant gained a share of the yield, or
paid a rent (often a third of the yield) to the chief. The terms of these
sharecrop arrangements varied in different areas and different periods.
Through sharecrop arrangements chiefly stools were able to acquire
considerable cocoa plantations without directly investing in labour.
After the cocoa plantation was created, it could be hired out to a mi-

grant caretaker who gained a third of the proceeds or harvest from the plantation, or an annual labourer who was paid a fixed sum after the cocoa was harvested and sold. The terms of arrangements on these lands have often changed, with chiefs introducing new arrangements as land became scarce and applying these arrangements retrospectively to other farmers, or creating new exactions, tributes, and rents on migrant farmers (Boni 2005). This often led to insecurity of tenure for migrant farmers.

With the attempts of paramount chiefs to claim a monopoly on the sale of land from the 1920s, sharecrop arrangements became popular. They often served as forms of disguised sales of land, through which farmers and town chiefs could transact land without being challenged by paramount chiefs or members of their lineages claiming the sale to be a violation of custom. In the cocoa belt sharecrop transactions became more frequent than land sales from the 1920s onwards.

The sale of land by chiefs to migrant cocoa farmers has resulted in land shortage for local youth, particularly in the Eastern and Western Regions. This has frequently led to resentment of migrants by local youth (Amanor 2001; Boni 2005). In many areas, the dominant rural populations are overwhelmingly migrants. In some situations, chiefs have been able to manipulate the local youth's resentment of migrant farmers to make increasing exactions from migrants. When the migrants resist these actions, chiefs mobilise local youth to take actions against them, often making claims that the migrants have abused the hospitality that was extended to them and have encroached into lands that they were not allocated. Boni (2005) recounts how the Sefwi District Council decided to register 'stranger farmers' in the early 1950s, with the aim of organising a more efficient system of land revenue collection in which the migrant tenants had to renegotiate land agreements. The migrants refused to comply and the chiefs sent in local youth to dispossess strangers of their farms. As violence spread, the government was forced to intervene.

The influx of migrant sharecrops and annual labourers often undermined the position of local youth among the rural poor. Farmers could play off family youth against sharecrop tenants, making more demands on youth labour and hiring sharecrop labour to replace family youth when youth were not compliant. This has led to an anti-youth discourse that rural youth are lazy and footloose and unwilling to help their parents on their farms. By the 1970s, youth participation in family cocoa production became increasingly insecure. As land became scarcer youth contributions of labour were devalued by elders. Okali (1983) records many grievances among youth, who worked with their fathers or matrilineal uncle's, only to find that on the death of their patron the plantations they had helped to establish were usurped by the brothers of their fathers. One son, who had managed his father's cocoa plantations, only to find himself displaced by his father's matrilineal heir, bitterly declared: 'If you follow your father you are a fool' (Okali 1983:107). Wary of working for their fathers only to be displaced by matrilineal kin, many sons abandoned their father's cocoa farms when they saw other relatives treated more favourably than them. However, the same fate also befell nephews, who worked on their uncle's plantations only to find themselves displaced from inheriting the land by junior brothers of their maternal uncle. Fathers' attempts to pass on land to heirs were often challenged by other lineage members, as lineage land became increasingly scarce with the decline of new frontier land. Increasing scarcity of land has hindered the transmission of land across generations, as well as the use of gifts of land within the family to build up family labour networks. While in the past farmers would allocate land to nephews and sons, the allocation of land is increasingly challenged. While this allocation is challenged on the basis of customary matrilineal norms, it often results in the breakdown of family relations and their replacement by commodified market relations. Increasing areas of family land are allocated as sharecrop arrangements to non-kin rather than being inherited by kin members.

Without secure access to family land, many youth have chosen to withdraw from the family farm, seek alternative livelihoods, or work as labourers or sharecrop tenants elsewhere. During the 1970s, long distance migrant labour from the Sahelian countries relocated to the Côte d'Ivoire, where the cocoa frontier was still in an expansionary state and land could be acquired on favourable terms. Youth in the Ghanaian forest zone have increasingly been transformed into labourers or sharecroppers, responding to the demand for labour but shortage of family land for redistribution to the new generation. In matrilineal areas, many fathers who work closely with their sons attempt to gain matrilineal land for their children (who do not have inheritance rights) on a sharecrop basis. While the access of the children to land involves payment for land in the form of a sharecrop rent, this creates more secure access which will not be challenged by the family. In areas where land is highly scarce and has acquired a high value, sharecropping has become the dominant form of transaction, and most young people, such as in the Kwaebibirem area of Akyem, gain land through sharecropping rather than through inheritance (Amanor and Diderutuah 2001). Oil palm plantations are recognised as highly profitable but expensive to establish. Rather than release land to family youth, farmers prefer to enter into sharecrop arrangements with those who have sufficient capital to develop oil palm plantations. Customary prestations for the allocation of land have been inflated to levels which prevent poor youth from getting access to land. This assures that those cultivating land are going to cultivate profitable cash crops to recover the costs of their investment in land (Amanor and Diderutuah 2001). Farming has become increasingly commodified. Land and labour are transacted on markets rather than offered or received on the basis of family solidarity.

Women and the commodification of land

The expansion of cocoa and the increasing commodification of land undermine women's rights to land. Prior to the development of cocoa, food crop production was an important activity for women, and men were responsible for clearing forests for their wives to cultivate. With the development of cocoa as a means of accumulation by the wealthy, and the rapid accumulation of land and plantations by wealthy male cocoa farmers, the security of women farmers was undermined. The customary framework of land, articulated in the colonial period, eroded women's rights to land and reinvented women farmers as the wives of male cocoa farmers, who migrated to the new frontier to help them establish cocoa farms. Frequently, women were not remunerated for their activities. One of the women farmers interviewed at Asafo and Maase by Hill during the 1950s commented 'in the olden times we used to help our husbands to get big, big farms; and when they died we got nothing' (Hill 1959:2). The women interviewed by Hill insisted that they worked together as women with daughters and granddaughters, and that women's land passed from mother to daughter. As Hill (1959:3) reports:

> Apart from the assistance given by school children in their holidays, some women are assisted by their elder sons, though they tended to play this down in an interview. It was mentioned that a particular helpful son might be given a farm by his mother during her lifetime. Usually, of course, a women's daughter succeeds to her property and it is considered more appropriate that they should provide for her brother's needs from her mother's farm than that the farm should actually pass to him.

During the 1970s, as land became increasingly scarce, many women who had worked on their husband's cocoa farms increasingly found themselves dispossessed of the cocoa farms by their husband's matrilineage. Okali (1983) found that women were making demands that the farm services they performed be reciprocated in immediate rights in land for themselves and their children. If these demands were not met, they were prepared to divorce their husbands.

With growing insecurity in access to land through marriage, many women are also insisting on their rights to matrilineal land in their

own right. In research carried out in the Akyem settlements of Apinaman and Dwenease during 1999-2000 (Amanor 2001), many women
insisted that they were the true purveyors of the matrilineal tradition,
and that men violated this by passing on land to their own children.
Under matrilineal inheritance, land is transmitted by men to their sis-
ter's children rather than their own children (although in the past, institutions have existed which allowed fathers to make gifts of property
to their own children and to other people who have served them). A
woman at Apinaman stated:

> Women usually pass on lands to their daughters and grand-
> daughters. That is the tradition here because men do not belong
> to the *abusua* [matrilineage]. If you give land to the son, it goes
> out of the *abusua*; but if it goes to the women, it will stay home.
> If you give land to the boys and they happen to give birth the
> land will go to the wife's children. A father can always give out
> his land as a gift to his children. In that case, it becomes the
> property of his children and they can sell it out or develop it for
> their own use.

Some women also controversially challenged the right of men to matrilineal family land. One young woman confided:

> We are three sisters and a brother. Our mother's brother (*wofa*)
> is dead, and he has left a large tract of land for us, which is lying
> fallow. We are planning to meet here to share the land among
> us. We are planning that we will not give our brother any part of
> the land because it will allow him to develop part of it and leave
> it to his children. So he has to find his own land elsewhere,
> since he is not going to marry from our family. We can develop
> what is there, little by little, for our children.

Young women at Apinaman aggressively asserted their rights to matrilineal land over their brothers. This becomes increasingly necessary, as
intergenerational conflicts exist between men. This serves to prevent
sons, who become increasingly estranged from their fathers and
mother's brothers, from approaching their mother for land, thus
further eroding land available to women. This assertion of a matrifocal
ideology serves to cast doubts on the legitimacy of men's customary
rights to control matrilineal property and their transparency in managing matrilineal property. It promotes female solidarity within the lineage, and consolidates women's defence of their property rights in land
and its erosion by male control of property and the increasing commodification of agricultural production. Many women farm in matrifocal

units consisting of three generations of women (grandmother, mother, and daughter). Divorce is high and many women look to these matrifocal units rather than to the conjugal family for security. Paradoxically, this matrifocal identity threatens the rights of married women to receive land from their husbands. Nevertheless, it is symptomatic of the pressures of commodification of agriculture on family relations, and the tensions that ensue within the family as customary forms of reciprocity break down.

The commodification of land and the rights of cultivators

In policy circles, customary land rights are frequently associated with the allodial rights of chiefs to land, or the rights of chiefs to sell land. However, these are very modern notions, which could only occur in the context of the development of land markets and migrant farmers willing to purchase land. Without the development of frontier markets for land for export crop production, the issue of allodial rights and clearly defined customary rights does not arise. The definition of the allodial only acquires economic significance in the context of the alienation of land. Where everyone has only a use right to land, allodial rights do not carry any significant economic connotation. Allodial rights only acquire significance where there is an influx of migrants without rights of use and where land is transacted with these categories of people. Allodial interests thus only arise at the juncture where land is being commodified. This was clearly recognised by Field (1948:7) when she commented:

> The new income from mines and land sales means that the land, originally valueless to the *oman* [state] and quite independent of it, has become linked to the *oman*. The *oman* does not control or own it, but has acquired a very acute interest (in the non-legal sense) in it.

Since chiefs cannot sell land to insiders the assertion of allodial interests only arises in the situation of demands on land by outsiders and investors, in the context of the commodification of land. This can be clearly understood if we examine conceptions of customary land in areas where the commodification of land is not highly developed.

In the northern transition zone of Brong Ahafo, population densities are low, frequently below twenty people per square kilometre. Land can be acquired by migrant farmers for nominal annual fees. These fees are not linked to the area cultivated; they merely establish permission to cultivate and recognition of the landlord. Citizens have rights to

farm anywhere in the land of their settlement where other people are
not actively farming or managing fallow. Farmers claim land according
to their labour power. They usually farm together along a line moving
forward, until the land they have left behind is well regenerated, when
they may chose to return to farm and begin a cycle of rotational bush
fallowing or shifting cultivation. When farmers meet other farmers
clearing from the opposite direction, they are forced to return to the
lands at their back, reorient their direction of clearing, or move to a
new area. Rights to land are established through the investment of labour in clearing vegetation. In this situation, farmers' lands are constantly changing in relation to farming strategies and available labour.
Rights to land are clearly recognised within the communities and determined by customary norms and conventions. However, these notions of land rights to the tiller do not fit easily into modern notions of
ownership of specific areas, which can be mapped, digitised, placed in
databases, and transacted in land markets and 'one stop shops'.

Figure 3.2   *Land management under rotational bush fallowing*

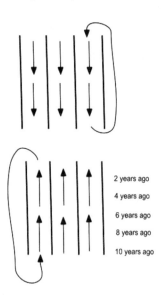

Rights to land are established through
clearance. Farmers move forwards, abreast
to each other, until they meet farmers clearing
from another direction. They will then return to
the land they originally cleared, which by then
will usually have regenerated well, and start
farming in the same direction. If they leave
the land they originally farmed on for too long
someone else may claim it. They claim
rights to the various lands they use
in their rotating fallow and cultivation cycles.

2 years ago

4 years ago

6 years ago

8 years ago

10 years ago

The security of landholdings within this system only breaks down
when chiefs begin to transact the land and allocate it to external investors. Unable to extract revenues from local cultivators, chiefs look to
the development of new high value crops and welcome external investors to develop the land, or when such investors move into their localities concepts of land begin to change. In the transition zone of Brong

Ahafo, chiefs are currently allocating large areas of land to investors in teak, cashew, and exotic mango. Eventually, these new investments will create land shortage for the food crop farmers and disrupt their fallow management strategies. Policymakers usually define the customary as occurring at this juncture, when chiefs begin to allocate land to external investors, and plots begin to be demarcated, rather than at the juncture where user rights in land prevails. The concept of the customary is used to empower chiefs to sell the land to the external investors and to create the necessary reforms to facilitate this transaction. The customary has thus from the early colonial period come to define the privilege of chiefs and their rights to alienate land to external investors as part of a process of commodification.

This is very apparent in the changes in land use in the grasslands of the southern Krobo areas situated in the Accra plains. Export mangoes are becoming a new crop, and external investors are now keen to acquire land in this area. This is transforming land values in a formerly highly marginal agricultural environment. An article in *Ghana Regional News* of 18 September 2005, states:

> The Eastern Regional Minister, Mr. Yaw Barimah, has suggested to the chiefs of Manya Krobo Traditional Area to take a second look at their land tenure system with a view to releasing land for commercial mango farming. He explained that mangoes grow well in the area and their cultivation could form the raw material base for the development of agro-industry to provide employment for the youth of the area.

This speech of the Regional Minister reveals many of the problems and concerns with current initiatives to strengthen customary tenure, defined as chiefly control over land. The empowerment of chiefs by the state to control land serves to enable chiefs to transform or re-invent tenure systems to serve the interests of elites. The chiefs are being asked to create reforms that will enable lands to be released to commercial mango farmers, presumably at the expense of the local population. The main role envisaged for youth is as providers of labour for agribusiness, which presumes their expropriation from the land and their inability to engage in independent livelihoods. In this context the phrase 'taking a second look' amplifies the process through which customary land tenure systems are recreated in the present. They are about commoditising land and creating the conditions under which land becomes transferred to investors with clear and undisputed ownership rights attached to them. While these land rights may have been appropriated from others, they cannot be challenged, since they are authenticated by customary authorities with power to define and redefine land rights. The customary (as represented by chiefs) thus serves to authenticate the commoditisation and appropriation of land and to transfer user rights into alienable rights.

Conclusion

In the present economic climate land and natural resources are increasingly being transacted in global markets and opened to investors. However, as new frontier areas decline, land resources are also becoming increasingly scarce and the source of competition. Future processes of accumulation and new investment are likely to take place through processes of dispossession of land users. The strengthening of chiefly control over land creates conditions for the expropriation of the peasantry. It enables chiefs to claim control over land and to redefine land relations. It absolves the state from blame for expropriating the rural poor. However, in reality, the state empowers chiefs to control land and enables them to define processes of appropriation, by insisting on mythical definitions of customary rights that serve to disempower individual cultivators of land, while promoting the customary as an egalitarian system which stands for the interests of the community. Without tacit support and recognition from the state and support for their version of customary tenure, chiefs would have little power to enforce their versions of customary tenure.

Although chiefs claim to be the customary custodians of land and of communities, in reality many chiefs form part of the modern elite. Many of them are businessmen in their own right. Modern and customary elites straddle each other. They intermarry; and they are members of the same political parties, religious associations and other elite associations. Businessmen use their wealth to gain chiefly titles and wealthy sections of chiefly families are able to wrest succession from poorer lines of the chiefly families (Arhin 2001). Chieftaincy is an institution that is closely associated with processes of accumulation and the redefinition of tradition to support accumulation. While strengthening of chieftaincy may promote processes of decentralised administration this often promotes highly unequal development.

The notion of customary land tenure has always been contested in Ghana. There are diverse concepts of the customary used by various groups to defend their rights against violation. This includes the rights of citizens to claim land through its transformation through their labour; the rights of women to create female property; the rights of youth to a livelihood; the rights of youth to hold elders accountable through demonstrations and threats of mob violence; the codes of conduct worked out by shifting cultivators as they move across the land. There are diverse interest groups in rural society and contested definitions of the customary and the ways in which social relations should be ordered and reformed. However, these interests are poorly represented in policy circles which, hark back to the era of Indirect Rule, associate customary rights with the rights of chiefs to define and redefine control over land and the power to allocate land on the market. In the policy world the notion of the customary functions as a rhetorical device in the context of social upheaval to justify attempts to impose control on fluid and changing situations by those with power, and to redefine dominant interests.

While chiefly rights and representations are being strengthened in the contemporary period in policy circles, the rural areas are characterised by considerable social turmoil and upheaval. The decline of new frontier areas, the inroads of agribusiness in the rural areas, and the commodification of agriculture and land is increasingly transforming existing social relations within the family in agricultural production. Family farming relations are increasingly replaced by individualised agriculture in which land and labour becomes increasingly commodified and subject to market relations. Youth are no longer guaranteed access to family land. These upheavals make it important to investigate the actual living conditions of people and the changing social relations of production, rather than to engage in abstract and dogmatic assertions and definition of the customary based on ideas deriving from colonial administrative frameworks. It is important to document changing social and production relations in agriculture and to address the implications of the increasing commodification of agriculture for peasant cultivators, for the rural poor, labourers, women, and youth. It is also important to open a debate in society about the ways in which people want their land relations to be structured, rather than leaving it to government and chiefs to jointly redefine and recreate new customary land tenure systems that meet the requirements of liberalised markets.

Notes

1   Lord Haldane presided over the Privy Council in London and in this role played an important role in defining customary land rights in the British Empire.
2   Ghana National Archives, ADM 11/457 case no 23 of 1913, Sale of Odometa.
3   This did not apply to the Northern Territories, which were mainly incorporated into the colonial administration as a labour reserve, and where land came directly under government control.

4 Traditional ambiguities and authoritarian interpretations in Sefwi land disputes

Stefano Boni

In the course of the twentieth century, academic literature, chiefly discourses, national legislation, government intervention, and court procedures have largely converged on a set of principles that is thought to provide the essential features of Akan land tenure. First, Akan land tenure is seen as grounded in tradition, which implies that a clear set of criteria of title allocation have persisted unchanged over centuries. Second, chiefs are said to hold land titles on behalf of the community, thus providing a general benefit and guaranteeing an equitable distribution (Addo-Fening 1987). Third, conflicts are considered the result of misunderstandings on the interpretation of tradition; courts and arbitration panels solve these quarrels and restore peace. These three principles have formed the axioms of the land tenure orthodoxy, which the prevalent and official discourse considers to be the correct distribution and management of titles. However, though the land tenure orthodoxy claims to be a faithful description, it does not, as we shall see, describe how land tenure dynamics are actually played out. The representation of land tenure contained in these three statements mystifies, in the sense that these land tenure assumptions systematically inhibit an understanding of facts and explanatory links. Rather, the production of a simplified and false land tenure representation – while not providing the tools to understand how land tenure is played out in villages – acts as a powerful normative and prescriptive statement, asserting how land tenure *should* be understood and managed, according to the wishes of those who put forward this particular representation of land tenure.

The mystifying discourse on Ghanaian land tenure is anonymous in the sense that it has involved, in various ways, different social actors: legal scholars principally writing down what they thought or were told was customary land tenure, focussing only on legal formulation and court proceedings with little attention to actual dynamics; politicians translating academic research – mostly by legal scholars – into legislation; judges and administrators selectively enforcing legal schema in people's lives through court houses and stool land administration; and of course chiefs and elders producing a persistent and abundant array of oral traditions to sustain their role as landowners. The interplay between these different agents – with convergent discourses – generated

a standardised land tenure orthodoxy that became the framework within which most land tenure issues were understood and addressed. I argue that different actors located in academia, in parliament, and in palaces across the country have converged on the utilisation of a certain
understanding of 'tradition' and on what are to be considered its legitimate contemporary applications. The prevalent use of the idiom of tradition has sustained the preservation of certain inequalities. There have
been social studies, based on in-depth fieldwork and on empirical evidence, stressing disputes, power relations, and negotiations (See Amanor 1999, 2001, 2002; Arhin 1986; Beckett 1944, 1945; Benneh 1970,
1988; Berry 2001; Chauveau 1982; Garceau 1982; Grier 1987; Hill
1963; Ninsin 1989). Overall, however, this empirical research has had
only a minor impact on prevalent and official land tenure discourses –
both at national and local levels – as well as on the formulation of
legislation.

This chapter questions the land tenure orthodoxy. It aims for a general reconsideration, not just of the details but of the overall framework
of land tenure studies, with two objectives. First, prevailing land tenure
discourses claim to provide a clear and reliable understanding of what
is happening on the ground, whereas these representations in fact
show wide divergence with local realities. This chapter advocates a rejection of notions such as 'tradition' and 'custom' to be able to grasp
the transformations, indeterminacy, negotiations, and conflicts. Second, the dominant land tenure rhetoric presents land tenure as communitarian and equitable, while the opposite is true. The 'traditionali-
sation' of land tenure, the representation of current dynamic as if these
have remained unchanged since an unspecified past, inhibits the focus
on conflicts except as legal confrontations aimed at establishing the
'true owner'. The overall organisation and distribution of land prerogatives has, however, been constantly questioned by marginalised groups.
Land disputes are, nevertheless, not seen as struggles produced by conflicting interests but inserted in the idiom of 'tradition' and judged according to presumed violations of custom.

In the first section of this chapter I critically review three key concepts: custom, ownership, and dispute. The definition of these notions
is crucial both to illustrate the flows of the prevalent land tenure discourse and to formulate a description accounting for the power struggles over land. In the second section, I describe the judiciary channels
active in the Sefwi Wiawso district. In the third section, I illustrate historically land disputes in the Sefwi Wiawso District of the Western Region with reference to four criteria: chiefly rank, ancestry, age, and gender. These criteria are both principles according to which land has been
unevenly distributed and the *loci* of land disputes. I demonstrate that
'customary' land tenure in the course of the twentieth century has

shifted constantly, elaborating new norms. These rules and their contextual application, moreover, change in relation to people's ancestral
identities, their gender, and their age. While norms have changed, the
key principles of the land tenure orthodoxy have remained unaltered
and have produced and perpetuated an unequal distribution of land
prerogatives. In the conclusion I return to the principal argument of
this chapter: the relation between power structures and the formulation
of an ambiguous land tenure discourse and legislation. Those with the
power to interpret custom (i.e. chiefs, elders, men, those identified as
'natives', and government officials) have been concerned with preserving this indeterminacy, as it guarantees the faculty to determine the allocation of land rights and revenues.

A critical review of crucial concepts in land disputes

Over the last century agricultural land in southern Ghana was a crucial
resource that became increasingly scarce, generating conflicts over the
attribution of titles. The continuous and dramatic land disputes that
emerged in the course of the twentieth century can hardly be understood within the framework of the existing land tenure orthodoxy. Both
the understanding and the organisation of land tenure urgently need
to undergo deconstructive public scrutiny. While the principal assumptions of current land tenure legislation are grounded in the conservative evocation of 'tradition' and ancestral rights, the actual management
of land tenure is best understood with reference to interest-driven politics. Before presenting ethnographic illustrations of conflicts concerning land, I show that the concepts of custom, ownership, and dispute
are often presented in ways that tend to obfuscate rather than promote
an understanding of the causes and unfolding of disputes.

Custom

Ghanaian land law – both legislation promoted by the government and
its 'ethnic' variants promoted by chiefs in the Traditional Councils –
has been conceptually and legally founded on the idea of a clear, stable
set of customary rules grounded in a past unspecified both historically
and geographically. Land legislation from the colonial period up to the
1992 Constitution is presented as the continuation of ancestral principles and values (Aidoo 1996; Kasanga 1988; Ollennu 1962; Woodman
1996). These are said to be characterised by the beneficial effects of a
hierarchical management of land. Crucial in this respect is the idea
that the head of a social unit (kingdom, village, lineage, household)
controls land rights for the general benefit: the chief is thus seen as

the custodian of the community's land; the lineage head as the custodian of the family land; and the household head as the custodian on
behalf of subordinate members. This fiction, upheld and justified by
the state and chiefs as 'custom', has largely been a legal fabrication
that, in village disputes, allows these prominent figures to preserve
their privileges and contextually adapt these to twentieth century economic transformations. Although 'custom' is presented as the foundation of fair land tenure legislation, it has not generated convenient and
equitable solutions at a local level. While the use of 'custom' claims to
clarify existing titles, it produces ambiguities for two reasons. First,
there have been multiple agents (the state, the Traditional Councils, individual chiefs, elders) that have competed in the formulation of
norms, all evoking tradition while defining it differently. Second, the
legal apparatus derived from the 'customary' understanding of land
prerogatives – transplanted in the 1992 Constitution – uses a conceptual framework and terminology that renders its application in villages
virtually impossible. The actual process of definition of property rights
over land in villages is irreducible to the legal idiom: the complex, dynamic, and multifaceted title negotiations that actually occur need to
be greatly simplified, frozen, and mutilated to be squeezed within the
legal conceptual schemes. Contemporary customary land tenure is a
contradiction yet to be acknowledged.

Ownership

It is well established that titles over land in Ghana involve a multiplicity of parties holding rights alongside each other. Some have proposed
the notion of stratified rights: according to this view, prerogatives are
clearly ranked (Aidoo 1996:3; Bentsi-Enchill 1964; Kasanga 1988:30-31;
Kyerematen 1971:24, 39-40, 97-123; Ollennu 1962:119). My view, however, is that land claims are exercised by each actor to an extent that is
determined by the outcome of confrontations, played out on the capacity to achieve recognition and the complicity of those recognised as
the rightful interpreters of land tenure, the two processes obviously
moving together (cf. Chauveau 1982; Lavigne Delville et al. 2002).
Rights are thus not static but continuously negotiated within structures
of power: there is no party that is inherently and eternally doomed to
hold a marginal right. Prerogatives are thus flexible and partial, as they
are shared with other parties. The legislative and scholarly codification
of traditional land tenure, however – clearly influenced by a colonial
setting aimed at preserving a powerful chieftaincy (Grier 1987) –
named the chiefly prerogative as 'complete' or 'ultimate' ownership,
(Kyerematen 1971:24, 39-40, 97-123) or as 'allodial' (Kasanga 1988:30-
31; Kasanga and Kotey 2001) and 'absolute' (Aidoo 1996:3) title. Along-

side the chiefs' title, the 'usufructuary rights', 'freehold interest' or 'determinable title' of community members was recognised (Aidoo 1996:3; Ollennu 1962:72). This static and codified notion of titles, however, clearly contradicts the existence of a multiple, dynamic, contextual exercise of prerogatives over land and seems intended to favour the imposition of a codified, ranked, and stable set of rights. The intended aim of the land tenure orthodoxy – that is to establish a clear and inalterable set of prerogatives over land – is far from being achieved in rural areas of southwestern Ghana: land prerogatives are continuously disputed and altered. Studies theorising an unequivocal set of land rights do not, in fact, describe the land tenure system as it is practiced in everyday life but make an effort to transform it in a direction that neglects derivative rights and ignores the multiplicity of prerogatives.

Dispute

In most legal studies and in chiefly discourses the causes of conflicts are downplayed. Disputes are presented as misunderstandings rather than the product of divergent interests. Some studies hold that land tenure disputes are resolved once the 'correct' historical precedent is unveiled and custom re-established (Bentsi-Enchill 1964: 23; Kasanga 1988: 48-53; Kyerematen 1971; Rattray 1969, first published 1929:351-352). If a dispute emerges within a kin group, the family elders preside over the hearing. In more important confrontations the village elders or the chief may hear the dispute. The Traditional Council hears all serious disputes, especially those concerning two or more chiefs. Each of these panels is said to be searching for the truth that is contained in custom and needs to be revealed. The self-legitimising idiom of tradition is used by all these panels to frame land disputes' conceptualisations and solutions. At the end of an hermeneutic process that sees men, elders, chiefs, and judges in privileged, monopolistic positions, the outcome is announced (Cutolo 1999). The arbitrators address this concern by offering a strategic interpretation of the ontological status of the parties involved (Who are they? To what kinship background do they belong? What is their rank in the political-parental structure of the kingdom?) and, consequently, of their rightful prerogatives. Conflict resolution is presented as the legitimate re-insertion within tradition rather than as a decision-making process that privileges specific views and interests. Parties are expected to abide by the authoritative decisions. The judgment is presented as aiming to restore peace and harmony. Those who do not abide with the decision of the courts are presented as menacing the unity of the community. The perception of conflicts as resulting from 'confusion' or non-adherence to custom, however, does not silence political conflict between groups. Individuals and groups systematically penalised by the shifting – yet traditional – interpretations of custom have voiced their concern. Land tenure canons have been, to a large extent, determined by chiefs and elders. The state, besides drawing a consistent share of the land revenues, has played its part through the courts, which, however, have addressed only a relatively low number of cases. More systematic land reforms, such as the review of migrants' taxation attempted by Nkrumah, or the land registration attempted in 1986, failed to materialise (Ninsin 1989; Woodman 1987).

Land justice administration in Sefwi

Everyday land practices are neither the product of state legislation nor the result of the mere application of what I have termed the land tenure orthodoxy. The management of land titles within agricultural villages has been continuously adapted to the shifting contexts in which power relations are played out, producing confrontations structured on persistent inequalities. With increased land commoditisation, conflicting interests have generated clashes managed within judiciary arenas that have varied according to the characteristics and importance of the confrontation.

In villages, most struggles are decided by 'family' elders or by a panel of elders, often senior men associated with the chief. House or family disputes, *awuro* or *abusua nsɛm*,[1] do not normally involve payments – if no compensation is decreed: the outcome of the arbitration often consists in an appeal to parties to live in peace indicating what the elders present as the correct solution. Even though house arbitrations are often presented as 'equitable' and 'genuine', elders' interpretations and decisions reflect and enforce gender and age inequalities in family relations. The enforcement of the 'house' arbitration's outcome does not rest on outright coercion but on social pressure and on the political dimension of kinship ties.

Most land cases are heard by village courts presided over by chiefs. This is not always the choice of the disputing parties. In 1957, the Sefwi Wiawso State Council decided to penalise what they termed 'refusal to arbitrate'.

> Councillors noted that Arbitration was a Die-Hard-Custom sought to actuate peaceful means of settling matters between two agrivied [sic] parties in order to avoid unnecessary and expensive Litigations at the Law Courts of Justice; [councillors] (...) felt that (...) this ancient Custom should still remain. It was therefore decided that any unscrupulous person who refuses to

attend the arbitration of his Local Chief with a view of disre-
specting or disparaging the Chief's position should be penalised.
It was decided that the following should form the bases of pun-
ishment: - (a) Before the Paramount Chief £2.8/-; (b) Before any
ordinary Chief £1.4/-.[2]

I am unable to tell the actual impact of this deliberation, but at the
turn of the millennium chiefly panels still controlled – at least in the
first stages of the judicial process – a large percentage of land confrontations in the Sefwi Wiawso district. In the late 1960s chiefly justice
was further enhanced through an amendment deliberated by the Traditional Council of Chiefs. A clause, which remained unaltered at least
until the late 1990s, was added to the effect that 'all farming disputes
between [immigrant] farmers shall first be determined by Arbitration
before the _Omanhene_ [the king] or his representatives (Other chiefs) before any further action is taken' (Boni 2006).

   In village courts the panel consists of the chief, linguists, local of-
fice-holders (_Kontihene_, _Gyaasehene_, etc.), and elders. Parties pay 'sum-
mons' or 'arbitration', 'hearing', and 'service' fees, as well as further
payments if surveyors are sent on the land to gather information and
observe boundaries. Each party will disburse approximately the equivalent of five euro, if the guilty party is not charged with 'compensation'.
The sum will be shared amongst the panel, witnesses, and surveyors.
If the guilty party is fined, the sum will go in part to the offended party
and, in part, to the court panel. The court makes a decree on the parties' title, on the legitimate boundaries, as well as on the fine to be paid
by the party found guilty. Chiefly courts are organised hierarchically:
appeal to judgments can be put forward up the ladder of 'traditional'
rulers, all the way to the king's, the _omanhene_'s court at Wiawso. The
amounts parties are asked to pay increase as the judgment of more
prominent panels is sought. Land confrontations involving chiefs are
judged by a superior chief. Disputes between sub-chiefs are therefore
heard by the Traditional Council, presided over by the _omanhene_; conflicts between _amanhene_ are heard by the Regional or National House
of Chiefs. The hierarchically superior party is both the legitimate inter-
preter of tradition and the one who establishes the adherence of land
narratives presented by the disputing parties to the required 'customary' schema.

   Farmers at times resort to state justice – especially for appeals from
chiefly courts; however, for several reasons, conflicts over prerogatives
are more often managed informally in villages. District Courts and
High Courts are located in the district capital and even large farming
villages in the two districts do not have a state court. Trials in state
courts involve the payment of large and unspecified amounts both for

procedures and for the payment of lawyers who need to be employed, at times from neighbouring regions. Often appeals follow the first judgment, and dealings are thus lengthy and uncertain. In the second half of the 1990s the village Committees for the Defence of the Revolution (CDR) heard some disputes, but land cases were normally sent to the chief. Even though few of the land quarrels that emerge in villages end up in government courts, the state has played a crucial – although often not fully recognised – role, providing judiciary procedures for appeals, deciding, until 1992, the withdrawals of chiefs' recognition, passing national land legislation, managing land tenure through the district administration and, as we shall see, being an active agent in times of crisis.

While confrontations between prominent stools are often heard in the _omanhene_'s court or in state courts, the disputes over the management of tenant farmers' land rights, and over the prerogatives of the youth and women, have – in most instances – been managed locally through procedures that seldom see state justice involved. Settlements of land disputes, in their multiple and multifaceted forms, are the locus in which the dominant discourse on land is continuously reframed and results in the allocation of titles. The interpretations of these panels, often defending partisan interests while evoking tradition, have often been challenged, generating continuous confrontations, before, during, and after the decision-making process.

Inequalities and struggles over land in Sefwi

The unequal distribution of land rights as well as the monopoly in certain social categories of the legitimate capacity to address land cases, to frame an interpretation, and to provide a judgment, reflect wider social canons of evaluation (Boni 2003). Dominant groups hold the capacity to produce land tenure norms, impose taxation, and establish the terms of title transferrals. This produces an unequal distribution of farming prerogatives, with those recognised as legitimate interpreters of correct land rights management benefiting in terms of land rights distribution. Pre-colonial canons of value attribution were adjusted, through the prevalent discourse on land tenure orthodoxy, to the ordering of the twentieth-century land tenure system, characterised by increasing population pressure on land and market-oriented productions. The elaboration of a twentieth-century land tenure system – with its ideological justifications, the redefinition of social taxonomies, and a new set of rules, etc. – transformed the attribution and management of power and value within Sefwi villages and inevitably produced confrontations over the management of a resource – land – that, in the course of the first half of the twentieth century, became both crucial and scarce. Disputes over land, thus, reflect and express wider canons of social inequality and are therefore examined, in the next paragraphs, according to four key criteria of value differentiation, namely the rank of the stool, the ancestry of farmers, their age, and their gender. These domains enable single confrontations to be located within wider patterns characterising Sefwi land disputes. The social position of the parties involved in the dispute determines to a large extent the causes and motivations of the conflict, the procedures activated, the judicial authority involved and, often, the outcome. Examined for each of these domains are the interplay between 'customary' justifications, diversified notions of ownership, avenues of negotiation, and the role played by the state. The ethnographic and archival evidence that follows is largely drawn from a previous work (Boni 2005), here refashioned with the aim of illustrating the sources of justification of land tenure prerogatives, the causes of land disputes, the available avenues of conflict resolution and the inequalities produced in the process of title attribution.

Chiefly disputes

Land quarrels between stools are amongst the most frequent topics addressed in the diverse district judicial arenas.[3] Endless territorial disputes have accompanied the process of demarcation of stool lands and the definition of the stool hierarchy. The relevance of chiefly status in land disputes is due to the fact that a large part of the incomes of 'traditional rulers' derives from the management of land, mostly by renting out prerogatives to entrepreneurs (farmers, loggers, miners). The determination of the rank of chiefs concerns land issues because it establishes the percentage of land revenues a stool should receive and the percentage that should to be conveyed up the hierarchical ladder to superior offices.[4]

In the early twentieth century land was abundant, and chiefs were concerned more with the affiliation of kin groups and settlements than with the definition of territorial titles. The extraction of gold and, later, cocoa production and timber felling produced key sources of revenue for chiefs, the importance of land titling clearly increased, and in the chiefly struggle to lay a claim on all possible territories, land disputes multiplied. Archival evidence shows that in the first half of the twentieth century the colonial administration was a crucial agency in promoting the transformation of a dynamic set of volatile titles into clearly demarcated and defined land rights. Colonial bureaucracy, rather than inventing boundaries, carried out in-depth surveys – with colonial agents sent to determine the extent of stool lands – that were aimed at ordering and stabilising what were, in pre-colonial times, mutable and uncertain attempts to establish territorial hegemony (Boni 1999). Evidence leading to the attribution of land rights was almost exclusively oral and the attribution of titles painstaking. Where was the boundary to be traced on maps when there was no clear demarcation on the ground? How was the rank of chiefs to be determined when conflicting narratives emerged?

The process of codification of ranked land titles was a complex issue but one that, nevertheless, was a crucial part of the colonial administration's work. Once the colonial administration decided that it would not administer land rights directly but – as part of the general deal implied in indirect rule – that chiefs would be recognised as having this prerogative, the clear allocation of land titles to stools was essential: only when land titles were attributed could these be allocated to European logging and mining firms (Grier 1987). The resources to be inserted on the world market (exotic agricultural products, timber, minerals) could be mobilised only if these had a clear owner who could rent out concessions. Uncertainty and the resulting land disputes retarded capitalist penetration presented in terms of 'development'. The extent of the alteration of land rights occurring in this process was not acknowledged: this exercise of fixation and codification was presented by the colonial administration as a mere continuation of pre-colonial custom. A close look at the context and motive of the demarcation indicate that the evocation of tradition was, from the start, a strategic and rhetorical mystification.

Chiefs understood readily that land titles were a source of quick cash and thus began to decipher colonial procedures for the allocation of prerogatives over the soil. Convincing 'traditional' histories – for the canons of the British administration – were formulated and presented in front of colonial officials to justify requests for the expansion of territorial prerogatives, as well as petitions for the elevation of the stool's rank. Obviously colonial administrators recorded incompatible chiefly claims with regard to both land boundaries and rank.

These trends appear clearly in the title dispute over the site of the Bibiani mines, in the South-East of what is today recognised as Sefwi. In the late nineteenth century the area was scarcely populated, worked periodically by miners with diverse ethnic backgrounds who paid tributes to the neighbouring stools. In 1891 three 'Sefwi' chiefs gave out a concession to the Sefwi Gold Mining Company Limited.[5] In 1898 production soared and the chief of 'Sankori' in Ahafo claimed a privileged title over the area and received £300 from the mining firm to renounce his rights. In 1902 the chief of Sankori advanced a fresh set of claims and was accorded a bulk sum of £1000 and a mining rent of £650. In 1909 the chief of Nkawie in Asante claimed a title over the area and was accorded half of the concession's rent.[6] With the suspension of mining operations in 1919, disputes focused on the right to tax cocoa farmers rather than the appropriation of mining rent.[7] To solve the confrontations, colonial administrators and judges recorded the narratives presented by the parties who claimed a title over the area and tried, with little success, to find a compromise between the conflicting claims.[8] The Bibiani case is just an example of a widespread and lengthy land dispute between stools: almost every stool in Sefwi has been involved in some sort of land dispute lasting decades rather than years.

Despite the belief that a clear map of 'customary' land rights could be achieved, colonial and post-colonial governments faced continuous claims to revise what was presented as 'traditional' in order to alter land title allocation. Some disputes emerging at the very beginning of the colonial administration are yet to be solved. For over a century, the Wiawso Paramount Stool has periodically claimed – with an abundant production of judicial proceedings – the village of Karlo. Wiawso claims its rights over the stool, population, and stool land of Karlo, while the settlement was inserted, in the early twentieth century, in the Aowin domains by the colonial government. Another interesting case is the claim by the Stool of Debiso, considered an *odikro* (village chief) from the early twentieth century up to the 1970s, to be recognised as an autonomous *omanhene* (paramount chief). Debiso has obtained some backing by neighbouring communities, can boast some favourable judgments in chiefly arbitration, and has successfully opposed attempts by Wiawso supporters to solve the issue through violent confrontations (Boni 2004). These diverse successes have enhanced the claims of Debiso and forced the Wiawso Paramount Stool to negotiate a solution.

Chiefly disputes indicate that land tenure in the twentieth century cannot be understood as a mere continuation of pre-colonial dynamics. The commoditisation of land enhanced by colonial intervention generated a drastic alteration of the legal framework aimed at inserting land resources on the market. This epochal change profoundly transformed the notion of land rights, its management, the terms of negotiations, the processes of title recognition, and the agents involved (cf. Austin 2005). While a scholar inevitably acknowledges the radical impact of transformations in all domains concerned with chiefly land disputes, these are debated by the state and the chiefs within the general framework of orthodox 'customary' discourse: tradition is the accepted rhetorical device which the disputing parties activate to enhance their claims (Boni 2000). Stool disputes are played out in courts by resorting to ancestral politics focused on the idiom of tradition. Each chief will try to show that the rank that he is claiming has historical evidence to support it, because this is the official criterion used by judges to attribute prerogatives. Even though it is clear to all parties that land conflicts are played out through political alliances and bribes, stools need to fabricate credible 'historical' narratives to sustain their claims.

Conflicts between immigrant farmers and 'indigenous' Sefwi

The distribution of agricultural rights reflects the ancestral origin of farmers. Members of the royal matrilineage tend to have larger plots. Chiefs and other prominent figures within the lineage have at times very large holdings, thus boosting the average holdings of the royal kin group. Data from a field survey carried out in 1996 and 1997 in Sefwi are significant.

The mode of acquisition of agricultural rights clarifies how this unequal distribution was produced. The royal lineage has had – in most locations – a privileged right to clear the forest and control the agricultural title on the deforested portions. Moreover, large holdings are normally passed on through succession. No member of the royal lineage has had to purchase agricultural prerogatives. Sefwi belonging to other kin groups and settled in the village exercised the right of first clearing, while also receiving land through gifts and succession: very few bought agricultural titles (Boni 2005). Immigrants – especially those from the North – have had to purchase most of their agricultural prerogatives.

Tenants, moreover, had to face a more fragile, uncertain and shifting regime of tenure.[9] The terms 'tenants' or 'settler farmers' were a part of a social taxonomy that emerged in the 1940s as a consequence of the increased commoditisation of land rights. Since then, local regulations were passed by the Traditional Council to limit and specify immigrants' conditions of tenure. Those who were identified as 'strangers' were taxed for their agricultural titles and were subject to norms limiting their right to sell and sublet their agricultural prerogatives. Immigrants, moreover, have had to clear their land within a few years or else their parcel would

Table 4.1 *Number of farmers, their holdings, and age according to ancestral origin*

	Number of farmers	Average holdings in acres	Average age in years
Members of royal matrilineage	33 (13%)	36	45
Sefwi relating in village	173 (66%)	14	41
Sefwi foreign to village	3 (1%)	15	47
Southern Ghanaian tenants	46 (18%)	14	50
Northern Ghanaian tenants	6 (2%)	13	42
Total	261	16.7	43

Source: Field Survey, Anglo and Fiafano 1996; Dedimendi 1997.

Table 4.2 *Percentage of farming rights acquired in last transfer by mode of acquisition and ancestral origin of owner*

	Succession, matrilineal land	First clearing	Gifts, inheritance[10]	Purchase or finished abunu
Members of royal matrilineage	16%	39%	43%	-
Sefwi relating in village	11%	16%	64%	2%
Sefwi foreign to village	-	-	100%	-
Southern Ghanaian Tenants	-	-	39%	61%
Northern Ghanaian Tenants	-	-	5%	95%

Source: Field Survey, Anglo and Fiafano 1996; Dedimendi 1997.

be confiscated. Titles of foreigners were in need of constant ratification. Next I focus on disputes which arise due to conflicting interpretations of the prerogatives of the tenants and on various forms of swindles.

Tenants' prerogatives, rather than being applied in strict adherence to local and national legislation, have been negotiated. With regard to foreigners' prerogatives, local 'ethnic' legislation passed by the Traditional Council was often more relevant than national regulations. Confrontations between tenants and the chiefly establishment were both produced and legitimised by divergent readings of titles and transactions. Chiefs – drawing their inspiration from governments' interpretation of tradition which was based largely on chiefly statements – evoke custom to present themselves as the custodians of the land on behalf of the 'indigenous' population. Land, they hold, cannot be sold and never could be. It was merely distributed temporarily to strangers for farming purposes. Immigrants need to accept the tenurial conditions imposed by their Sefwi hosts. Chiefs also claim that tenants seldom acquired their title through the proper written contracts that chiefs have drafted since the 1950s, termed 'memorandums of agreement' (Boni 2005, appendix). Immigrant farmers, on the other hand, state that money was paid to chiefs and land bought. Even though most tenants state that their devolutions should be understood as a form of purchase, and that the title acquired should be considered full ownership, it is clear that tenants' rights have fallen short of legal notions of private property. Tenants have acquired farming rights which have not been encroached upon only when a series of demands were met. The divergent notions of the title held by each party result in recurrent tensions which are often solved in villages through panels of arbitration, often presided over by the chief's kin and associates. Let us examine the perceptions and accusations of chiefs and tenants.

Chiefs fiercely oppose tenants' liberty to sell or sub-let part of their plots. In farming contracts of the late colonial period it is stated that tenants acquired the 'bona fide property' after the tripartite sharing of the farm: they could therefore legitimately dispose of their plot how they wished. Most of the tripartite agreements, according to which chiefs were to receive a third of the farm once the plantation was fully developed, however, never resulted in the division of plantations. Since the 1960s, memorandums of agreement sanctioning transfers of farming rights from chiefs to migrants have no longer contained any reference to the right of tenants to alienate their share. In the 1990s tenants' alienation of their title without chiefly consent is explicitly listed as a breach of contract. Chiefs have frequently complained that tenants, especially those who acquired very large tracts of land around the middle of the century, have illegally sold or sub-let their holdings to other tenants making extraordinary profits (cf. Hill 1963:38-74).[11] Chiefs feel that, since tenants have failed to abide by the terms of the memorandum, they may review the agreement themselves or seek additional payments. One of the principal chiefly concerns was that by allotting their plots to other immigrants, tenants were acting as grantors of land interests, which was solely the privilege of chiefs. Discord over tenants' subletting inevitably exacerbated in the 1980s when Sefwi youth faced problems of land access, while some immigrants controlled tracts of primary forest they had acquired decades earlier but had not yet cleared.[12]

A second major chiefly complaint concerns the tenants' failure to pay a yearly tribute. Chiefly revenue collection has been scarcely effective, and tenants have managed to dodge, in several ways, an annual tax payment, fixed by the chiefs, since 1967, at 10 per cent of the value of their cocoa production. While chiefs actually received the 'customary consideration money', upon the demarcation of the plot allotted to the tenant farmer, the collection of the yearly tribute, termed *afrishia tuo* in official documents and *nton* by tenants, proved more difficult. Chiefs did not keep a reliable record of the allocation of farming rights to tenants and therefore had trouble tracing the immigrants who were supposed to pay. Moreover, revenue collectors often collected bribes from tenants instead of receiving the required tribute for the chiefly apparatus. Since the 1960s the inability to receive stool revenue was addressed repeatedly in chiefly circles but failed to produce a more efficient solution.[13] Lately the Stool Lands Secretariat/Lands Commission was involved in the revenue collection exercise and an acreage system substituted the one-tenth fee on cocoa production; however, no significant improvement was achieved.

Chiefs have also accused tenants of not having a contract or memorandum of agreement to sanction their rights, of delaying cultivation, and of expanding their holdings beyond the boundaries allotted to them.[14] One of the problems with chiefs' complaints is understanding what contract they accuse tenants of breaking. Three contracts may be relevant in sanctioning the cession of the cultivation title: the written 'memorandum of agreement' current at the time in which the accusation is made; the written agreement that was actually signed by the chief and the tenant; or the verbal, 'customary' one that was sanctioned when farming prerogatives were conveyed. The contents of these contracts are, almost invariably, different. Chiefs have progressively expanded their prerogatives over the years, and it appears that chiefs often refer to recent norms that they expect tenants to abide by regardless of the fact that many strangers acquired their title decades ago, on more liberal terms.

Tenants have also voiced their concerns in courts and through petitions to the government: about the lack of security of their title; the reiteration of monetary demands by Sefwi landlords; and swindles. Both the clauses of the 'memorandums of agreement' and actual practice show that strangers in Sefwi do not acquire ownership but only uninterrupted use of the land. Overall tenants' prerogatives *vis à vis* those of Sefwi are more fragile, in need of periodic confirmation, limited, and taxable. The status of the title acquired by strangers is continuously subject to redefinitions, which are mostly resolved in villages but which may end up in court. The initial agreement for the acquisition of agricultural rights between tenants and chiefs is usually oral. Typically no contract is signed when the farmer produces the first payment, the *ase-da*. This leaves immigrants with a set of volatile rights since they lack documentation of their title (cf. Koné 2002:33-35; Lavigne Delville et al. 2002:85-86; Lavigne Delville 2003). Tenant farmers who seek to ratify and confirm their interests by acquiring written documents, some years after purchase, need to pay. The king and local chiefs demand cash before signing written contracts, indentures and maps (cf. Arhin 1986:24-33; Benneh 1988:233).[15] In 1986, the Ghanaian government tried to secure tenants' land rights stimulating the registration of agricultural titles, but the law has had little practical impact on farmers' lives (Agbosu 1990; Aidoo 1996; Takane 2002:50-54; Woodman 1987). Tenants attempting to secure their title through documents often end up being further exploited while not obtaining an ultimate guarantee. Strangers who have made the effort to acquire written stipulations face extortions as well as encroachment on their land. Moreover, both the local government institutions and chiefs have, over the last decades, questioned the validity of these documents or have sought to redefine their terms. Having documents thus minimises but does not prevent swindles.

Tenants have complained of continuous land frauds. As the state's judicial system is remote, expensive, and frequently corrupt, chiefs judge most small-scale land cases. Since the mid-1970s agricultural contracts contain a clause stating that all land cases should be brought, in a first instance, to the chiefs who granted the farming rights. 'Traditional' rulers are thus often both land grantors and judges. As a result, tenants' titles may be discretionally questioned or confirmed by chiefs. This results, on the one hand, in swindles carried out by Sefwi – usually chiefs – against tenants and, on the other, in a continuous effort on the part of the tenants to have their land rights further confirmed and secured.

Many tenants have been cheated due to a lack of documentation of their prerogatives. Allotments are undefined and what tenants consider swindles are justified by chiefs as misunderstandings on the location and size of the land, or are attributed to the tenants' encroachment on land that had not been allotted to them. Chiefs have often explained confrontations as follows: 'some of the tenants/farmers are greedy and selfish and they want to grab more lands, even pieces of lands which have not been granted to them. Hence incidents of encroachment'.[16] From the tenants' perspective, chiefs frequently refuse to acknowledge the first payment, ask them to enter into new agreements, and thus require them to pay again to confirm their title. Frauds are frequent and most tenants operating in Sefwi underwent some sort of land swindle: various tricks are used to extort further payments (cf. Arhin 1986:24-31), including the following.

First, immigrant farmers are led to reach agreements with false land owners. After the payment of the *aseda*, the tenant is informed that the one who received the money had no title over the land; and later the 'rightful' owner asks the tenant to negotiate a new contract and to pay again.[17]

Second, chiefs send messengers to 'remeasure' tenant farmers' land boundaries some years after the stipulation and invariably find that immigrants trespassed beyond the land originally granted to them. Tenants deny the accusation but are asked to pay additional amounts for the part which, according to the chief, was illegally cultivated. If the tiller does not abide with the chiefly intimation, the land deemed cultivated in excess may be expropriated – even when already developed – and reallocated.[18]

Third, Sefwi may encroach on land allotted to a tenant and claim portions of the plot as their own. These incidents are very frequent even though they normally involve small stretches of land and are therefore seldom brought to court.[19]

Fourth, the same parcel may be allotted to a number of tenant farmers as different chiefs sell the cultivation title over the same land. This is very often the case when an area is disputed between various stoolholders. It is not uncommon, however, for the same chief to alienate

farming titles over the same plot to numerous tenants.[20] In such instances, Sefwi witnesses who showed the land to the tenants and were
present at the oral agreement, simply refuse to acknowledge the con-
veyance. Immigrants dispute over the land amongst themselves, the
chief acting as judge. Typically the tenant who is ready to pay an additional amount is recognised as the rightful owner of the title. At times
this trick is used on Sefwi farmers as well.[21]

Strangers have repeatedly complained that there are periodic incur-
sions on their holdings. At times cocoa pods are found missing from
branches, at times the tenant finds that an animal caught in a game
trap set on his land has been removed prior to his arrival. Thefts are often of minor importance but tend to be reiterated, as a constant remin-
der of the immigrant's judicial impotence and limited tenurial security.
Tenants have also been asked to disburse additional sums for the funerals of Sefwi royals; upon the annual festival; to sponsor road constructions and the building of the palace at Wiawso; and to contribute
to chiefly expenses upon enstoolment or land disputes. These payments are indirectly linked to tenants' farming rights: those who refuse
to comply with the chiefs' demands are often harassed, and some are
chased out of their holdings (cf. Benneh 1988:235-236).

A further chiefly privilege, not stated in any contract but related to
the chiefs' capacity as 'ultimate landlord', is their right to draw a share
of the property of strangers who leave the area forever or die in Sefwi.
The successor needs to cede part of the land or pay a fee to the local
chief. If upon the death of a tenant no successor is forthcoming, the
chief collects the whole property (cf. Ollennu 1962:87-88; Rattray
1969, first published 1929:356-357). If the deceased is said to have
been a slave, chiefs take over the whole property even when the children or a successor are present.[22] In 1970, with the introduction of the
Aliens Compilation Act, chiefs took over the property of non-Gha-
naians who were forcefully repatriated.[23]

There is a general understanding of the rights of chiefs, Sefwi commoners, and tenants. There are also, however, areas of ambiguity and
therefore, on certain issues, the claims of the various actors clash. Tenants usually come off worst as they have had few weapons to challenge
chiefly interpretations and impositions of 'custom'. They are usually in-
ferior to Sefwi in numbers, internally fragmented on ethnic lines, and
lack a structured political organisation and the capacity to render hege-
monic the ideological validation of their claims. Tenants end up com-
plying with chiefly demands in most instances for fear that the consequences of their refusals will exceed the burden of chiefly requirements.

When tenants feel chiefly obligations are excessive, they appeal to
the national government or try to take advantage of divisions amongst

chiefs. There have been some periods in which the government backed tenants' requests and tried to expand their agricultural rights. This happened in two periods in particular: in the last years of Nkrumah's leadership (1962-1966) and during the early years of Provisional National Defence Council's rule (1983-1986). These governments presented themselves as socialist or revolutionary, defending farmers' interests against chiefly descent privileges: their policies were supported by tenants who felt they could now challenge chiefly harassment and claim an extended set of land rights with the backing of the national administration. Government support for tenants' requests gave them the strength to oppose swindles, disobey chiefs, and ameliorate their conditions of tenure, albeit for short periods.

While contestations over farming rights were exercised peacefully or with limited, localised violence in most periods, in 1986 the tension between chiefs and tenants matured into generalised violence in Sefwi.[24] Each party was exasperated by decades of low intensity conflict over what both tenants and landlords considered breaches of contracts, swindles, and lack of respect for lawful prerogatives. Throughout the 1970s and early 1980s, chiefs tried to impose new taxes on tenants. In 1986 the Traditional Council of chiefs, with the support of the recently appointed government representative, began a new and more serious operation to register tenants' holdings. As the government opposed the reform, the District Secretary was advised by the Provisional National Defence Council's Regional Secretary not to support the king's attempt to register tenant farmers. The District Secretary, however, did not back down. Posters were hung on cocoa sheds throughout Sefwi announcing the registration policy.[25] Immigrant farmers saw the exercise as the latest strategy to extort money. They feared that portions of their land on which cocoa had not yet been planted would be expropriated and reallotted to Sefwi.

Until then, most of chiefs' extortions of tenants' resources had been personal and informal, in the sense that tenants faced chiefly demands for money individually, either in traditional court proceedings or when summoned to palaces. In 1986, the situation was rather different: an official act was passed by the Sefwi Wiawso Traditional Council applicable to all tenants. This brought unity amongst them, and immigrant farmers firmly refused to comply with the ordinance. The king notified tenants to submit or stop cultivation altogether. Immigrants disregarded the order and continued their agricultural activities. Violence ensued as Sefwi chiefs sent villagers to dispossess strangers of what the former considered land illegally occupied. Some immigrants fled. A settler farmers' union was established to protect tenants and oppose the registration.[26] In its membership card those days are recalled.

The perfidy of the traditional rulers was at its zenith and in the open and made no secret of their intentions. In the wake of various acts of provocation by the traditional rulers and their agents which include outright confiscation of fully developed farms, encroachment upon lawfully acquired farmlands[,] the exaction of the ten percent levy on all cocoa produced by tenant farmers, unnecessary invocation of the traditional Oath *'Takwa e Asantewa'* against settler farmers, and the extortion of large sums of money from tenant farmers.[27]

The government stepped in to mediate between the parties. The Asare Committee was hastily formed and sent to investigate the matter. The results of the enquiry, sympathetic with the position of tenants, documented the violence committed on immigrant farmers and recommended a fairer treatment of tenants.[28] In May 1987, the government posted the District Secretary elsewhere and passed the 'Sefwi Wiawso Settler Farms Law', temporarily prohibiting proceedings by chiefs' courts on land issues.[29] In June and July 1987, several tenants who had fled returned to their plantations making explicit reference to the newly enacted law and the findings of the Asare Committee. Sefwi youth and chiefs established an association to safeguard their privileges on Sefwi land. The Association wrote to the Asare Committee:

We wish to bring to the notice of the [Asare] Committee that the lands so brotherly and generously leased out to Tenant Farmers for the production of food, cocoa and other valuable crops, remain the inalienable birth rights of the Sefwi Ghanaians whose ancestors fought with their sweat and blood and that the present generation will never toy with the land so bequeathed to us.[30]

Sefwi attempts to rationalise and increase the exploitation of immigrant farmers in the 1980s were not successful. However, even though chiefs appeared defeated at the time, they continued to exercise considerable authority locally and maintained their privileges with regards to land rights and tenants' taxation.[31] Harassment of farmers continued in the 1990s, but in a more contained and subtle fashion. Over the last decade, there has been an attempt by chiefs to transform what was, at first, 'bona fide property' and then 'uninterrupted use' of land by tenants to a time-limited lease. While tenants feel they have acquired permanent farming rights that may be passed on to their children and nephews, chiefs increasingly question the unlimited time extension of immigrants' title. In 1999 a 'Committee on tenant/settler farmers' established by the government produced a report in which the need for the documentation of tenants' rights through site plans, the establish-

ment of an acreage system of yearly tribute payment, and the elimina-
tion of land swindles are recommended.[32] The causes of the strained
relations between chiefs and immigrant farmers have, however, remained unchanged: the tenants' title is weak and uncertain, and this
ambiguity allows swindles that benefit those who hold the authority to
voice tradition and utter judgement.

Age-related confrontations

The distribution of cultivation rights is strongly associated with age.
Holdings increase as farmers receive agricultural titles as gifts from elder kin and through succession. In the second half of the twentieth
century, the youth faced a shortage of land for cultivation, while elders
accumulated prerogatives over large tracts through first clearing operations in previous decades. Youngsters had to wait for elders to pass on
their rights over some of their holdings. The alienation of agricultural
rights to immigrant tenants further increased land scarcity for young
'indigenous' cultivators.

   In the early twentieth century Sefwi villagers backed chiefs in their
alienation of cultivation rights to immigrants. The compliance of Sefwi
villagers suggests that chiefs used at least part of their money for communal purposes and that some revenue was usually redistributed within communities (Hill and McGlade 1957:9-10). When available farming
land began to grow scarce, conflicts emerged: the most sensitive political issue was a triangular dispute between Sefwi commoners, chiefs,
and immigrant farmers. As Sefwi commoners rushed into cocoa production, a competition developed between them and the chiefs, as the
former began to clear as much forest as possible while the latter intensified alienation of cultivation titles to immigrant tenants.

   When land began to grow scarce and the control of agricultural titles
became crucial, the youth managed to exercise very little influence on

Table 4.3 *Percentage and number (in brackets) of farmers in age group per size of holding*

Landholdings (acres)	Age groups				Percentage of farmers
	10-24	*25-39*	*40-59*	*Over 60*	
Small (< 5)	74% (21)	23% (24)	24% (19)	6% (3)	26% (67)
Medium (5 to 10)	18% (5)	33% (34)	22% (18)	23% (11)	26% (68)
Large (10 to 20)	4% (1)	32% (33)	27% (22)	29% (14)	27% (70)
Very large (< 20)	4% (1)	12% (13)	27% (22)	42% (20)	21% (56)
Average acreage	4.6 (28)	11.8 (104)	22.3 (81)	24.7 (48)	16.7 (261)

Source: Field Survey, Anglo and Fiafano 1996; Dedimendi 1997. Landless farmers were
excluded.

chiefly administration of stool lands. The younger generations, since the 1960s, tried to halt alienation of agricultural prerogatives to immigrants and asked for a more equitable distribution of titles as well as an increased clarity and security of their prerogatives. These issues seldom became cause for concern in official politics: conflicts between chiefs and youngsters concerning the overall management of land rights failed to have a wider national or class resolution. The question raised by young farmers concerning the legitimacy of chiefs – who were supposed and claimed to be custodians of rights on behalf of the community – selling the agricultural titles without accounting for the profits, remained unanswered. The youth had limited means of influencing the decision-making processes. As chiefs managed to label youth concerns as illegitimate, arguing that the management of land was not their prerogative, the diverse views became a cause of outright confrontations.

The youth voted and took the sides of political parties that promised a more equitable land tenure regime. In Sefwi Wiawso, the electoral success of the Convention People's Party can largely be attributed to the youth. In the 1960s chiefs' indiscriminate alienation of agricultural titles to immigrants began to be questioned by young men who found access to land for agricultural purposes increasingly problematic. Chiefs found themselves under pressure to put an end to a major source of revenue, the *aseda*, the amount received by chiefs when selling agricultural rights to immigrant tenants. The chiefly establishment reacted by taking a formal pro-youth stance while the alienation of farming rights to immigrants continued to be practiced up to the time that land ran out, and indeed beyond. The manoeuvre failed to convince the youth. In 1965 a Convention People's Party councillor of the Wiawso Local Council urged the appointment of a committee to look

> (...) into rampant indiscriminate granting of Forest Lands (...) by people who are financially exclusively benefited [sic] with heavy sums of customary consideration monies [*aseda*] unduly exacted from the prospective farmers.[33]

The reference to chiefly abuse of their role as custodians of communal land is clear. The containment of the chiefly establishment's privileges – with regard to the administration of land rights and the cashing of land revenues – however, was on the political agenda for just a few years. Younger generations tried other means to halt the alienation of land titles. In 1970, the intellectual elite of the youth, organised in the Sefwi Wiawso District Scholars' Association 'resolved that (...) our chiefs, elders, and young men stop selling land to stranger-farmers forthwith' and asked chiefs: 'What provisions are we, the natural owners of the land, making for posterity?'[34] Protests and appeals, however, seldom produced tangible transformations in the chiefs' attitude and thus the youth in villages, at times, resorted to menace and violence to make their concerns heard. Youth unrest has been common especially in support of attempts to oust chiefs who failed to procure general benefits for the community with land revenues. The formulation of charges against the 'traditional ruler' was managed by elders and often indirect: dissatisfaction has been expressed in terms of 'stealing of stool property', 'impoverishes his own subjects', 'ignore maintenance and care of Stool Wives and children, directly under your care'.[35]

While chiefly political rhetoric was on the side of landless Sefwi farmers, the alienation of agricultural titles to immigrants rendered land access a real problem for Sefwi youth (cf. Amanor 2001:105-110). In the 1970s a struggle developed as Sefwi farmers and chiefs were both trying to control the remaining portions of virgin forest: commoners deforested large areas, as they knew agricultural land would soon no longer be available, chiefs responded by speeding up the alienation of cultivation rights to immigrants. By the late 1970s, even though there was no change in local legislation, chiefs decreed their agricultural prerogatives over most tracts of remaining virgin forest: Sefwi commoners could no longer acquire farming titles through deforestation. Since then an increasing number of Sefwi youngsters has been forced to purchase farming prerogatives.

The state did not take any legal initiative to promote youth control of land rights, and protests could therefore be solved only in the arena of local politics, managed by the elders of the Sefwi Wiawso State. The issue of equity raised by the youth was channelled into village arbitrations in which chiefs showed their ability to maintain their privileges over both the alienation of land rights and dispute management. Young farmers did not have the legal, political, institutional, or 'traditional' avenues to convey their concerns. The youth's struggle to redirect the overall policy of land administration – with the focus on new generations' right to land – was largely ignored or neutralised. In Sefwi Wiawso youth associations were attacked by chiefs and some prominent members were forced into exile. Once again the diverse power to conceptualise the terms of the confrontation and thus manage its outcome appears linked to the overall privileges in agricultural rights' distribution. The youth's weakness is manifest in the overall allotment of land rights; in their loss of rights to the benefit of chiefs and elders; in their inability to block the alienation of titles to immigrant farmers; in their incapacity to channel their concerns through institutions; and in their failure to activate a favourable judiciary or political settlement.

Table 4.4 *Acres of farming rights owned by sex and age of owner*

| | Age groups | | | | Average acreage | Total no. of farmers |
	10-24	25-39	40-59	Over 60		
Male	4.8 (22)	12.3 (80)	33.3 (42)	33.9 (27)	19.9	171
Female	3.8 (6)	10.2 (24)	10.4 (39)	12.9 (21)	10.5	90
Average	4.6	11.8	22.3	24.7	16.7	-

Source: Field Survey, Anglo and Fiafano 1996; Dedimendi 1997. The number in brackets indicates the number of farmers in the age group. Landless farmers were excluded.

Conflicts concerning the determination of the appropriate compensation for wives' marital toil

The data gathered in the course of a field survey shows that there is a marked inequality in the distribution of farming rights between men and women, both with regard to the total acreage controlled and the age of acquisition.

Women's acquisition of titles has been limited in comparison to men's from the very beginning of commercial agriculture. Historical evidence from Sefwi shows that gender imbalance in the control of agricultural products is due to the increased individualisation of rights as a consequence of the spread of cocoa. Even though forest clearings involved both men and women, men were seen as the righteous controllers of the land title in most instances. This pattern of male accumulation of valuable resources was a partial innovation in gender relations, extending established practices in gold and rubber extraction to agriculture (Boni 2001; cf. Alden Wily and Hammond 2001). The unequal distribution of agricultural prerogatives was perpetuated by a system of succession and inheritance that tends to transfer male property to men. As a consequence both of the shortage of women's title over land and of marital dispositions, most wives in rural areas perform most of their agricultural labour on their husband's plots. Benefits from the cultivation of cash crops (arrangements for food crops may be somehow different) are controlled by men who should use part of their incomes to cater for members of their household.

Women acquire agricultural rights by gifts from kin – mostly uterine relatives though fathers are a relevant percentage of donors – and through succession. Most rights controlled by women are, however, acquired through the husband who should compensate the wife for her working effort. Men carefully arrange transfers of agricultural title to wives during their lifetime to provide them with what men consider an adequate reward and to prevent conflicts after their death. Promises of future gifts are a veiled, dissimulated form of bond and control. Men

Table 4.5 *Number of plots, acreage, and percentual importance of last mode of acquisition of farming rights according to sex of owner*

	Land receiver	
	Women	Men
Gift from father	36 (100; 17%)	76 (243; 13%)
Gift from mother	12 (66; 11%)	42 (158; 9%)
Gift from maternal uncle	12 (33; 6%)	52 (212; 12%)
Gift from spouse	28 (131; 22%)	-
Gift from other male matrilineal kin	11 (50; 8%)	28 (135; 8%)
Gift from other female matrilineal kin	11 (38; 7%)	17 (74; 4%)
Gift from non-lineage kin	-	16 (75; 4%)
Use of matrilineal land	9 (38; 7%)	7 (44; 2%)
Succession	5 (21; 4%)	31 (147; 8%)
Inheritance	11 (38; 7%)	13 (47; 3%)
Divorce	2 (5; 1%)	-
First clearing	5 (19; 3%)	48 (415; 23%)
Purchase	8 (43; 7%)	22 (208; 12%)
Finished abunu contract	-	1 (4)
Access to wife's land	-	9 (19; 1%)
Unknown	-	4 (26; 1%)
Total	151 (582; 100%)	366 (1807, 100%)

Source: Field Survey, Anglo and Fiafano 1996; Dedimendi 1997.

usually point out that the lineage had done little to help them establish their farm, while the services of children and wives are acknowledged as crucial. When speaking of their own estate, Sefwi men state that giving self-acquired estates to children and wives is the righteous choice, but when discussing the fate of the property of their maternal uncles the view seems to change drastically and the matrilineal principle is often defended.

A man normally transfers the bulk of the property he has acquired during his lifetime to his wife and children as gifts. Drinks and money are provided by the one who receives the farming rights and passed, through the donor, to his uterine kin. If lineage elders recognise that the estate being conveyed is self-acquired property, the drink is accepted and the uterine group agrees to forgo all prerogatives over the plot being passed over. The ritual and the provision of drinks are essential. At times men perform the ceremony just before death to make sure that a certain parcel will be transferred to their spouses or offspring. If the husband/father dies unexpectedly, before officially allocating portions of his farms to his wife and children, the deceased's lineage usually tries to get a hold of all the property, even when aware of the deceased's intention to convey some of the rights to the children or the wife (cf. Roberts 1987:54-56). Such instances are repeatedly discussed and narrated in Sefwi as they are a cause of anxiety before the death of the husband/father and of anger afterwards.[36]

Gifts of agricultural titles are offered to wives after years, usually decades, of marriage. Transfers are viewed as gifts which show the husband's appreciation of his wife's agricultural toil and as a form of anticipated inheritance: men state that they do not want trouble to break out after their death between their wife and their lineage (cf. Amanor 2001:78-88). Procedures are decided by the donor. Wives may be assigned portions of cocoa farms or secondary forest, which may or may not be suitable for cocoa planting: they frequently end up acquiring small portions of their husbands' least productive land. Data from Sefwi show that women generally acquire land at a more advanced age than men; plots received from husbands as gifts or inheritance are obtained at a particularly high age. The age of acquisition is crucial because cocoa plantations take several years to enter into full production. Acquiring land titles beyond the age of forty renders cultivation both more problematic due to decreasing physical strength, and less attractive because the farmer feels that she may not benefit from the full cocoa cycle.

There is social pressure on husbands to perform these devolutions, but no obligation. Tashjian (1996:214) describes husbands' responsibilities towards their wives as 'so nebulous as to be unenforceable'. If wives work for several years without obtaining gifts in land, they may bring the spouse in front of a panel of elders, divorce him, or stop working on his farms (cf. Palumbo 1991:292-301). The 'compensation' for women's toil on husband's farms produces tension, especially in instances of divorce and inheritance.

On divorce, spouses usually claim what Tsikata (1996:112-115) terms a 'send-off' fee for their work performed in domestic enterprises with their husbands. As jointly worked plots are normally cultivated on the husbands' land, men are supposed to provide a suitable compensation for the labour performed by their wives towards the establishment of these farms. In 1953, Abu Yaw divorced Adwua, a Sefwi woman, after she had worked alongside him to establish nineteen cocoa farms. She did not receive compensation upon divorce and therefore appealed to a government officer to seek relief. In her petition she explained the wife's rights on divorce:

> That it is obvious in the Government service, when one is grown of age Government grants the one a compensation or pensions the one. So do to [sic] we Africans, if a wife serves the husband and the husband prospers out of his wife's services the wife ought to gain her share of one or two farms. But in my case the relatives of Abu Yaw [the husband] have overlooked me.[37]

Table 4.6 *Average age at acquisition of farming rights by sex of owner and mode of acquisition*

	Land receiver	
	Female	Male
All gifts	34	23
Gifts from spouse only	46	-
Inheritance	51	25
Succession	44	37
Purchase	32	35
First clearing	30	31
All modes	36	27

Source: Field Survey, Anglo and Fiafano 1996; Dedimendi 1997.

Husbands usually comply with their wives' kin requests for compensation, which habitually consist of agricultural title over parcels planted with food crop or cocoa farms. The share is not predetermined but negotiated according to the woman's labour contribution on the particular farm, the cause of divorce, and the negotiating strength of the woman's and the man's kin groups. The amount of land passed over is typically small.

The determination of the 'compensation' to the woman rests on the assumption that women and not men should be compensated. The assumption is confirmed by the objective structures of unequal gendered distribution of agricultural titles: in most cases women work on the husband's land rather than the opposite. While wives who work on their husbands' land receive small portions of the estate as compensation, husbands who jointly developed a cocoa plantation on the wives' land, frequently claim half the farm (cf. Mensah-Brown 1968:84; Mikell 1989:118-119; Okali 1983:118-123; Vellenga 1986:70-71).

In most cases tension concerning the determination of the compensation to be given to divorcees and widows is solved through panels of male village elders. Should one of the parties be unsatisfied – normally the woman – recourse can be advanced at the government's administration. The first step is normally the recourse to the Social Welfare Office, and if this fails, court procedures may be started. The 'Intestate Succession Law' of 1985 is the state's most serious attempt to safeguard the recognition of women's agricultural contribution. This law is one of the better known in rural areas: it is evoked in village settlements, and women appeal to it when talking to government officials. In Social Welfare Offices and court houses in rural areas the law, however, is negotiated rather than being rigidly applied, for the following reasons. First, the law applies only to the self-acquired property of the deceased. The deceased's matrilineal kin tends to assert that a large part of what was cultivated was actually only in the custody of the deceased while still belonging to the matrilineage and should thus be returned before dividing the remaining assets according to the legal criterion.[38] Second, the deceased's debts should be settled before sharing the properties. Matrilineal kin often state that they had lent money and covered some of the deceased's debts (typically a debt occurs as a result of funeral rituals). The money should be returned before the assets of the deceased are divided. As the wife and children do not have ready cash, the family keeps hold of the deceased's farms for years claiming that the profits are used to repay the debt.[39] Third, matrilineal successors at times successfully argue that, notwithstanding the 'Intestate Succession Law', their role requires them to cater for the deceased's wife and children and that the deceased's property should be transferred to them to allow them to do so, even though the obligations are seldom seriously met.[40]

Conclusion

Far from being managed clearly by a set of traditional norms, land tenure in southern Ghana in the course of the twentieth century has undergone profound transformations. Contemporary Ghanaian land tenure is traditional in the sense that there has been a tradition – not a pre-colonial but a twentieth century tradition – aimed at preserving a good deal of indeterminacy in land tenure dynamics (cf. Alden Wily and Hammond 2001). The ambiguity lies in ever-shifting, multiple, and unclear normative sets tolerated by the state, promoted by the Sefwi Wiawso State/Traditional Council of chiefs, and reshaped and applied locally by chiefs and elders. All these parties have acted as legitimate enforcers of laws they had themselves formulated within a discourse of unchanging traditions. The state has occasionally intervened in land issues but most of the time has accepted rules decreed by chiefs on land tenure which have been enforced, with a varied degree of success, in individual villages or in the whole Sefwi Wiawso Traditional Area. Further uncertainty was produced by the fact that norms were differentiated according to people's ethnicity and ancestry, thus transplanting all the ambiguities of identitarian determination into land tenure management (Boni 2005).

Rules of 'traditional' or 'customary' land tenure, as formulated in the land tenure orthodoxy, thus often prove to be neither applied by the state nor applicable to concrete settings that shape farmers' daily lives. They are not applied by the state, as most land disputes are addressed and solved outside state institutions: recourse to government courts and the Social Welfare Office is limited, while most confrontations are solved by panels of elders and chiefs. They are, moreover, inapplicable, because their conceptual framework rests on assumptions, centred on the notion of 'tradition', without taking into account the dynamism, multiplicity, and ambiguity of titles actually exercised in disputes within Sefwi agricultural villages.

In this dynamic and uncertain context, some actors have been recognised as having the authority to determine how the ambiguities were to be understood and solved. The panels of arbitration in villages, and to a lesser extent the government and State/Traditional Council courts, selectively applied the multiple and shifting norms to concrete settings, determining what was due to each party with regards to titles, boundaries, prerogatives, fees, compensations, and taxations, while referring to unchanging custom. The perpetuation of insecurity and uncertainty in land-related procedures required and strengthened the existence of authoritarian figures at a local level – elders, the chiefly establishment, government officials – who, on the one hand, created and transformed norms and, on the other, contextually employed rules (national, written 'ethnic' norms, oral directives) to address disputes. Those recognised as the legitimate interpreters of custom have invariably been the prominent figures (indigenous, elders, male) who – as we have seen – control the bulk of land titles and who impose the framework of understanding of property relations, appropriate procedures for title transfer, and standards of documentation which preserve unequal relations. Moreover, local 'judges' are often involved in disputes as interested parties. Partisan interpretations have, however, been presented – in line with prevalent discourses on land tenure – both as beneficial for the community as a whole and based on tradition.

The idiom of tradition, even though continuously evoked by those recognised as the legitimate interpreters, has produced only partial adherence by residents. Weaker categories have constantly questioned and disputed both reference to tradition and specific interpretations of what was to be considered customary. Far from being the peaceful application of equitable norms elaborated by past wisdom, traditional norms concerning land have been the strategic imposition of partisan interests leaving large sectors of the population dissatisfied.

Conflicts over land rights have been largely presented by those who judge land disputes not as struggles produced by conflicting interests but as the breaking of immemorial rules: the determination of titles by the panels that have judged land confrontations, at all levels and in the diverse contexts, has thus been largely seen as a technical issue. If one considers that tradition and law have been continuously reshaped, it becomes clear that there is nothing technical in the adjudication of prerogatives: the determination of land titles has been and is inserted in the realm of political relations between parties in shifting contexts. The state could very well intervene through practical measures to establish recognised procedures of land title certification; to reduce costs for peasants who seek to secure their rights; and to protect weaker categories in court proceedings. The state legislation has done so to a very limited extent and this has had a very limited effect; thus strong inequalities in the distribution of land rights according to chiefly status, 'ethnic belonging', age, and gender still persist. The lack of clear advancements in policies of equitable and clear land rights' distribution, combined with the application of the customary idiom in the 1992 Constitution, shows the state's unwillingness to address the ambiguity of land practices and thus reveals the intention to continue sponsoring the current interpreters of an ambiguous land tenure 'custom'.

Notes

1   Local terms are written in Sefwi. Sefwi orthography is variable and therefore I follow what seems the prevalent spelling. Orthographic note: closed e: ɛ; open e: e; closed o: o̱; open o: o.

2   SWTCA, State Council 1956-59, Minutes of Meeting 26 June 1957.

3   SWTCA/GF/LD, Land Disputes; SWTCA/F32, Land dispute internal.

4   SWTCA, Minutes of the Meeting of the Finance Committee of the Sefwi Wiawso Traditional Council held at the *Ahenefie* on 5 June 1972. One should, however, bear in mind that deviations from this norm have probably been numerous; see SWTCA/GF/TF/53-96, Submissions and suggestions, p. 3.

5   NAG Accra ADM 11/1/1130, Mr. Vroom to H.C.S., Elmina 6 September 1893; ADM 48/1/4, Copy of No. 328/H 37, 20 December 1901.

6   NAG Kumasi ARG 1/5/2/6, ARG 1/3/1/185.

7   NAG Accra ADM 48/1/4, Arbitration held at Bibiani on October 18th, 19th and 20th [1928].

8   See NAG Kumasi ARG 1/3/1/185.

9   I have addressed the intricacies of immigrants' conditions of tenure elsewhere (Boni 2005; 2006).

10   By inheritance I mean transferals of land rights from deceased to kin other than the matrilineal successor.

11   NAG Sekondi WRG 13/2/60, Kwadwo *Aduhene* II to The Secretary, National Liberation Council, 4 April 1967; SWTCA, Loose Papers, Statement (n.d. but probably 1969); SWTCA/F.13 Memorandum, 10 May 1974.

12   NAG Sekondi WRG 13/2/138, Campaign of falsehood... (not dated but May 1987).

13   SWTCA, 22 Administration of Stool Lands, Stool Lands Administration Act 123, 5 June 1967. SWTCA/GF7/71-73, Registration of stranger farmers, 19 October 1972; SWTCA 2B Esahiemae, Release 18 December 1975. Cf. SWTCA/F26/vol.2; SWTCA, Minutes of Meeting of the Sefwi Wiawso Traditional Council, 25 August 1975, 13 June 1980; SWTCA, 26, Tenant Farmers, September 1979. In 1983 the chief of Boako carried out his own local 'registration' of tenants; see NAG Sekondi WRG 13/2/127, Complaint against..., 12 February 1984. Cf. SWTCA/GF11, Minutes of anti-cocoa smuggling meeting, 18 October 1985.

14   SWTCA 7. Miscellaneous, A Resolution, 28 August 1970; cf. SWTCA, Loose Papers, Statement (not dated but probably 1969).

15 NAG Sekondi WRG 13/2/60; NAG Sekondi WRG 13/2/127, Complaint against collection of money..., 12 February 1984; NAG Sekondi WRG 13/2/113.

16 SWTCA/GF/TF, Submissions, not dated but late 1980s, p. 9.

17 NAG Sekondi WRG 13/2/127, Complaint/Report, 10 March 1982.

18 NAG Sekondi WRG 13/2/60, Cocoa Farmers Association to The Regional Chief Executive Officer, 5 February 1970; Petition Cocoa Farmers Association, 15 May 1972; Notes of Meeting..., 11 August 1972; Petition by George Opare..., 17 January 1973. See SWTCA/F1, Kwasi Boakye to *Aduhene* II, 8 March 1972; SWTCA/F32, Kwahu Chambers to Nana Yao Ntaadu II, 16 March 1984; SWTCA/F26, Arbitrary and Forcible Seizures, 6 May 1988; SWLCS, White Paper on the Report of the Committee..., February 1990, pp. 3-4; SWTCA, 26 Tenant Farmers, Chorichori Tenant Farmers Association, 7 March 1980; SWTCA/GF5, *Aduhene* II to Mr. Biney, 5 June 1967.

19 NAG Sekondi WRG 13/2/60, Petition of *Opanyin* Samuel Kwabena, 21 December 1972; SWLCS, White Paper pp. 6-10.

20 See SWTCA 7. Miscellaneous, A Resolution, 28 August 1970, Threats on my life, 30 November 1970; SWTCA, 26, Tenant Farmers, Petition for Land Dispute, 10 December 1982; NAG Sekondi WRG 13/2/127, Report against Nana Kwame Nkrumah, 12 July 1982, Petition against Land Dispute, 16 March 1982, A.A. Acheampong to Office of the PNDC, 16 March 1982.

21 See, for example, SWTCA/GF6, Retraction of agreement, 25 October 1969; NAG Sekondi WRG 13/2/64, Petition by Abusa Tenants at Suiano Village, 1969; Complaint, 4 September 1969; NAG Sekondi WRG 13/2/127, Subject Matter..., 28 March 1983; In the Matter..., 12 April 1983.

22 Native Courts were often called upon to hear such cases: see, for example, Pepe Roberts Papers, Sefwi Native Tribunal Court Archives, Kwesi Armah vs Nana Kweku Asante, 25 June 1958 and 30 January 1959. Cf. SWTCA, 12. Letters Personal, Kwame Abosi to Otumfo, 16 April 1962; SWTCA, 9. Cocoa Tribute, _Omanhene_ vs Kwabina Donkor, 25 March 1965; SWTCA, Miscellaneous, Late Ebiaku's Estate, 19 August 1970; NAG Sekondi WRG 13/2/60, A Petition, 7 January 1974.

23 SWTCA 7. Miscellaneous, Claims of Ownership, 7 April 1970, 8 April 1970.

24 Relations between immigrant and autochthonous farmers have periodically produced violent 'ethnic' clashes throughout southern Ghana (Akwabi-Ameyaw 1974: 192; Austin 1987: 273-275).

25 NAG Sekondi WRG 13/2/138, Registration tenant farmers/ demarcation of tenant farms, 13 November 1986.

26 On the events of 1986 and 1987 see various documents in NAG Sekondi 13/2/138.

27 Western Region Settler Farmers Union, Membership Card- Brief History of the..., not dated but probably 1987.

28 NAG Sekondi WRG 13/2/138; SWLCS, White Paper.

29 NAG Sekondi WRG 13/2/138, Sefwi Wiawso Settler Farms Law, 1987.

30 NAG Sekondi WRG 13/2/138, Memo, 12 November 1986.

31 SWTCA/F5/vol.1.

32 See SWTCA, Report of the Committee on tenant/settler farmers, 1999.

33 NAG Sekondi WRG 13/2/53, Minutes Local Council Meeting, 12 April 1965.

34 SWTCA 7. Miscellaneous, A Resolution, 28 August 1970.

35 SWTCA/GF/ASM/53-55; State Council, Constitutional charges preferred against Nana Kwame Kesse, 30 November 1960.

36 Similar dynamics have been described throughout the Akan world (Adomako-Sarfoh 1974; Allman and Tashjian 2000:105-110; Okali 1983:103-107; Tashjian 1995:300-313; Vellenga 1977: 204-205).

37 NAG Accra ADM 47/1/1, Petition on cocoa farms, 23 January 1953.

38 SWDSW, George Acquah vs Thomas Ashie, 23 February 2005; Thomas Asante vs Yaw Mensah 23 June 2005.
39 SWDSW, Kwasi Sirikye vs Kofi Tiah, 18 March 2005; Angelina Donkor vs Simon Bae, 9 October 1995 to 12 December 1995.
40 SWDSW, Faustina Gyabeng vs Taw Asante, 15 February 1995 to 19 June 1995; Yaa Fosua vs Yaw Mensah, 27 May 2005; Nana Burukye vs Kwasi Adjei, 26 May 2005.

5 Chiefs, earth priests and the state: Irrigation agriculture, competing institutions and the transformation of land tenure arrangements in Northeastern Ghana

Steve Tonah

Introduction

During the 1970s and 80s the construction of large-scale irrigation projects was a central part of the government's agricultural policies in Ghana. In this period, successive Ghanaian governments, but in particular the National Redemption Council (NRC) government (1972-'77), mobilised large sections of the population to actively participate in the development of irrigation projects throughout the country. The government established irrigation projects at Dawhenya, Okyereko, Akumadan, Mankesim and Asutuare in the south of the country and in Botanga, Vea and Tono in Northern Ghana. The aim of these irrigation projects was to make the country self-sufficient in the production of food and provide raw materials to Ghana's infant industries (Hansen 1989; Ninsin 1989; Nyanteng and Seini 2000). In Northern Ghana, the irrigation projects were also to provide economic opportunities and employment to large sections of the population, alleviate the perennial food shortages that have been part of the rural livelihood for several decades and stem the high rate of migration to Southern Ghana (Cleveland 1991; Goody 1980; Shepherd 1981).

The introduction of irrigation agricultural projects in Northern Ghana did not only affect the economic activities of individuals and households in the beneficiary communities but also transformed the social and political institutions in the area. This paper examines the impact of state-sponsored irrigation agriculture on the lives of the people of Biu and its neighbouring communities in the Kassena-Nankana District (KND) of Northeastern Ghana. In particular, the paper will analyse how the intervention of the state in agricultural production has transformed the land tenure system in the area. One major effect of the peculiar nature of state intervention in the agricultural sector in the area, which is still manifest today, is the continuing struggle amongst earth

priests, chiefs and state agencies for control, allocation and management of household and communal lands in the area.

This paper is based on detailed ethnographic research work conducted at different periods in the KND over a period of nearly two decades. Initial fieldwork was carried out in the area between 1988 and
1991 (see Tonah 1993, 1994). Subsequent field visits to the area were
undertaken in 1994 and 2002. The author has also benefited from a
number of studies carried out under his supervision in Biu and the
KND between 1994 and 1998.[1] Several secondary materials were also
reviewed by the author. A recent study undertaken between 2002 and
2005 in Biu that analyses the impact of irrigation agriculture on the local resource regime in the settlement has been quite useful for purposes of comparison (see Laube 2005). Thus, the author has been able
to follow developments and changes in the land tenure system in Biu
and the KND during the early years following the introduction of irrigation agriculture and the changes in the land tenure system in the
area.

This paper is divided into sections. It first provides an overview of
the livelihood of the inhabitants of Biu and adjoining communities.
The next section focusses on the land tenure system in the settlements
prior to the introduction of irrigation agriculture during the mid-
1980s. This is followed by an analysis of the state-sponsored Tono Irrigation Project and how the expropriation of land by the government
has transformed economic and social activities in the area, changed the
land tenure system and altered power relations in the community. This
section also examines the struggle among earth priests, chiefs and the
project management to control land in the irrigation project and in
areas where land is managed under customary laws. Furthermore, this
section will show how smallholder farmers and households whose ancestral lands were expropriated by the state are struggling with commercial farmers and the project management for increasingly scarce
land on the irrigation project site and beyond.

Study area and population

This study was carried out in Biu and the surrounding settlements of
Kolnaba and Kologo. Biu lies eighteen kilometres south of Navrongo,
the district capital of the KND in Northeastern Ghana. Biu, with a population of 2,748 inhabitants, is amongst the largest settlement in the
KND (GSS 2002). A total of 269 compound houses (in which 485
households reside) were found in the settlement. The average household size in 2000 was 5.7 persons, while 10.2 persons lived in each
compound (Laube 2005:114). Biu lies close to the main trunk road be-

tween Navrongo and Naga in the East and is bordered in the west by the Tono River and the southernmost portions of the Tono Irrigation Project. Though essentially rural, the settlement is, in comparison with many villages in the KND, quite well served with infrastructural facilities. Biu has primary and junior secondary schools, a clinic, market, churches, stalls, and shops at the centre of the settlement. The settlement also boasts of a number of trained professionals including teachers, health workers, carpenters, seamstresses, hairdressers, masons, drivers, and mechanics.

Climatic conditions in this part of Northeastern Ghana are similar to those found in the Guinea savanna region. The vegetation consists of scattered, widely spaced trees and shrubs. In areas with high population density and with extensive human activities, the tree landscape has been replaced by high-growing grasses. The Biu area has a comparatively low population density. Forests and bushes are found south of the settlement and cover the entire stretch of land between Biu and the White Volta River. The area has a single rainfall pattern with annual rainfall ranging between 850 mm and 1200 mm. Most of the rain falls between August and October. This is followed by a long dry season (December to May) during which temperatures are as high as 45°C. Soils are generally of poor quality except in the alluvial valleys of riverine areas (IFAD 1989).

Biu is somewhat of an aberration in terms of the ethnic categorisation of the population. The inhabitants speak the Buli language, a language of residents in the neighbouring Builsa District, but their customary practices are in many ways similar to those of the Nankana, another ethnic group that occupies the area south of the KND. There is also at least one section of the settlement which traces its root to the Kassena, the major ethnic group in the KND. This essentially means that many residents speak, in addition to Buli, the Nankani and Kasem languages. Some residents have a rudimentary command of the English language while residents who have sojourned in Southern Ghana speak Twi and Hausa.

The inhabitants of Biu can be categorised into two main clans or sections – Seenza and Agobiza – which are further divided into several lineages locally referred to as 'houses'. Clans in Biu, just as amongst the neighbouring Kassena and Nankana, are patrilineal and exogamous. Descent is traced through the male line. The residence pattern is patrilocal with the man maintaining close relations with his in-laws. The typical residence pattern is a compound house with persons of three or more generations living together. Some compounds, however, have two or more households, with each household operating as a separate economic unit. The head of the compound (*Yidana*) represents the compound at sectional/clan meetings, performs religious sacrifices on behalf of its members, settles quarrels among them, and is responsible for their social and economic well-being (Becher 1996; Gutschmidt 1996).

Prior to colonial rule, the settlement was under the headship of the earth priest (*Tengnyono*)[2] who was the religious and political leader of the settlement. Each clan within the settlement was autonomous and the clan head governed the activities of its members. Clan heads would, however, consult with the *Tengnyono* in cases of intra- and inter-clan disputes and for general directions on the administration of the clan. During the period of colonial rule, the various clans or sectional heads were transformed into headmen, and later chiefs, who served as representatives of their communities in the Native Administration. The transformation of clan heads into chiefs (and the creation of chiefs where there were none) by the colonial government has altered the balance of power in Biu and indeed throughout the KND (cf. Der 2000). The various chiefs in the KND were later grouped into a hierarchy with the creation of village, divisional and paramount chiefs. The transformation of clan heads into chiefs, or rather the establishment of a hierarchy amongst hitherto independent and autonomous chiefs, is a major factor accounting for many of the conflicts that were later to engulf Biu and the KND in general. From the period of colonial rule until the present, chiefs are still considered by government officials to be the official representatives of the inhabitants.[3] Most of the earth priests who used to govern these settlements have been sidelined, although they still perform their religious rites and lay claim to the ownership, control and management of land in the KND.

Farming practices and the land tenure system[4]

Residents of Biu and surrounding villages can be described as being agro-pastoralists. Besides their farming activities, most households keep livestock and poultry. Trading, involving the sale of food crops and livestock, also constitutes a major economic activity (cf. Gutschmidt 1996). The main crops grown include grain (mainly millet, rice, and sorghum), cowpea, groundnuts and vegetables. All households keep poultry and small stock but the ownership of cattle is increasingly becoming the preserve of wealthy individuals and households. Farming is typically done with simple equipment (like the hoe, cutlass, sticks etc.) although the use of the bullock in the completion of agricultural tasks has become common. A few households have purchased tractors which they use on their own fields and hire out to neighbouring farmers. Since the mid-1980s when dry season irrigation farming was gradually introduced into the community, increasing numbers of individuals and households have taken to irrigation farming where they cultivate rice, soybeans and tomatoes mainly for household consumption and for sale on the market. The majority of households in Biu have remained subsistence farmers who cultivate less than five hectares of land on farms located around the compound, in the village, the bush area and on the irrigated fields.

The land tenure system in Biu, just as in all Kasena-Nankani settlements, has been shaped both by the pattern of arrival and settlement of the various clans and the social organisation of these clans. Traditionally, the first clan to settle on a particular piece of land claimed ownership of the land and the area immediately surrounding the settlement.[5] The eldest male member of the clan was typically appointed as the *Tengnyono*, that is, the spiritual, political and administrative head of the settlement. Subsequently, the allodial title[6] to land remains within the 'first-comer' clan and a *Tengnyono* is chosen from amongst members of the clan to succeed a deceased leader (cf. DaRocha and Lodoh 1995; Pogucki 1955; Woodman 1996).

A *Tengnyono* never owns the land but only holds land in trust or custodianship for the members of the community. He allocates land to members of the various clans and sections in the settlement and to newly-arrived migrants. The *Tengnyono* remains only a custodian of land and can hardly refuse a native land on which he wishes to settle or farm. He may, however, express his dissatisfaction with a native seeking farmland by not giving him enough land or by offering him an infertile area. Land may be allocated only to adult males and females have no rights of usufruct. In practice, unmarried, divorced, or widowed women are always allocated a portion of the household land for farming purposes (cf. Becher 1996). Strangers, on the other hand, may be refused land if they are known to be of doubtful character or suspected of being able to destabilise the community. The *Tengnyono* may also reallocate bush land which has been abandoned or is left fallow for several seasons (usually for more than 5 years) to another household or individual willing to cultivate it. Virgin lands can only be acquired through the *Tengnyono*. This involves having to send him small amounts of cola nuts, oil, millet-flour, salt, tobacco, and alcoholic drinks to be used in sacrifices to the ancestors, in prayers for a good harvest and for the protection of the individual acquiring the land. All items found on such acquired lands, including strayed livestock, metals, bangles, axes, hoes etc. remain the property of the *Tengnyono*. After the harvest, it is customary for individuals who have been given farmlands to send a small part of the harvest (typically, two or three bowls of maize or millet) to the *Tengnyono* to be 'given to the ancestors'. This practice is often waived when grain harvests during a particular season are poor (Tonah 1993; 2002).

Land lying fallow, virgin lands, forests and indeed all land not allocated to a particular individual or household are regarded as communal
property. Usable resources on these plots of land may be used by any
member of the community. Livestock may graze freely as long as they
do not destroy crops or property. Forests and bush resources may be
exploited for their fruits, wood, vegetables and meat. Rivers and ponds
may be used for minor irrigation and fishing.

An individual who acquires land from the *Tengnyono* may transfer it
to his descendants for farming purposes. Once a household or lineage
has established its right over a piece of land, no one can dispossess that
household/lineage of the usufructory right unless it acts contrary to
the conditions under which the land was given to the household. Currently, most of the compound and in-village plots have been allocated
to the various households and lineages. The use and control of these
plots are subsequently transferred to the male children within the
household. Land for farming purposes is, however, available in the
bush and forest areas far away from the settlement.

Generally, the *Tengnyono* of Biu still has considerable authority within the community and has maintained control over the administration
of land. He is regarded as the legitimate authority over land matters by
the vast majority of the inhabitants. His exclusive right to perform the
numerous religious rites associated with the use of land and the belief
that the non-performance of these rites has serious implications for the
community has contributed to strengthening the position of the *Tengnyono* vis-à-vis other individuals and groups. While the *Tengnyono* has
largely retained his authority over land in Biu, he has over the years
lost control over a vast stretch of land in the KND (Laube 2005:137).
Two major factors were responsible for the *Tengnyono's* gradual loss of
power and control over land in the Kassena-Nankana area. The first
was a result of the imposition of colonial rule in the area. This resulted
in the transformation of clan heads into chiefs and the creation of a
hierarchy among the chiefs. The chiefs later on became the political representatives of their communities and eventually constituted themselves into a powerful group meddling in land issues (cf. Berry
2006:256). The second was the negative impact that colonial land policy had on the authority of the *Tengnyono*.

Since the period of colonial rule, the *Tengnyono* of Biu has seen his
authority over land being challenged by several paramount chiefs in
the KND. Prior to colonial rule, the *Tengnyono* was in charge of the entire territory stretching from Biu to Paga, along the border with Burkina Faso. This includes all the land in Paga, Pungu, Navrongo and parts
of Chuchuliga. However, with the creation of divisional and paramount
chiefs in areas that did not have any hierarchical leadership structure
prior to colonial rule and the provision of such chiefs with powers by

the colonial authority, such 'government-sponsored' chiefs gradually became more powerful than the *Tengnyono*. The power and authority of the *Tengnyono* as the 'owner of the land' has been systematically eroded.

The various colonial administrations did not recognise the authority of the *Tengnyono* of Biu. Instead they created divisional and paramount chiefs in the neighbouring settlements including Kologo and Naga. Biu, on the other hand, was provided with only a headman, who became the political representative of the community with the colonial government. Similarly, the colonial authorities recognised the chief of Navrongo (*Navro-pio*) as the leader of his community. The *Navro-pio* utilised his closeness to the colonial administrators to enhance his status and power. In subsequent years, the chiefs of Kologo, Naga, and many other settlements were made paramount chiefs while the *Navro-pio* also became the paramount chief of Navrongo. Residents of Biu, on the other hand, lost out in the colonial administrative set-up and had to content themselves with a divisional chief. In recent times, as a result of their elevated status and their close connections with persons in central government, chiefs have been claiming to hold the allodial title to land in areas where they traditionally did not have such powers (cf. Lund 2006). For example, during the period of colonial rule, the chief of Kologo (*Kologonaba*) successfully wrestled control over land in the Kologo settlement and in the neighbouring bush area from the *Tengnyono* of Biu and this situation has been maintained until today. Similarly, the *Navro-pio*, using his position as the paramount chief of Navrongo and his closeness and influence amongst top government leaders claims allodial title to lands in Navrongo and its environs. His claim is hotly contested by the *Tengnyam* in the various settlements. Currently, all persons wishing to acquire land for non-agricultural purposes in the Navrongo area have to seek the consent of the *Navro-pio* as well as that of the *Tengnyono* of Navrongo (Konings 1986:243). This has resulted in some confusion over the ownership and control of land in Navrongo and the surrounding settlements. There are reported cases of some *Tengnyam* contesting the claim by the *Navro-pio* to be solely responsible for administering lands in Navrongo and its environs. Some of the *Tengnyam* are demanding that compensation paid by the government with respect to lands acquired by government agencies in the area be given to them instead of the *Navro-pio*.[7] Generally, one can conclude that the colonial government, while strengthening the powers of chiefs, weakened the position of the *Tengnyono* in many parts of Northeastern Ghana.

The land policies of the colonial and post-colonial governments have also curtailed the powers of the *Tengnyono*. A Land and Native Right Ordinance introduced by the colonial government in 1927 declared all

lands in Ghana 'public lands'. Such lands subsequently came under
the management and control of the Governor. The Ordinance empowered the colonial government to claim land in any part of Northern
Ghana for 'development purposes' without the payment of any compensation to the original landowners. Similarly, the government could
grant rights of occupancy to any persons who required the use of land
and charge the appropriate fees (Agbosu 1978; Konings 1986). In this
way the powers of chiefs and the *Tengnyono* with respect to the management of land were rather limited and made subordinate to that of
the colonial government. After the attainment of independence, all
lands in Northern Ghana continued to be vested in the President who
held them in trust for the people of the area. This remained the case
until 1979 when the state finally relinquished its authority over lands
in Northern Ghana and returned the ownership and control of such
lands to their traditional owners. Given the different land tenure regimes in Northern Ghana and the changes that have taken place since
the expropriation of these lands by the colonial government, it has become increasingly difficult for the government to determine the 'traditional owners' of lands in parts of Northern Ghana as a result of conflicting claims by different persons and groups to ownership of a particular land. This is particularly the case in the towns and major
settlements where there is considerable rent to be obtained from the
ownership and control of such lands. Since 1979, there has been an intense competition in many parts of Northeastern Ghana between the
Tengnyam and chiefs over who has allodial title to land. During the colonial and post-colonial period, many chiefs were able to use their privileged position and power to wrestle control over land from the *Tengnyam*. However, it appears that the *Tengnyam* are beginning to fight
back and are re-claiming their rights to control land and reverse their
loss of authority over land (Laube 2005; Lund 2006).

In the next section, I examine in detail how the introduction of
large-scale irrigation farming in Northeastern Ghana during the 1980s
has intensified the conflict over land between chiefs, the *Tengnyam* and
the Ghanaian state. I shall also indicate how commercial irrigation
farming has changed the environment under which farming takes
place, transformed the land tenure system as well as the authority of
the *Tengnyono* in Biu. Today, residents move between commercial irrigation agriculture that largely ignores the social and religious rules in
the area and rain-fed agriculture on household/communal land that is
embedded in and regulated by the social and religious practices of the
population.

Irrigation agriculture and the transformation of land tenure and rural livelihood

The Tono Irrigation Project, located in the KND, was initiated in the early 1960s but was abandoned following the overthrow of President Nkrumah in 1966. It was not until 1974 that the National Redemption Council (NRC) government decided to construct the irrigation project. The Project was expected to provide the raw materials required by the newly-refurbished Pwalugu tomato factory. Furthermore, it was expected to improve the livelihood of farmers in this impoverished part of Ghana and contribute substantially towards the NRC government's 'Operation Feed Yourself' and 'Operation Feed Your Industries' campaigns (Hansen 1989; Ninsin 1989).

The irrigation project itself consists of an embankment across the Tono River to form a 1,860 hectare reservoir capable of providing water for irrigation purposes. The reservoir is linked to the irrigated lands by a canal network of about 250 kilometres with 100 kilometres of access roads. The Tono Project was financed by the Ghana government with loans obtained from the Canadian and British governments. Besides developing irrigation lands, the Tono Project developed a reservoir that facilitated fishing activities, installed a scour pipe that provides Navrongo with potable water, and built housing facilities for the staff of the project. Farming commenced in 1979 and the project was initially managed by a foreign-owned company (Tate and Lyle). The project management was transferred to the Irrigation Company of Upper Region (ICOUR) in 1981 (ICOUR n.d; Kasanga 1992; Konings 1986).

During the construction phase of the irrigation project, all lands in Northern Ghana were vested in the President of Ghana. Land used for the construction of the irrigation facility was expropriated by the government without extensive consultations with the stakeholders and the inhabitants and without the payment of adequate compensation to the landowners. Settlements, farms, religious and sacred sites, forest reserves and groves in communities including Bonia, Korania, Tono, and Yobgania were destroyed. The administration of the meagre compensation paid to the landowners was handled by the *Navro-pio* without the involvement of the *Tengnyam* in the area. Here again, although the *Tengnyam* were traditionally responsible for land matters, the post-colonial government, just like the colonial government, worked through chiefs and imposed its decisions on the communities. By dealing exclusively with chiefs on land matters and elevating them above the *Tengnyam* the government effectively took the side of chiefs in the struggle for the control of land in the district. The *Navro-pio* and other chiefs in the area were thus able to gradually legitimise their hold on land in their traditional areas with the connivance and active support of the state (Konings 1986).

Household, lineage and communal lands in Biu were also expropriated by the state for the construction of the irrigation facility. As elsewhere, neither the *Tengnyono* nor the landowners were consulted prior to the demolition of their property. Landowners in Biu still claim that they did not receive any compensation from the government for property destroyed during the construction phase. Many residents in Biu were initially hesitant about participating in irrigation farming partly due to the grievances they had against the project. There was still abundant fertile land in the area and many households did not see the reason why they should pay to work on land that originally belonged to them. Other farmers feared that the non-observance of religious rites and the destruction of holy sites were bound to bring calamity unto participating households and the entire community.

Villages whose lands were expropriated by the government were allocated plots in the irrigation project area on which to farm. Zones Q, S, U, V and X which are located at the tail end of the irrigation scheme were allocated to residents of Biu. Besides the communities, smallholders, commercial farmers and workers of ICOUR were also allocated farming areas in the project area. Until 1989, only a few young men and women in Biu participated in dry season irrigation farming. Some residents could not mobilise the labour and funds required to participate in irrigation farming. Others were discouraged by the fact that only commercial crops such as tomatoes, soybean and rice were allowed on the irrigation facility. The Village Management Committee therefore decided to give part of its unused irrigation land to commercial farmers and ICOUR workers (Tonah 1993). However, by 1995 the number of households participating in irrigation farming in Biu had increased three-fold and the average size of land under cultivation had also increased (Gutschmidt 1996:59). By the 2004 farming season, residents of Biu were fully using their portion of land under the project and irrigable land had become very scarce (Laube 2005).

During the initial phase of the project, the Land Allocation Committee of ICOUR was responsible for the allocation of zones and plots of land on the project. Members of the Committee included the Regional and District Administration staff, chiefs and the ICOUR project management. The Upper East Regional Commissioner was the Chairman of the Committee. The membership of the Committee was itself an indication of the extent to which chiefs had entrenched their influence and interests in land matters in the district. While the *Tengnyam* were not part of the Land Allocation Committee, chiefs were well represented on it. Many of the administrators, prominent chiefs, top civil servants and military officers were able to use their position on the

Land Allocation Committee and their influence on the project management to obtain land in the most fertile areas on the irrigation project. As the cost of irrigation farming grew following the withdrawal of agricultural subsidies by the Ghanaian government, ICOUR was compelled to cut its staff and transfer part of its activities to the communities (Tonah 1993:185-6). In 1987, ICOUR set up Village Committees (VC) in all the participating communities to allocate irrigation land to residents, repair canals, clean laterals, distribute water, handle credits provided to smallholders and collect debts from farmers (Laube 2005:102). ICOUR had no clear cut criteria for determining the membership of the VC. Members are, however, expected to reflect a cross-section of the community. Individuals chosen are also expected to be honest, hardworking and fair in the execution of their duties. For practical purposes the VC executives in Biu typically include a representative of the *Tengnyono* and two other members selected from the two main clans in the community. Due to the influence that members of the VC wield in the allocation of project lands, the two chiefs of Biu[8] are often at loggerheads as to who should be on the committee. Disputes between the two chiefs over land and the quest to represent the village on the VC were partly responsible for the 'Biu war' in 1997 during which sympathisers of the two chiefs and their clan members clashed (Laube 2005:137-141). Members of the VC typically use their position not only to ensure that they get a sizeable plot on the irrigation scheme but also to secure the interests of their friends and supporters. Allocation of irrigation plots has thus become a means of ensuring political support and patronage within the community.

The establishment of the VC and the involvement of communities whose lands were expropriated by the state in the management of land have increased rivalry among the chiefs and the *Tengnyam* in the area. In Biu, there is a fierce competition for power and irrigated land among the two chiefs, the *Tengnyono* and other landowners. Prior to the involvement of the communities in the management of land, the Land Allocation Committee of ICOUR was the main institution allocating land on the project site and had exclusive management control over the irrigation project. ICOUR was also responsible for meeting the land and water needs of commercial farmers, smallholders and the project staff. The project management could thus more easily hold in check the activities of chiefs and the *Tengnyam* who have long claimed ownership and control of communal land in the project site. With the increasing participation of the communities in the project, the *Tengnyam* appear to be regaining their authority and control over part of the land that they lost to the state and the chiefs. The *Tengnyam* are still very much revered by large sections of the population and still play significant social, economic and religious functions in their communities. They have tried to maintain the traditions of their people and are not associated with the institutions of the modern state. Chiefs, on the other hand, are directly associated with politicians and the state apparatus and institutions. They benefit considerably from the largesse and support of politicians and the government. Chiefs are therefore sometimes viewed with suspicion by their subjects. However, chiefs are able to influence the decisions of the project management by using their links with government officials and top civil servants in the area.

In Biu, farmers sometimes seek the permission of the *Tengnyono* to work on abandoned plots or waste lands on the irrigation project under the pretext that these lands should be given back to their original owners in the community. Plots under the cultivation of the expropriated communities are increasingly coming under the influence of chiefs and *Tengnyam* who are systematically influencing and interfering with the allocation of land within their communities. This has resulted in the development of a parallel land management regime, especially on the so-called waste lands within the irrigation project. These waste lands are managed according to customary laws that sometimes contradict official ICOUR regulations. Farmers who cultivate areas declared as waste lands by ICOUR end up using the project's facilities on their fields without having to pay any land and water levies. The project management often turn a blind eye to some of the negative activities of beneficiary communities because they do not want to estrange these communities. Although backed by state power that has vested ownership of all land in the Tono project in ICOUR, the authority of ICOUR appears increasingly limited to areas cultivated by small-scale and commercial farmers. The management of zones and plots allocated to the communities are increasingly left with the Village Committees. However, ICOUR does intervene directly in the affairs of the VC when the VC is unable to manage its affairs as a result of conflicts or when the communities are highly indebted to ICOUR. The project management appears not very keen to dabble in land politics within the communities. Instead, ICOUR prefers to indirectly control the use of land in the project area by controlling the provision of water. ICOUR can and intermittently does withhold the provision of water to recalcitrant communities and individual farmers indebted to the organisation, thereby preventing them from undertaking irrigation farming.

While most residents contest ICOUR's claims over the ownership of land, they do accept the fact that the irrigation water belongs to ICOUR. ICOUR has, so far, been able to maintain its authority over land use in the irrigation project through its unassailable monopoly over the control and distribution of water. Individual farmers and the communities, on the other hand, do employ the 'weapons of the weak' (Scott 1985) in putting pressure on ICOUR. They may damage or steal irrigation property, steal crops from the fields, divert irrigation water courses, burn the fields, etc. in protest against any unfair treatment by the project management. Chiefs also commonly employ their links with politicians to expand their influence on the project management. They typically use their influence to obtain a large acreage of land in the best farming areas. They usually have access to any credit packages provided by the government and donor agencies in support of the agricultural sector. Commercial farmers are another powerful group operating on the irrigation scheme. They are usually members of the local and regional elite with links to persons in high authority in the government or in government agencies. They work to protect their interests in the project. In view of their enormous contributions to the viability of the project, they tend to have very close relations with the project management. Generally, the irrigation project therefore provides the environment where the various actors and institutions can compete for land and other resources, and ultimately for influence and power in the area.

Three decades of state-sponsored irrigation farming have resulted in the creation of two land and resource management regimes in the KND that operate alongside each other in an often contradictory and confused fashion. One set of rules operates on the irrigation project while another operates in areas under customary land laws and social conventions. This is in spite of increasing and subtle attempts by the *Tengnyam*, chiefs and other traditional leaders to introduce customary rules and practices into irrigation farming. The rules and social conditions under which individuals and households participate in irrigation farming remain very different from those that operate within the traditional rain-fed farming environment.

On the irrigation project, plots are allocated by members of the Village Committee upon the payment of water and other levies. The farming season is regulated by the ICOUR project management and is subject to the availability of water. Some zones may be closed and farmers denied access to their plots when there is too little water in the dam. Hired labour is commonly used for the execution of several agricultural tasks, including land preparation, transplanting of crops, weeding, harvesting and threshing of produce. Crops that are planted on irrigated fields are mainly those with high economic value such as rice, tomatoes and soybeans. These crops have little social or religious value in the community. Generally, farming on the irrigated plots involves the use of modern equipment and machinery for several stages of farming. Irrigation agriculture is essentially individualistic in nature. Women can acquire, own and use plots on the irrigation projects in their own right and do not have to depend on their male relatives for access to land and labour, as long as they can afford the cost involved. The har-

vest belongs exclusively to the farmer and s/he can market the produce
and keep the proceeds from the sale of the harvest. Harvests are commonly stored in jute sacks and hidden from other members of the
household or the extended family to ensure their exclusive use by the
farmer.

Farming on household or communal lands, on the other hand, takes
place under very different social conditions and land tenure arrangements. Farming typically commences with a religious ceremony and
sacrifices are made to the ancestors to announce the commencement
of the farming season. Farming takes place on household or lineage
land, or on plots provided by the *Tengnyono*. Farming on household
plots involves the extensive use of family and kin labour. The labour of
relatives and in-laws is commonly used in the completion of all agricultural tasks. Similarly, communal labour may be organised, during
which the host provides food and drinks for persons who participate in
the work. Contrary to practices that prevail under irrigation agriculture,
crops with social and religious significance, such as millet and sorghum, are commonly planted on household lands. Traditional agriculture involves expectations of reciprocity on the part of relatives and
community members. A small part of the proceeds from the harvest is
given to the *Tengnyono* to be used in sacrifices, for the performance of
funerals, weddings and other community activities. Part of the harvest
is frequently shared with relatives and neighbours, especially during
the lean season or in case of a drought. Harvested crops are traditionally kept in barns and shared amongst households within a compound.
While farming under irrigation conditions is largely profit-motivated
and self-centred, farming on household land is mainly of a subsistence
nature and driven by reciprocal relations.

Dry season irrigation farming was slow to catch up in Biu and other
communities in the KND. The commencement of irrigation farming
was associated with the expropriation of land and the destruction of
the economic, social, and religious property of the affected communities. Some communities lost all their farmlands and the basis of their
livelihood in this largely impoverished part of Northern Ghana. Others
had to be relocated to make way for the building of the dam and the canals. The non-payment of compensation to the landowners and residents whose farms and property were destroyed also contributed to the
initial frustration and despondency found among large sections of the
rural population in the KND. During the 1970s the bulk of the farmlands on the project was allocated to commercial farmers, most of
whom were government officials, military officers, civil servants and
large scale farmers. Most of them had ventured into irrigation rice
farming to take advantage of the huge subsidies that the government
provided to the agricultural sector. During this period the level of parti-

cipation of the rural smallholder farmer in the Tono Irrigation Project was very low. Only those communities without adequate bush farms felt compelled to participate in irrigation farming.

During the early 1990s the level of participation of smallholder farmers in the project increased considerably. This was partly because the benefits to be derived from dry season irrigation farming became evident to more farmers but also because of a new policy that placed emphasis on increasing community participation in irrigation farming. Irrigation farming has greatly alleviated poverty in Biu and the KND in general: it provides grain (especially rice) needed by poor households to survive the long and harsh dry season in the savanna region. Irrigation farming has also been beneficial to the poorest households, especially female-headed households, who did not own livestock that could be exchanged for grain during the lean season. Furthermore, it has provided the opportunity for women to acquire farmlands in their own right. Single women, widows, and female-headed households can now acquire land without having to depend on their male relatives. Women may also keep the proceeds from the sale of crops for the use of their family members. Under the traditional farming practices, crop harvests are usually managed by the male head of the household and any cash income from the sale of grain belongs to him.

Irrigation agriculture has also been a major source of employment and income for the poorest households in Biu and neighbouring communities. Persons from poor households form the majority of those employed as labourers on the fields of commercial farmers. Women as well as young boys and girls constitute the bulk of the agricultural labour on the irrigation project. Women are frequently employed to transplant rice, weed fields and harvest crops. Young boys and girls are typically employed to scare away birds from the rice fields. Irrigation farming has also reduced the level of migration of the youth to Southern Ghana. Persons who leave their communities to do menial jobs in Southern Ghana often return to their home villages during the dry season because of the possibility of undertaking irrigation farming.

The availability of employment in the irrigation facility has, however, resulted in an increase in the incidence of child labour and truancy in the district. Many children who should be in school are found working on the irrigation fields, especially during periods of peak demand for labour. Another negative effect of the introduction of irrigation farming in the KND is the high level of social differentiation within the participating rural communities (cf. Kasanga 1992). Households that can mobilise adequate material and human resources and possess the necessary power to influence the decisions of the project management have been able to secure large acreages of land for irrigation farming. They have, with time, been able to make a fortune from irrigation farming.

Such households have invested part of their wealth in the renovation of their buildings and the purchase of solar panels, motorbikes, bicycles, tractors and other farming equipment. Poor households, on the other hand, have to eke out a living from small irrigation plots. A large number of those working as wage labourers on the irrigation project come from the poorest households.

Summary and conclusion

This paper has examined the changing land tenure arrangements in Biu and the KND before and after the introduction of irrigation agriculture by the state in the 1970s and '80s. It has shown that prior to the construction of the Tono Irrigation Project there was a stiff contest between the *Tengnyam* and the chiefs for the control over land in the area. Developments during the colonial period favoured the chiefs who were considered to be the political representatives of the communities in the Native Administration. The Land and Native Right Ordinance introduced by the colonial government in 1927 declared all lands in Ghana 'public lands' and placed them under the control and management of the Governor. This law enabled the colonial government to obtain access to land without hindrance or the payment of compensation. However, the control of land by the government was only effective in the major towns. In the rural areas, landowners and *Tengnyam* continued to administer land according to customary laws. Chiefs used their powers and closeness to the colonial administration to gain some control over land, especially in the urban areas. Some of the paramount chiefs later claimed allodial title over land in their traditional areas. The contest for control over land thus intensified with the chiefs gradually gaining the upper hand due to their influence in national politics. The *Tengnyam* gradually lost effective control over some lands that had hitherto been under their control. By and large, the various post-colonial governments in Ghana maintained the status quo by leaving all lands in Northern Ghana as 'public lands' until 1979 when these lands were returned to their traditional owners. The return of northern lands to their traditional owners further heightened the struggle for control of land between the *Tengnyam* and the chiefs, as the former began to reassert their authority over land that apparently had come under the administration of the chiefs.

It was against the background of the ongoing struggle for the control of land that the Tono Irrigation Project was constructed. The National Redemption Council government with the support and connivance of the chiefs expropriated land from communities lying along the Tono River for the construction of the irrigation project. The *Tengnyam* who were traditionally accepted to have authority over community lands were largely ignored during the process. The Ghanaian government paid a meagre compensation to the chiefs to be distributed amongst households and communities whose lands were expropriated, but many residents claimed they did not receive their share of the compensation. The Tono Irrigation Project has further intensified the struggle for the control of land between the chiefs, the *Tengnyam* and the state since the introduction of community management of irrigation fields. The *Tengnyam* or their representatives have almost everywhere been made part of the Village Committees created to manage the allocation of irrigated land to individuals and households participating in the Tono project. This has resulted in attempts by the *Tengnyam* to *reassert* their claim and control over land expropriated by the state. They have tried to bring part of the irrigation project indirectly under their control by introducing traditional religious practices in areas under the control of the VCs. Chiefs have also used their influence with the project management and government officials to secure access to large acreages of irrigated lands on the project. They have also strived to be members of the Village Committee to ensure that their supporters have access to irrigation plots. They often use irrigation land for patronage purposes. The contest for land and power between chiefs and the *Tengnyam* in Biu and the surrounding communities has had a disastrous impact on these communities. It has polarised the inhabitants along their various sections and interest groups. It has also intensified chieftaincy succession conflicts and politicised the life of the residents. The competition for chieftaincy has become intense as the various sections in the settlement support different candidates for the chieftaincy position. Indeed, these animosities were partly responsible for the 'Biu war' in 1997 and the continuing tension within the community.

While the ICOUR has lost some control over land allocation in areas under the management of the VCs, it still controls the use of land by commercial farmers, smallholder farmers, public and civil servants, as well as politicians. Besides, ICOUR maintains a certain amount of control over the use of land in the project area through the control of water. ICOUR exerts its influence by refusing to provide water to indebted farmers and communities. This has enabled it to maintain its fragile hold over lands in the irrigation project. The Tono Irrigation Project provides a good example of the changing land tenure system in the KND and the on-going struggle between chiefs, earth priests and the state for the control over land in Northeastern Ghana. The Project also shows the considerable extent to which rural livelihood in the KND has been transformed through the introduction of irrigation agriculture.

Notes

1   See Becher 1996; Gutschmidt 1996; Lachenmann 1995; Rabbe 2004.
2   The local name for the earth priest varies amongst the different ethnic groups in Northeastern Ghana. He is called *Tindana* and *Tegatu* amongst the neighbouring Nankani and the Kassena respectively. I will use the Buli word *Tengnyono* (pl. *Tengnyam*) which is the language of the residents of Biu and the neighbouring Builsa District.
3   Some of the important roles of chiefs, including being the main link between the government and the inhabitants, have since the introduction of the local government system in 1988 been taken over by the Assemblyman. Nevertheless, chiefs still represent their communities and have remained influential in national life and politics.
4   This section relies heavily on earlier fieldwork in Biu. See Tonah 1993:69-82.
5   See Kunbuor 2003 and Lentz 2006a for an extensive discussion on the relationship between 'first-comers' to a particular locality and 'late-comers' with respect to the type of rights a group or individual asserts over land and the security of tenure associated with such rights.
6   According to Kunbuor 2003, the allodial title is 'the highest proprietary interest known to customary schemes of interest in land. It is sometimes referred to as the paramount title, absolute title or radical title'. See also Kasanga 1988.
7   In the neighbouring Builsa District, for example, the paramount chief of the area (the *Sandemnab*) and his elders are claiming that the allodial title to land in the Builsa area is vested in the paramount chief who holds land in trust for the people. The paramount chief has succeeded in displacing the *Tengnyam* who previously held the allodial title to land in the area (Konings 1986: 154). Similarly, the paramount chief of Bolgatanga (the *Bolganaba*) is also claiming allodial title to land in the Bolgatanga area although this is being contested by the *Tindana* (earth priest) who apparently had authority over land in Bolgatanga prior to the colonial era (see Lund 2006).
8   The Biu community has the unenviable situation of having two chiefs. Each of the two clans/sections has its own chief and both of them are laying claim to being the direct descendant of the first settler in the settlement.

6   Customary justice institutions and local Alternative Dispute Resolution: What kind of protection can they offer to customary landholders?

Richard C. Crook

Introduction: Chiefs, customary landholding and legal pluralism in Ghana

In Ghana, as in most of tropical Africa, the majority of landholdings are based on customary forms of tenure which are either unwritten or are at best only informally recorded. Landholders' rights depend on agreements embedded in local society and derive from their social relations with family, lineage, and community (Berry 1993). Ghana is special, however, in the extent to which customary chiefs in the dominant Akan cultural areas are legally recognised as 'trustees' or allodial owners of community land, and in the extent to which customary land law has been incorporated into the common law of the state courts and recognised by the Constitution.[1] In the non-Akan areas chiefs were not traditionally recognised as having such extensive claims over land, but the impact of colonial rule encouraged chiefs especially in the north to develop such claims, leading to contemporary conflicts with land priests (*tendana*) and family heads. The chiefs' Native Courts were abolished throughout Ghana in 1958, after independence, and the chieftaincy has since been progressively stripped of virtually all of its formal judicial and administrative powers including the collection of land revenues. Nevertheless, chiefs continue to be the *de facto* land managers of most customary landholdings even in the urban areas, allocating plots and selling leases for 'drinks money' (fees) at market rates, and running 'customary courts' for the settlement of land and other disputes.

Most customary landholders are, therefore, still very much dependent on chiefly and local or family institutions to uphold their right of access to land, and for protection against unlawful dispossession of their customary landholdings, especially if they cannot afford to go through the state's land sector agencies (Lands Commission, Survey Department, District Physical Planning Departments, Deeds Registry,

Land Title Registry), or to engage with surveyors, lawyers, and courts. What happens if those rights are threatened – by the state, local government or the community itself through the chief – or if they come into conflict with other parties? If they cannot be resolved amicably, the situation of legal pluralism which prevails in Ghana means that there is a wide range of possible dispute settlement institutions to which they can turn, ranging from state courts and administrative agencies through superior chiefs' customary 'courts' or tribunals to village level arbitrations by village chiefs, family heads, elders, and community leaders. But whether those different fora or 'Dispute Settlement Institutions' (DSIs) offer equally good protection of customary rights is by no means certain; the norms or legal codes used in each DSI can differ quite markedly, and the legitimacy, authority and fairness of the procedures used may also lead to quite different outcomes according to the status of the parties. Nevertheless, given the reality that most landholders in practice use mainly local and customary forms of dispute resolution, and given the congestion and huge backlogs in the state courts, state policy in Ghana now favours an emphasis on encouraging these local and customary DSIs. Current policy discourses also tend to equate such local and customary DSIs with the fashion for using 'Alternative Dispute Resolution' (ADR) mechanisms as a way to deal with the crisis in the state courts. The intention of this paper is therefore to address two main issues:

• How legitimate, effective and inclusive are these customary and informal local level systems of land dispute settlement?

• To what extent can they really be promoted as ADR-type solutions to the land case backlog facing the state courts?

Evidence will be drawn from research on land disputes and DSIs carried out in peri-urban Kumasi, Brong-Ahafo and Upper West Regions during the 2001-2005 period (Crook et al. 2007).

ADR and its transposition to Africa

Alternative Dispute Resolution (ADR), is currently extremely popular in justice sector reform programmes throughout the developing world, and has been officially introduced in India, Bangladesh, and various Latin American and African states in recent years (see PRI 2001). It is primarily seen as a method for relieving the crisis of overburdened state courts facing impossible backlogs of unresolved cases. More positively it is also advocated as offering a cheaper, faster and more accessible form of justice for ordinary citizens, particularly the rural and urban poor, who do not have access to state justice either because of lack of resources, social exclusion or lack of physical access (distance).

The essence of the modern ADR concept, as developed by its European and North American advocates, is the idea that a better form of justice can be obtained by focussing on mediation or the search for an agreed settlement, rather than on binding adjudication by an external (usually state) authority. Both state and non-state institutions or mediators can offer ADR; what makes it different from the practice in formal courts is the procedure, which is 'de-legalised', relying on an informal search for an agreed and just solution, as opposed to deciding who has won or lost. This emphasis on 'better' and 'non-compulsory' justice distinguishes the recent ADR movement from the already well-established contractual forms of commercial ADR, which rely on binding arbitration and may exclude the right to go to court (Ryan 2000).

In European and North American states, the ADR concept is based on three main assumptions:

- Disputes are about individual rights and agreement between the individual parties, which is appropriate in urban societies where one cannot assume a 'community public' with an interest in social harmony or groups which will somehow police the settlement between the parties.

- ADR will be monitored so as to ensure fair procedure, and should not lead to denial of the right to trial under the law (Ryan 2000:1869).

- ADR is based on finding a neutral mediator who will help the parties to bargain freely to reach an agreed settlement without pressure or intimidation – an assumption which has provoked much criticism from those who argue that ADR enthusiasts too often ignore differences in status and power between the parties (Nader 2001).

The idea that ADR could be a powerful reform tool in developing countries may well have emerged from the ideals of some of the original campaigners for ADR, who were predominantly anti-state and pro-community empowerment. They sought justification in the popular, community-based or rural traditions of their own societies; but they also drew inspiration from what they saw as the virtues of traditional approaches to dispute settlement in African and some Asian societies. These were praised for emphasising consensus and socially-sanctioned compromise; hence ADR became linked with a rhetoric of 'harmony law' (Brown and Marriott 1999; Nader 2001; Silbey and Sarat 1989).

This strong 'communitarian' strand in the ADR concept underpins a strong tendency in many of the justice sector reform programmes adopted by donors to equate ADR with customary forms of justice or chiefs' courts, an equation which has become widely adopted by African advocates of ADR themselves. An ideal of African village justice – the 'meeting under the tree' in which a dispute is resolved through a search for community consensus – is often cited as a basic inspiration for ADR in Africa. But this idealised picture may conceal a real misunderstanding of the nature of community and traditional dispute settlement procedures in African societies (Grande 1999). The analysis of the Ghana cases which follows will illustrate some of the real differences which exist between the practice of customary DSIs in particular, and the principles of ADR.

Policy responses to the land conflict issues in Ghana

In Ghana, as elsewhere in Africa, policy responses to the issue of how to deal with the increasingly serious levels of conflict over land and the associated rise in both individual and communal land disputes have been driven by two main assumptions:

- It is assumed that the ambiguity, uncertainty and flexibility of customary land tenure cannot deal with conflicts caused by land shortage and urban development, and must therefore be made more certain through various modernising measures such as mapping and documentation of titles. Even with the current 'adaptation paradigm', which aims to recognise and formalise customary tenures, the basic assumption remains that greater certainty through mapping and documentation of titles will help to reduce conflict and therefore the numbers of cases coming before the courts or other DSIs (Atwood 1990; Bruce et al. 1994; Platteau 1996).

- The inability of state courts to deal with an ever increasing flood of land cases is seen as a capacity problem which can be dealt with by diverting them to a range of alternatives to the state judicial system, such as customary and informal local institutions, and ADR. The situation in Ghana is undoubtedly serious; it has been estimated that land cases accounted for around 42 per cent of all pending High Court cases in 2002 (Kotey 2004) and in the Kumasi High Court, for instance, the rate at which new land cases were being filed during the period 1997-2002 was on average four times the number being settled, so that the settlement rate fell from 1.5 per cent per annum to 0.6 per cent per annum (Crook et al. 2007). In Accra, the settlement rate fell from 4.2 per cent to 2.6 per cent between 1998 and 2001 (Wood 2002).

The Ghana Land Administration Project (LAP) incorporates both of these assumptions in its main components, which are strongly supported by various bi-lateral donors and the World Bank. Institutional reforms such as the restructuring of the state land sector agencies (LSAs), decentralisation of land management, and documentation to Customary Land Secretariats (CLSs) under the aegis of customary authorities all address the need for more effective and certain dispute resolution as an accompaniment to the development of greater certainty of title. The LAP therefore suggests a two-pronged approach: the creation of special Land Courts (Divisions of the High Court) in regional capitals, to try to deal with backlogs in the state system; and the development of ADR. But what type of ADR mechanisms these should be and where they should be located is the subject of some variation in the different official and donor memoranda. There are three different kinds of proposal on the table:

- It is proposed that ADR be set up as an integral element of the new CLSs, in order to resolve disputes over land allocation and recording of land rights at the local level. Thus the chiefs and their customary tribunals will be recognised as a form of ADR.

- There are plans to introduce an ADR bill in Parliament which will empower the courts, the judicial service and the legal profession to use (perhaps impose?) court-supported ADR.

- Other proposals focus on the role of the elected local authorities and NGOs: for instance, the LAP Appraisal Document of April 2003 envisages that Local Advisory Committees of 'community elders' be organised by the elected District Assemblies to resolve cases where the parties have not been able to reach agreement in any of the chiefs' tribunals (a form of proto–District Lands Tribunal). And some District Assemblies have supported local 'dispute settlement' NGOs organised by respected community leaders, often with the help of retired members of the legal profession.

These various proposals for the introduction of ADR reflect differing and in some respects contradictory understandings of what ADR mechanisms are, and how they are supposed to operate. There is (perhaps

deliberate) confusion over whether ADR mechanisms are 'non-state' alternatives or whether they can and should be state-supported. But the
differing institutional locations proposed also reflect different political
interests within the current regime, and 'bureaucratic politics' among
rival agencies: the chiefs, various ministries, the LSAs, and the Judicial
Service.

The policy for reviving customary justice under the banner of ADR
is, however, of particular interest to the chiefs. Since the NPP government came to power, the leading chiefs in the country, mainly from
the Eastern and Ashanti Regions, have pursued an open political campaign to reverse as many as possible of the legislative measures
brought in by the Nkrumah (CPP) government and successive governments since 1952, measures which not only took away the chiefs' official judicial and administrative functions but also gave most of their
powers to collect revenue from stool land, and to manage the development of land, to the LSAs.[2] Chiefs welcome the titling programme insofar as it may lead to the registering of their stool land allodial titles
as the first stage of the process (see World Bank 2003a).[3] The chiefs
quite naturally see policies for recognising and strengthening customary land law and management as an opportunity also to revive their
customary judicial powers, formerly exercised in the Native Courts.
They therefore claim that their customary tribunals are an authentic
form of 'ADR', which should rightly be located in the proposed CLSs,
not within the 'modern' elected local government or judicial service institutions.

Customary and local forms of DSI: The institutional and historical context

Essential in any discussion of customary and local forms of land dispute resolution in Ghana is recognising their wide variety, in terms of
scale or level of operation, degree of formality, and the kinds of codes
or legal norms utilised. At the most intimate and informal level, many
disputes are settled by family heads and elders, or by mutually respected persons such as an elder, an educated community leader, traditional priest, or modern church leader. Family heads are most likely to
use 'traditional' norms of obligation and conventions when it comes to
the issues surrounding the use and inheritance of land. Also at the
very local level, village chiefs are resorted to as repositories of customary knowledge and norms. At the community level, leaders of modern
political institutions such as Unit Committee chairpersons or District
Assembly members are used, as well as associational leaders (ethnic,
neighbourhood, even NGOs); they will tend to use commonsense

norms of fairness and search for mediation and consensual agreement. A clear distinction must be made between these forms of dispute settlement and the more formal customary hearings offered by higher ranking chiefs within the traditional hierarchy – divisional and sub-chiefs of the established Traditional Councils, who may be located in particular towns, and paramount chiefs who are heads of the Traditional Councils.[4] In these hearings, chiefs apply customary law and procedure as they understand it.

The difference between the dispute resolution offered by village chiefs and that offered in the customary hearings or 'courts' of the superior chiefs is highly significant and reflects not just the traditional political hierarchies of Ghana's pre-colonial states, but also the legacy of colonial rule and its impact on the political and economic roles of the chiefs. The superior chiefs in Ghana continue to wield a political authority which until recently was a formal part of the governmental system of Native Authorities (NAs) and Native Courts (NCs) created by the British. The NA gave an institutional, legal and economic basis to the chieftaincy which both consolidated the political identities of the pre-colonial entities upon which they were (more or less) based and produced a powerful 'neo-traditional' elite of wealthy and western-educated chiefs who were a major bulwark of colonial society. The power of these rulers was recognised formally in the colonial system through the role given to the territorial councils of the ruling chiefs (the Joint Provincial Council of the Colony, the Asanteman Council and the Northern Territories Council). Recognition of the concept of 'allodial ownership' of stool lands by the chiefs also underpinned the power of the chiefs to manage and allocate land, a power which became highly significant economically as the growth of the cocoa industry in Southern Ghana and urbanisation throughout the colonial period led to the wholesale commercialisation of land values. The contemporary role of the chiefs in the control and management of land and their ability to profit from its market value are a direct legacy of the law and institutions developed during the colonial period; this legacy is particularly strong in the Akan areas, where political jurisdiction has long been conflated with allodial land ownership or 'trusteeship' and management rights.[5]

The most powerful chiefs today are the heirs of the largest NA chiefs and include the rulers of large traditional states such as the Asante Confederacy or Akyem Abuakwa who are 'modern monarchs' of political entities with populations in their millions. The current *Asantehene*, the *Okyenhene*, or the *Ya Na* of Dagbon are figures of national political importance who, whatever the formal rule which prohibits chiefs from participating in 'party politics', have in fact played key roles in Ghana's political history since independence.

The customary courts which the superior chiefs continue to run are the direct descendants of the Native Courts, in which customary land law was formalised and developed over a period of 60-70 years. The current campaign to give the superior chiefs more formal powers to adjudicate land disputes is, in effect, little more than an attempt to revive the old Native Courts. The Native Authorities in colonial times were empowered to administer their own customary law through Native Tribunals, renamed Native Courts in the 1935 Ashanti Native Courts Ordinance and the 1944 Colony Native Courts Ordinance. The Native Courts, as the lowest level of first instance courts, not only had the power to administer the customary law of family, inheritance, land and religious customs; they also had jurisdiction over minor criminal cases, local bye-laws and various offences against colonial regulations (markets, licenses, health and sanitary rules etc.). The grade 'A' and 'B' courts set up by the 1935 and 1944 Ordinances had unlimited jurisdiction in land cases – in Ashanti, the Asantehene's court was the only grade 'A' court, in recognition of the *Asantehene*'s jurisdiction over the whole of the recently restored Asante Confederacy. The judges of customary law in the Native Courts were the chiefs and elders who formed their benches. Until the 1944 reforms in the Colony, the benches were formed as of right by the chiefs and their hereditary office holders and elders, with the paramount chief as president; there was therefore no distinction between political or executive office and judicial functions. Lawyers were not allowed to plead in the Native Courts, although their influence was undoubtedly felt in the litigations which engulfed many of the large chieftaincies during the 1920s and '30s.

Even more importantly, the Native Courts were regarded by the British as part of the hierarchy of state courts; customary laws could be pleaded and 'judicially recognised' in the state courts, both on appeal and at first instance. Over time it was established that a customary rule would be accepted as a legal rule if it could be shown that it had been applied by a Native Court; the resulting decision then became part of the common law under the normal rules of *stare decisis* (Allott 1994; Woodman 1996:45). Thus 'customary law' developed during the colonial period as a body of written, court-developed law, or what Woodman calls 'lawyers' customary law'.

In spite of their crucial role in the development of customary land law and the colonial judicial system, the Native Courts did not have a good reputation during the colonial period. Criticisms of corruption, oppressive procedures and lack of accountability for funds came not just from administrators and lawyers but also from litigants and increasingly from local 'youth associations' and emergent nationalist movements led by new generations of educated Ghanaians. The fact that members of the panels derived personal income from sharing out

fees and fines was one of the most obvious areas of abuse which encouraged the proliferation of tribunals and excessively large benches.
They also 'fomented' litigation, even as 'informal' costs to litigants spir-
alled. The Blackall Committee of Enquiry in 1943 described their procedures as 'amounting to a denial of justice' and noted that expendi-
ture by litigants in the Gold Coast was 'without parallel in native Africa' (Hailey 1951). Although the reforms of 1944 regularised payments
and appointments to panels, the move to 'democratise' colonial rule in
the late 1940s/early '50s signalled the end of the indirect rule institutions of which the NCs were so much a part (Crook 1986). In 1951 the
Korsah Committee recommended their abolition and replacement by
Local Courts under the control of the Chief Justice, with appointed lay
and stipendiary magistrates. But it took another seven years for them
to finally disappear, with the passing of the Local Courts Act in 1958.
During those seven years, which coincided with the transfer of power
to Nkrumah's CPP government, their reputation was further undermined through the systematic replacement of traditional panel members by 'politically reliable' government appointees whose behaviour
was no better (Rathbone 2000; cf. Gocking 1993).

   The legacy of the Native Courts is therefore an ambiguous one, insofar as the justice offered by the superior ranking chiefs is concerned.
Their development up to 1958 undoubtedly produced an uneasy synthesis of traditional procedures and concepts with those imported from
British law and justice. Scholars disagree on the outcomes; Woodman
argues that living custom or social practice inevitably diverges from formalised (written) 'lawyer's customary law', to the extent that real contradictions can emerge on what the 'authentic' rules are (Woodman
1988, 1996; cf. Ubink 2002-2004). Insofar as the chiefs and elders are
both the custodians of customary law and holders of political and economic power over land, customary rules are bound to be reinterpreted
by each generation in the light of their own interests and changing
socio-economic circumstances. Customary courts in the past provided
an institutional setting within which social and economic conflicts
could be played out. But the decoupling of the chiefs' tribunals from
the formal legal system over the past 48 years or more has probably
contributed to an increasing divergence between the chiefs' vision of
customary law and that of the common law courts.[6] Woodman also
points out that the customary forms of justice clung to quite different
processes of reasoning and offered different remedies; one obvious example is the key role which discourses or political ideologies of genea-
logical legitimacy and histories of settlement still play in customary dispute hearings (Berry 1997, 2001; Crook 1973). Although these arguments are still brought before the state courts, the way in which the
court comes to a decision will probably be different, not least because

of the basic common law practice of discussing a case in terms of the *ratio decidendi* of the relevant precedents.[7]

Gocking on the other hand, argues that the Native Courts incorporated a large number of British legal practices which were absorbed in such a way that they soon came to be viewed as authentically traditional – for instance the alternate cross examination of witnesses, defendants' statements, the taking of surety from litigants, and of course, the writing down of proceedings and decisions. Much of this happened under pressure from administrative officers and then, perhaps more importantly, from the influence of the post-1927 formally trained Native Court Registrars or court clerks, who became pivotal figures dispensing advice to the chiefs and even influencing case outcomes. Customary law was therefore subtly mediated and modified over a long period of time through its interface with British common law, and this legacy has been thoroughly incorporated into what are thought of as 'traditional' procedures (Gocking 1993).

Arguments about the 'authenticity' of the Native Courts and their successors, the superior chiefs' customary or traditional tribunals are probably fruitless in that they can never now be resolved. What is clear is that they cannot be described as informal, surrounded as they are by the trappings of traditional office, ancient rituals of spiritual significance, and the legacy of their recent colonial past. Nor can they be seen as mediations in which the parties have equal bargaining power and the judges are neutral 'arbitrators' with no coercive or other social power. On the contrary, the chiefs still wield significant political and economic power, particularly with respect to land, which is highly likely to lay them open to accusations of having an interest in the cases they may be hearing.

The courts of the biggest chiefs are very formal and 'theatrical' affairs where the large number of 'judges' or those attending can produce an intimidating effect. Appearing before an important Ashanti chief and his councillors (e.g. a divisional chief, or an *omanhene*) is, for village people, to appear before officials who must be shown the full respect due to persons of high status and power. Although the public can observe, their opinion is not sought, and deliberation is the prerogative of the chief and his council. Order is strictly maintained by the Linguists. The *Asantehene*'s full court, which is both a court of first instance for large cases and an appeal court for the whole of the Asante kingdom, is highly formal and traditionally accessed through the solemn swearing of the 'Great Oath of Asante' followed by payment of fees and sureties by the parties.[8] In colonial times, the *Asantehene*'s Court A included the *Asantehene* himself as president, his twenty divisional or head chiefs, the Kumasi clan chiefs and Linguists through whom all discourse was passed. The setup today is little different; the full court may number two hundred chiefs and take all day to assemble. The procedure is extremely lengthy as all counsellors can cross examine parties and witnesses. The traditional procedure aims at persuading the winning party to publicly accept an apology and reconciliation or 'pacification' from the other party, and Yeboah argues that it is basically non-adversarial and conciliatory in character (Yeboah 2005). Nevertheless, the format, especially in Ashanti, gives a very strong sense of 'winner and loser', as embodied in the traditional concepts and language used. A loser is deemed to have 'wasted the time' of the chiefs and has to 'purchase his head' by paying a fine (the equivalent of slaughtering sheep) and pay a 'thank you', in addition to any fines or compensations to the winner. Overall, it can be argued that the high status and wealth of the royal judges, and the fact that it is an enforced procedure not a voluntary mediation, indeed make the experience somewhat intimidating.

With respect to land cases, the *Asantehene* has recently introduced various innovations, following on his edict in 2000 that all disputes should be withdrawn from court and from the Regional House of Chiefs and sent to him for settlement. It is clear from the research done at the Kumasi High Court that not all land cases have in fact been withdrawn and remitted to the *Asantehene*. This is because the likelihood of them being heard more quickly at the *Asantehene*'s palace is in current circumstances even less than in the state court system. In November 2004 the *Asantehene* set up four new courts (labelled A - D) to deal with the hundreds of outstanding land cases; for each court, there are Lands Sub-Committees of five sub-chiefs and officials appointed to carry out all the preliminary investigation work and report to the court. It is envisaged that the proceedings in the courts (which have only deliberative functions) will be videotaped and then the notes of the decision and the tape sent to the *Asantehene* and his eleven Councillors for review and final decision. A decision is pronounced with the parties present at a full *Asantehene*'s traditional court with all his Councillors and sub-chiefs present. So far, however, few cases have been actually tried through this new procedure which has been in gestation since 2004, and little evidence could be obtained on how many cases had been heard. The *Asantehene*'s Lands Secretariat, located in the palace (*Manyhia*) is still a small and very traditional office with few professional staff and no modern recording systems (Crook et al. 2007).

The legitimacy and accessibility of customary and local forms of justice

Arguments about the legitimacy and accessibility of customary justice can only really be resolved, however, by looking at empirical evidence of the ways in which it is viewed and used by ordinary people or litigants. Research conducted between 2001 and 2005 in Ghana and Côte d'Ivoire looked at customary and local forms of justice within the framework of a wider study of the whole range of dispute settlement institutions (DSIs), ranging from informal types of arbitration at family and local levels to administrative actions and formal state courts. The key question addressed was whether, in situations of legal pluralism, the land rights of the poor and vulnerable are best protected through sustaining the mix of legal codes and procedures characteristic of legal pluralism, or whether an integrated system of state justice affords better protection. The different DSIs were analysed and compared with reference to their effectiveness, legitimacy and inclusiveness (see Crook et al. 2007 for a full account of the research results). The evidence presented below is drawn from studies of land disputes and DSIs in three areas of Ghana: Asunafo District (Brong-Ahafo Region), Nadowli South District (Upper West Region) and peri-urban Kumasi (Ashanti Region). A village-level survey of 676 respondents was carried out in selected villages, in order to find out what kinds of disputes were most common, how people resolved them and what they felt about the different kinds of dispute settlement which they had experienced.

Causes of land disputes at the local level

In the three case-study areas, 22.6 per cent of respondents in the village-level surveys said that they had personally experienced a land dispute.[9] (This group of 153 respondents will hereafter be referred to as the 'popular survey sub-set'). The largest group of disputes concerned trespass (encroachment on or misuse of the owner's land), or some kind of difference with a neighbouring farmer (Table 6.1). The experience of disputes came disproportionately from villages in the Asunafo area, which accounted for 63 per cent of the sub-set. To some extent this can be attributed to the fact that this is a cocoa growing agricultural area with a large population of migrants, although the Kumasi peri-urban areas might have been expected to have been even more conflictual. But Asunafo is also an area where migrants have been established for a long time, and the survey tends to show that relations with the host communities are, at the present time at least, relatively peaceful. Thus there were surprisingly few cases of disputes with a 'landlord'.

Table 6.1 *Popular survey sub-set: cause of dispute*

Cause of dispute	Valid percent
Trespass	34.6
Unlawful sale	3.9
Inheritance	2.6
Disposition of rights	11.1
Family dispute	23.5
Dispute with another farmer	13.1
None specified	9.2
Dispute with landlord	1.3
Other	0.7
Total	100.0 (n= 153)

The choice of local dispute settlement institutions (DSIs)

When the sub-set of respondents (those who had experienced a dispute) were asked where they had *first* gone to resolve their dispute, a surprisingly wide range of DSIs was revealed (Table 6.2). The contrast between these village level disputants and those who had become litigants in the state courts was striking; of the latter, 46 per cent overall (and over 50 per cent in Kumasi) had gone straight to court without using any other procedure, compared with the village disputants, of whom only 10.5 per cent had gone to court (Crook et al. 2007:46). But particularly noteworthy is that only a minority of the village respondents – just over a quarter overall (26 per cent) – had used a 'traditional' court (superior or village chief, chief and elders, or land priest [*tendana*]). And there were significant differences between the Kumasi

Table 6.2 *Popular survey sub-set: dispute settlement institution by location*

Dispute settlement institution	Location			Totals %
	Kumasi %	Asunafo %	Nadowli %	
Not specified	3.3	14.4	19.2	13.1
Court	13.3	11.3	3.8	10.5
Traditional court	40.0	22.7	23.1	26.1
Family gathering	20.0	22.7	15.4	20.9
Police	3.3	0.0	0.0	0.7
Not resolved	6.7	1.0	0.0	2.0
Between concerned parties	3.3	10.3	15.4	9.8
Arbitration	10.0	16.5	23.1	16.3
CHRAJ[10]	0.0	1.0	0.0	0.7
Total	100	100	100	100

peri-urban villages and the other locations: in Kumasi, chiefs' courts
were much more popular (40 per cent) as opposed to Asunafo and Nadowli (23 per cent). In spite of the generally good relations between
host and migrant communities, strangers or non-locals were also much
less likely to use a chief's court – 16 per cent of non-locals had used a
chief's court as opposed to 31 per cent of the locals. This can be interpreted as a preference for using their own community leaders or for resolving matters between themselves, as well as a lack of trust, to a degree, in the local chiefs.

The next most-used types of DSI were in fact a family gathering (21
per cent) and an informal arbitration (16.3 per cent) – that is, the parties sought the help of 'informed' or respected persons which could for
instance be an elder, their landlord, or the local elected Unit Committee Chair or a respected District Assembly member.[11] An unusual case
was the predominantly migrant village of Ahenkro in Asunafo, where
the Unit Committee Chair was also the head of the Pentecostal Church
which incorporated the main elected leaders of the community (Kro-
bos, Ewes, and Kwahus from the Eastern Region) and effectively combined religious and secular leadership. The socially-embedded authority of the Chairman was consequently both legitimate and strong, and
the community was peaceful and well run.

As to why they chose the DSI they had used, the most frequently cited reason amongst villagers was to 'maintain peace and harmony with
neighbours'; but a close second was the need for a 'final' settlement
(most of those who had gone to court), followed by the need to 'respect'
the elders and respect local norms of behaviour.

The legitimacy of the different forms of DSI

All respondents (not just those who had had a dispute) were asked
who they would most trust to settle any problem they might have concerning their land. The people named most frequently as 'trusted a lot'
(an unambiguously positive choice) were: first, village chiefs; second,
family heads; and third, court judges, with Unit Committee Chairmen
coming a close fourth (Table 6.3). Even more surprisingly, lawyers figured on the list at a respectable number 8! If we add in the 'to some
extent' responses, to get an aggregated positive scoring, we find village
chiefs and family heads in first and second places with virtually equal
scores, named by 80.6 and 80.5 per cent of respondents; Unit Committee Chairmen third with 65.6 per cent; and court judges fourth
with 58.5 per cent. On the other hand, the people they were most *unlikely* to trust were village school headteachers and the police (except in
the Upper West Region) (Table 6.4).

Table 6.3   *Whom would you most trust to settle any land dispute? 'Trust a lot'*

Trust in	% choices	Ranking
Village chief	62.1	1
Head of family	61.4	2
Court judge	35.4	3
Unit Committee Chairman	34.2	4
Paramount chief	32.1	5
Divisional chief	28.8	6
Tendana	26.2	7
Lawyer	19.8	8
Police	14.2	9
Agriculture Department officer	13.8	10
District Commissioner	13.2	11
School headmaster	11.4	12
Lands Commission officer	11.1	13
Town and Country Planning Officer	10.4	14
CHRAJ	8.6	15
Church leader	3.4	16
Elder	1.6	17

Table 6.4   *Whom would you most trust to settle any land dispute? 'Not at all'*

Trust in:	% choices	Ranking
School headmaster	47.6	1
Police	38.2	2
Agriculture Department officer	28.0	3
District Commissioner	25.4	4
CHRAJ	22.0	5
Town and Country Planning Officer	19.2	6
Unit Committee Chairman	18.3	7
Lands Commission officer	17.2	8
Lawyer	16.9	9
Court Judge	15.1	10
Paramount chief	12.0	11
Divisional chief	8.1	12
Head of family	7.0	13
Village chief	6.5	14
Tendana	0.3	15
Church leader	0.3	15

The legitimacy of chiefs' courts

Although it is clear that chiefs remain an important source of dispute settlement at the local level and enjoy high levels of respect and trust, there are important ambiguities and difficulties surrounding their role, as well as differences amongst the three areas of study (Table 6.5).

Respondents in all areas made a clear distinction between the village chief and paramount and other important chiefs. Everywhere the vil-

Table 6.5 *'Trust a lot' rankings by location*

'Trust a lot'	Location		
	Kumasi % / rank	Asunafo % / rank	Nadowli % / rank
Village chief	61.2/ 1	55.6/ 2	71.3/ 3
Head of family	52.7/ 2	47.7/ 3	87.1/ 1
Court judge	20.9/ 5	57.1/ 1	21.5/ 6
Unit Committee Chairman	37.8/ 3	27.4/ 4	39.2/ 5
Paramount chief	28.4/ 4	15.8/ 5	56.5/4
Tendana	n/a	n/a	84.7/ 2

lage chief was highly trusted, although in Nadowli the family heads and *tendana* were recognised as most appropriate for settling land issues. In the Asunafo district, however, the big chiefs were ranked lowest, and the popularity of the district judge was confirmed by a top ranking, above even the village chief. As might be expected there was a difference between expressions of trust in response to a general opinion question, and what people actually did when they had a dispute – 62 per cent overall saying they trusted a village chief to settle disputes compared to 26 per cent of the sub-set who had experienced a dispute saying they had used a traditional court. Nevertheless, the lower general trust expressed in chiefs in Asunafo compared with Kumasi (see Table 6.5) was in fact reflected in the sub-set figures – only 23 per cent in Asunafo had used a traditional court, compared to 40 per cent in Kumasi. In peri-urban Kumasi, chiefs have a more powerful and prominent role but even here the paramount and big chiefs were not so trusted. One explanation for these figures could be the involvement of chiefs in land management allocation, and the politics of chieftaincy in the Brong-Ahafo Region.

In Asunafo, there have been and continue to be long standing disputes between the major chiefs of the Ahafo Traditional Council and the *Asantehene*'s Kumasi 'caretaker chiefs', and between big paramountcies such as Mim and Kukuom (see Dunn and Robertson 1973). Although the lands have all been vested in the government, ordinary citizens are fearful of coming up against or being involved in any kind of a dispute that might engage these 'major players'. As regards the position of the many migrants in the area, since the crisis over the Busia Government's Aliens Expulsion Order of 1971 relations between hosts and migrants have settled down and are relatively peaceful. But it is clear that trust in the chiefs depends on a 'virtuous circle'; it is maintained so long as relations are good and there are no major problems; migrants are happy to acknowledge the rights and status of the allodial owners. The new government of the NPP is perceived to be, and is in fact, a direct heir to the Busia government of 1969-1972, and some

fears were aroused in many southern 'Akan' areas about the future position of migrants. Some of the chiefs interviewed in Asunafo (and
chiefs at government seminars on land management – see GTZ 2002)
referred to the new Constitution of 1992 as giving them the right to
turn all tenancies granted to strangers and foreigners into 'leases' –
something which the Lands Commission has been doing, even though
it is legally suspect. But migrants in the village focus groups all regarded their customary tenancies as giving them the land in perpetuity
and heritable by their heirs. They do not see this as threatened at the
moment, but this could change depending on the progress of the legal
reforms associated with the LAP. Hence the greater reluctance of non-
locals in the Asunafo area to use a chief's court to resolve an actual dispute (see below, Table 6.8).

Although people in Kumasi (as elsewhere in Ashanti) look to the
Asantehene to resolve these issues, the new *Asantehene*'s attempt to deal
with the land dispute problem in the region by ordering that all disputes should be withdrawn from the court and sent to him for settlement, has not so far produced many results (see above). In the peri-urban areas of Kumasi, there is continuing conflict over the role which
the chiefs play in the appropriation of village lands for sale as urban
plots. Where a Land or Plot Allocation Committee (as recommended
by the *Asantehene*) has been set up and works effectively, the community (the customary landholders) can ensure that some of the capital
raised (and the plots) are retained for the benefit of the citizens themselves. But in many places this does not work – for instance, in one of
the case study villages in Kumasi, Esereso, the Land Allocation Committee collapsed after a dispute over the succession to the queenmother
post, and the queenmother herself was selling plots illicitly in the teeth
of resistance and opposition from other factions in the village.[12] In
some villages (e.g. Appiadu) the chief is trusted; but the system is fragile and accountability structures are generally not robust enough to
avert the constant danger of abuse, or rumours and suspicions of
abuse. This is strongly supported by comparative evidence from
Ubink's linked studies of peri-urban villages in the Ejisu paramountcy
south of Kumasi (Ubink 2008, in press). She shows that in such situations, the chief is often regarded as having too much personal interest
to be trusted as an impartial judge of a local land case.

Even in Nadowli, where the respect for traditional institutions is still
apparently very high, the legitimacy of a chief's court is not always sufficient to ensure acceptance or enforcement of a decision. In one of the
case-study villages, Loho (on the northern border of Wa) a serious land
dispute with a neighbouring village, Charia, has been through various
stages of arbitration, beginning with elders and land chiefs, a Committee of Enquiry chaired by a chief of the Regional House of Chiefs (the

Lambussie Kuoro) and finally the High Court, all of which found in favour of the Loho claim.[13] Yet the Charia people continue to contest the
results, including the 'wrath of the gods' which was called down upon
them when they flouted the traditional ruling. The Loho people, however, claim the moral high ground in that they have refused to retaliate,
either with direct action or a new court case (Hammond 2003).

Another case involving urban land in Wa has been even more resistant to resolution. Here, some land was acquired by the Ghana SSNIT
(the government Social Security and National Insurance Trust) for an
office building, generating significant financial returns for whoever
could establish their claim to be the 'customary owners'. Again, the dispute between rival traditional claimants (descendants of rival 'settler'
lineages) has gone through every form of dispute resolution ending in
the Supreme Court. The faction which lost in the arbitration offered by
the Waala Traditional Council (the Kabanye) refused to accept the
chiefs' verdict, went to court and won all appeals up to the Supreme
Court. The losing faction (the Danaayiri), feeling they had traditional
right on their side, broadcast on local radio after the Supreme Court's
decision to announce that they had won, and were the true owners of
the land. There are political overtones to the case, in that the faction
which won in court (Kabanye) has long been associated with the former ruling party, Rawlings' NDC, which is now in opposition. The losing faction, although associated with a minor opposition party, the
PNC, engaged an NPP lawyer to fight their case, a man who subsequently became a Deputy Minister of Lands in the NPP government. It
is likely that they imagine that a connection with the governing party
may help to overturn all previous verdicts and they have submitted a
petition to Parliament.

Overall, in this area a professed respect for traditional norms is not
carried out in practice, primarily because of the chaotic legacy of the
de-vesting of northern lands in 1979.[14] There is little or no agreement
on who owns particular parcels of land and an almost total absence of
historical records. Traditional norms quickly crumble in the face of the
growing marketisation of land, and factions defy all authority, whether
traditional or state, where there is the prospect of making some money
from a claimed right of land ownership.

The inclusiveness of different DSIs

Although traditional institutions such as chiefs' courts are frequently
criticised for being gender biased (against women), the general trust
rankings showed very little difference in levels of trust between men
and women (Table 6.6). And not many significant differences emerged
by age or education, except that of the very small number of post-sec-

ondary educated respondents (eight out of 676), only two (25 per cent) said they trusted the village chief a lot. Only the origin of respondents produced interesting differences in the extent to which they trusted paramount chiefs and judges; migrants from a different district or region showed much less propensity to trust a paramount chief and were more likely to trust a judge (Table 6.7). (The figures for foreigners refer to only seven respondents, so they cannot be relied upon too heavily).

These small differences in attitudes to the traditional authorities were once again confirmed more conclusively through analysis of the sub-set of those who had experienced an actual dispute. Here, origin was the most significant predictor of the choice of a dispute settlement institution, rather than sex or education. Non-locals were only half as likely to have used a traditional or chief's court, and were much more likely to have used arbitration by respected persons or to have sorted out the issue through negotiation with the other party (Table 6.8).

Conclusion

How inclusive and legitimate are customary and informal local DSIs in Ghana? The village level research shows that a lot of potential conflict, particularly over boundaries and land use, is typically solved by very lo-

Table 6.6 *'Trust a lot' rankings by sex*

'Trust a lot'	Sex	
	Male % / rank	Female % / rank
Village chief	60.7/ 2	63.9/ 1
Head of family	62.8/ 1	59.4/ 2
Court judge	39.0/ 3	30.6/ 4
Unit Committee Chairman	33.6/ 5	35.1/ 3
Paramount chief	34.1/ 4	29.5/ 5

Table 6.7 *'Trust a lot' selected rankings by origin*

'Trust a lot'	Origin				
	Locality %	District %	Region %	Other Region %	Foreign %
Court judge	31.2	29.3	27.5	57.4	100.0
Unit Committee Chairman	35.6	36	25.5	30.6	57.1
Paramount chief	34.7	41.3	21.6	22.2	0.0

Table 6.8   *Popular survey sub-set: choice of DSI by origin*

Dispute Settlement Institution	Origin		
	Local %	Non-local %	Total %
Not specified	11.7	16.3	13.1
Court	11.7	8.2	10.5
Traditional court	31.1	16.3	26.1
Family gathering	20.4	20.4	20.9
Police	0.0	2.0	0.7
Not resolved	1.9	2.0	2.0
Between concerned parties	7.8	14.3	9.8
Arbitration	14.6	20.4	16.3
CHRAJ	1.0	0.0	0.7
Total	100	100	100

cal forms of conflict resolution involving family heads and village chiefs or elders and other respected persons including elected opinion leaders. These are trusted because they are not co-opted by, or associated with, unpredictable external forces. Nevertheless, even these community-based DSIs can suffer from many well-acknowledged problems, such as perfunctory or summary procedure, unequal power relations, or 'crony justice' dominated by local power holders.

The research evidence also shows that if a case cannot be solved peaceably at the local level there is certainly a thirst for a legitimate authority (a trusted external arbiter) and some certainty – a need which is often fulfilled by going to the state courts or institutions such as the CHRAJ. But beyond the village level, the customary courts of the superior chiefs are not necessarily more trusted or user friendly than the state courts. Many, especially in the Asunafo District, clearly trusted the court judges, particularly the District Magistrate, more than they trusted the chiefs. This is partly because historically the chiefs have an association with the colonial state, and are still regarded as part of the political power hierarchy. Another reason, however, lies in the power which chiefs have in local land allocation and management, and the development of customary law in response to marketisation and urbanisation. Chiefs have been using their allodial claims to attempt to gain control over the value of urban development land (and thus challenging the security of the 'customary freeholds' held by citizens of the political community). In the cocoa areas, there is a growing fear that apparently secure landholdings of migrant farmers could be converted to 'leaseholds' by chiefs citing the new laws. Yet the accountability mechanisms linking chiefs to their communities are fragile and frequently ineffective. Thus chiefs can be accused of defining the rules for their own benefit and of being 'interested parties' who cannot necessarily be trusted to offer impartial justice in local land disputes.

Whether local and customary DSIs can be promoted as an ADR-type solution to the crisis of land cases in Ghana depends very much on the kind of power held by the chosen arbitrators, their role in the community, and the kinds of procedures adopted. As noted above, ADR as developed in Europe or North America assumes that disputes are between individual parties and need the services of a 'neutral mediator'. But in Ghana, as in many other parts of West Africa, customary dispute settlement ideally involves building the consensus of the whole relevant community, and the individuals in dispute are not seen as abstract individuals but as members of groups – families, clans, age sets, ethnicities – with a particular status and known position within the community (both gender and age as well as wealth and office may be relevant). Even if mediators are not chiefs or elders, they are not expected to be strangers or unknown to the parties, and therefore 'impartiality' may be less valued than intimate knowledge of the circumstances of the case (cf. Grande 1999; Van Donge 1999). In the case of a chief's court, the chief's decision should take account of the need to reflect a broader agreement between the groups behind the disputing parties, which will ensure social harmony and avoid feuding in the future. In doing so he will be fully aware of the power, status, and social position of those groups. This is because the effectiveness of the agreement – its acceptance and enforcement – depends upon social sanctions, such as shame, hostility, and social pressure on the parties. Indeed, some scholars regard the 'community harmony' model itself as idealised or even mythical, and suggest that community-based customary justice simply 'reinforces local power relations', including those related to gender (Khadiagala 2001).

Nor does the requirement for a balance of power and a non-coercive mediator necessarily correspond to the reality of a community-based customary adjudication, especially if the case is being heard by one of the superior chiefs' courts described above. These chiefs have high authority and status, and the procedures are often very formal, even intimidating. As the history of the customary courts in Ghana indicates, the idea that parties who come before a superior chief's customary court have equal bargaining power, or that the mediator or 'judge' is somebody without coercive power over them, is not a necessary or realistic element of the situation. And this is reflected quite strongly in our survey-based evidence of popular perceptions of customary justice institutions, which suggest that a state policy to bolster chiefs' courts as an ADR alternative to the state courts is fraught with many difficulties and will not necessarily produce either a more popular or more just form of land dispute settlement.

Is there a more effective way in which the potential of local and customary forms of land dispute resolution can be harnessed? The state courts are clearly under enormous pressure, and even the state does not possess the necessary legitimacy, as some of our cases from the Upper West demonstrate. Perhaps one way to improve the form of justice offered, and to enhance the accountability of the chiefs, is to give more formal recognition to the dispute resolution tribunals which chiefs will be given with the new Customary Land Secretariats proposed in the LAP. As customary law is already a fully recognised part of the formal law of Ghana (as embodied in common law precedents) then any DSIs empowered to administer it should be (as in colonial times) part of the state court system and subjected to the normal rules of public accountability. Otherwise the CLS tribunals will suffer from the same problems as the existing chiefs' customary courts, which can apply whatever procedures and legal codes they choose without any reference either to established norms of customary law or the requirements of 'natural justice' (let alone ADR principles). If a fuller training in both customary law and in ADR procedures could be offered, it might be possible to create a very local popular court system as has been done in many other African countries. Any system which purports to offer ADR must somehow provide an informal but authoritative and impartial dispute resolution system; the chiefs' courts can only provide that if they combine socially and culturally-rooted legitimacy with more effective and respected procedures, while applying recognised laws. It may be that the time has come to recognise that customary law *has* been formalised and can no longer be permitted to develop spontaneously and randomly at local level, subject in practice to the dictates of the most powerful interests in local society. According to the Constitution, the National House of Chiefs has in any case been charged with the duty to codify and 'harmonize' customary laws throughout the nation. If undertaken seriously, such an enterprise would at least have to confront the serious contradictions which have emerged between 'lawyer's customary law' and the reinterpretations being created in chiefs' tribunals and other DSIs, and deal with them in a systematic and transparent manner.

Notes

1   Chiefs generally hold the ultimate or 'allodial' title to the land of the political community over which they rule in their official capacity as occupants of the Stool (the sacred symbol of their office, in the same way as the 'Crown' refers to the institution of the British monarchy). The concept of 'trustee' (borrowed from English law) is used to express the idea that the chief is a 'fiduciary' who has to manage the lands of his state for the benefit of his political community and can only act with the consent

of his councillors and his subjects (Constitution of Ghana, 1992, Articles 36(8) and 267(1); Woodman 1996:191, 200). Customary law is now recognised as an integral part of the laws of Ghana in the 1992 Constitution, Article 11(2).

2 The most powerful chiefs from the Akan-speaking traditional states of Ghana are located in the Eastern and Ashanti Regions. The 'stool' in Akan states is both a sacred physical object representing the ancestors of a chief's family, and a term used to refer to the chief's office (like 'the Crown' in the UK). The body of land law, which developed under British colonial rule, came to accept the principle that there is 'no land without an owner' and therefore that all unused or 'unallocated' land in a particular political community belonged ultimately to that community, and, insofar as it remained within customary tenure, was managed by the chief – or stool – on their behalf. This is the origin of the term 'stool land'; the ambiguity of the concept remains in the unspoken question: which community? The paramount chiefs eventually claimed that title to all the lands of a state was vested in the paramount stool and that all other customary rights were usufructory, but this is frequently contested by subordinate chiefs, and chiefs generally have tried to blur the distinction between stool lands meaning 'all the unallocated lands of the community', and lands belonging to the stool family (see Crook 1986). Article 295 (1) of the 1992 Constitution defines 'stool lands' as 'any land or interest in or right over land controlled by a stool or skin, the head of a particular community or the captain of a company for the benefit of the subjects of the stool or the members of that community or company'.

3 This registration would greatly strengthen the claims of the chiefs as against those of 'customary freeholders' (indigenous community members who hold land through their family membership and whose rights have not – so far – been reduced to the leaseholds provided under Article 267(5) of the Constitution).

4 The Traditional Councils are based on the pre-colonial political entities which were recognised and in many cases reorganised and even aggregated or 'created' by the British during the colonial period.

5 See footnote 2.

6 One of the most significant examples is the contemporary claim by the chiefs that the rights of customary freeholders are extinguished when land is needed for urban development. As in colonial times, customary law as practised is a process of constant negotiation and renegotiation amongst changing social interests; but the power of the chiefs to define customary law lies not only in their *de facto* control over land allocations, but also in the fact that the 1992 Constitution (Article 272) gives the National and Regional Houses of Chiefs the power to interpret and codify customary law.

7 The *ratio decidendi* is the rule of law emerging from the particular facts of a case and the judgment given on them.

8 In pre-colonial times, use of the Oath could bring death to the one who used it wrongly.

9 Defined as a non-trivial problem with the potential to become a 'justiciable event' (See Genn 1999).

10 Commission for Human Rights and Administrative Justice.

11 The Unit Committee is the lowest level of the District Assembly elected local government system, created in 1989 as amended by the Local Government Act of 1993 and Legislative Instrument (L.I.) 1589 of 1994. In theory based on population units of around 500-1000 people instead of 'villages', they are partly nominated (one-third) by the political boss of the District, the District Chief Executive, and partly elected. They replaced the former Village Development Committees which formally incorporated both traditional authorities and local citizens. But they have never attracted much electoral competition and in many areas exist on paper only – over 65 per cent

of the UCs were uncontested in the 1998 elections. But where they do function, they tend to be composed of leading members of the community who are co-opted or self-selected rather than elected and, depending on their political affiliation, may represent a counter-balancing force or even rival to the chief (see Crook 1999).

12 Queenmother is an official position in the Akan political hierarchy; she is head of the royal matrilineage and one of the key 'kingmakers' in the selection of a chief.

13 The Lambussie Kuoro Committee of Enquiry into the Charia-Loho Dispute, Final Report, 1 October 1995.

14 Under British rule, all land in the former Northern Territories was declared to be 'public land', vested in the Governor, who was empowered by the Northern Territories Land and Native Rights Ordinance 1927 to dispose of land 'for the use and common benefit of the African people'. Under the Ordinance, 'existing titles' had to be proved to the Governor within three years. In practice, very little land was registered in this way and according to Lands Commission officials in Wa, no records were kept of government land use and no attempt was ever made to map out landholdings. The low density of population and the lack of commercial exploitation of land meant that land was simply not regarded as an issue, and traditional institutions (unlike in southern Ghana) did not exercise strong control over land except informally at the local community level. A legacy of trouble was stored up, however, through colonial indirect rule institutions which created chiefs who began to claim Akan-like rights over land. The 1979 Constitution (Article 188) attempted to undo colonial history by simply stating that all lands in the former Northern Territories vested in the government were 'de-vested' and deemed to be returned to those who had owned the land prior to the 1927 legislation. This provision was consolidated in the 1992 Constitution, Article 257(3).

7 Struggles for land in peri-urban Kumasi and their effect on popular perceptions of chiefs and chieftaincy

Janine Ubink

Introduction

In recent years land in peri-urban Ghana has become increasingly commoditised as a result of the growing value of real estate and the expansion of urban residential areas. These new developments and the changing values in land that they create result in attempts to redefine land ownership and tenure and contestation of rights to land by citizens, traditional authorities and the state. At the heart of these contestations lie the issues of control over land and the authority to convert farmland to residential land and the entitlements to the proceeds from this conversion. The rapid conversion of farmland to residential land causes considerable unrest and distress in the peri-urban communities. Many families are losing their farmland and with that their jobs and income base. Since chiefs play a central and often negative role in the conversion of farmland, this could be expected to affect popular perceptions of chiefs and their various functions, and as a consequence have a bearing on the institution of chieftaincy. Especially, since claims of an institution to define property are also claims to the institution's legitimacy itself (Lund 2002:14; Shipton 2002: xi).

This chapter examines the struggles and negotiations over land in nine villages in peri-urban Kumasi[1] and poses the question to what extent the commoditisation of land and the role of chiefs in this process affects the way chiefs and chieftaincy are perceived by local citizens. The first part focusses on how Ashanti chiefs try to legitimise their actions through appeal to customary law, and how community members try to resist their chiefs' actions and claims. It shows that the success of local resistance against chiefs' maladministration of land is often very limited and that chiefs are making much personal profit from communal land. Three factors explain this 'local power balance', which lie respectively in the position of chiefs as guardians of stool land and authorities in the field of customary law, the lack of traditional checks and balances, and the government's present 'policy of non-interference' with regard to chieftaincy matters. After a description of the local contestations of land rights, the second part of this chapter focusses on

the effects of current land management practices on popular perceptions of chiefs and chieftaincy. A number of fundamental questions
have been formulated to study this issue: How do people feel about the
chief's role in land conversions? How does it influence their perceptions of other functions of the chief? What roles and tasks do they want
him to perform, and what are the limits to his powers? How do the activities of chiefs relate to the tasks and functions of local government?
How do people assess chiefs' performances? After studying these questions, this chapter concludes with some observations on the effects of
the performance of chiefs on the institution of chieftaincy. Data for this
research were gathered through participant observation, semi-struc-
tured interviews, and a survey, during a year of fieldwork in 2003-
2004.[2]

Struggles for land in peri-urban Kumasi, Ashanti

A royal attack on usufructuary rights?

In Ashanti, a large proportion of the land is so-called 'stool land',
which the Constitution describes as land vested in a stool[3] – a customary community – on behalf of and in trust for the subjects of a stool in
accordance with customary law and usage.[4] According to customary
law as represented in case law and textbooks, the ultimate or allodial
title of every portion of land is held in common by the members of a
community, and traditional authorities are regarded as custodians of
such land. Community members and families have so-called usufructuary interests in the land, which they have acquired by farming or
building on vacant communal land. These interests are heritable[5] and
are extinguished only through abandonment, forfeiture[6] or with consent and concurrence of the interest holder. The usufructuary cannot
be deprived of any of the rights constituting the interest. Not even the
chief can lay an adverse claim to the land (Asante 1969:105-106; Danquah 1928b:197-200, 206, 221; Ollennu 1962:29, 55-56; Ollennu 1967:
252-255; Pogucki 1962:180; Sarbah 1968:64-67; Woodman 1996:53,
66, 107).[7]

These customary rules date from the days when communities were
involved in subsistence farming in land-abundant areas, when not
land, but people were of value to chief and community. Now that market production, population growth and urbanisation have enhanced the
economic value of land, many chiefs in peri-urban Kumasi claim that
these rules are outdated and need to be adjusted to modern circumstances. Two kinds of legitimising discourses were found among the
chiefs in the area. One group of chiefs argues that the conversion of
farmland into residential land cannot be avoided and that communal

land that can be used in a more productive way should be brought back into chiefly administration (cf. Kotey and Yeboah 2003:20). According to the *Beseasehene*, 'It is a law that when the town is growing and it comes to your farm, you do not have any land. Because the land is for the chief.'[8] The *Kontihene* of the *Ejisuhene* agrees: 'When the town reaches the farm, people lose their rights.'[9] 'Only the chief can sell,'[10] says the *Kontihene* of the *Beseasehene*. However he takes a more moderate point of view: 'You must compensate the farmer for his loss of livelihood if he approaches you with respect. How much? That depends on when the farmer is satisfied. You don't want trouble in the family. It's a process of negotiation.'[11] The argument of this group of chiefs – that communal land which can be used in a more productive way should be brought back into chiefly administration – is only convincing, however, when the proceeds of the conversion are used for community development such as infrastructure, investments in education and alternative livelihood projects. That might ensure that the inhabitants of the village would still be able to make a living after the loss of their agricultural land. Although all interviewed chiefs acknowledged that they have at least a *moral* obligation to use part of the stool land revenue for compensation of the farmer and/or for community development, the actual practices differ considerably and substantial amounts of land revenue disappear in the coffers of the chiefs.

A second group of chiefs claims that their rights to administer the land do not derive from their function as caretakers on behalf of the community. Instead they assert that 'land belongs to the royal family, since it was members of the royal family who fought for the land'.[12] As leader of the royal family, the chief has administrative powers over the land. According to these chiefs, the royal family had only given this land out for farming purposes, to temporary caretakers, and can reclaim it when its use is changed to residential. And since the people were only temporary caretakers of the land, they have no right to compensation, save for the crops on the land.[13]

At the heart of the struggles over the authority to convert land lies a tension in the definition of what constitutes communal land and the concepts of allodial and usufructuary rights that make up this definition. Now that there is hardly any vacant communal land left in peri-urban Kumasi, the only way that chiefs can make money from the land is to cancel out the usufructuary rights of the citizens. They therefore attempt to transform usufructuary rights into permissive rights of tenant-like character, based on the leniency of the chief instead of on the communal ownership of the land. The consequences of this transformation are drastic for most people.[14] In peri-urban Kumasi farming is still a major occupation. In the eight villages surveyed, farming was the main occupation of 31.8 per cent of the people, and an additional

25.6 per cent farmed besides pursuing another occupation (N=242).[15] However, this situation is rapidly changing. Of the people that were either still farming themselves or whose family members in the village were still farming (N=171), 58.5 per cent stated that they or their farming family members had less farmland than ten years ago. Most of this lost farmland has been converted into residential land. Farmers and families who lose their land without appropriate compensation become poorer and in time lose the basis of their livelihood strategies. They are no longer able to grow their own food and generate some income by selling the surplus at the market. The loss of farmlands forces the landless to try and change occupation from farming to trading and other non-farm activities, such as working in the construction industry and other related industries, to earn a living. Many of the poorly educated farmers also become jobless. Through lack of farmland food prices rise in these communities, making life even harder for the poor. Social stratification increases and social cohesiveness has been reported to decline.[16]

Resisting the land appropriation

Villagers' views with regard to the right to convert and sell land vary widely, from acknowledging the chief's right to sell the land to a full denial of any such right. 'The chief decides to sell land. Farmers can't say no, but they can negotiate a price. But the bulk of the money goes to the chief, since he has full power'[17] is one view. While others feel that '(...) the chief cannot sell land without the family's consent because someone is farming there now. The money will go to the farmer, the chief only gets some of it.'[18] Considering the severe effects on the livelihoods of the people, it is understandable that many villagers undertake some kind of action to resist the reallocation of their farmlands or to influence the way the revenues are spent. All study villages witnessed various kinds of on-going struggles and negotiations between the land-owning chiefs and their people, ranging from direct confrontations with the chief, to bringing in other people or agencies, to more evasive techniques to 'get around' the chief.[19]

When tension about the chief's land administration rose, community members often first attempted to talk to the chief – either in private or at public village meetings – to persuade him to let farmers and families sell their own land with merely a signing fee paid to the chief, or to ask him to allocate a larger part of the revenue to farmer, family, and village. Such attempts were undertaken by a wide range of persons, such as elders, royal family members, local government representatives, otherwise influential persons in the village, or one or more of the farmers or families who were losing their farmland. In a number of villages, one of the popular solutions advocated to control administration of stool land was the establishment of a Plot Allocation Committee. Such a committee should consist of representatives of the chief and representatives of the village, often people from the Unit Committee (UC), the lowest level of local government in Ghana.[20] The Plot Allocation Committee should check concurrence of the site plan with the planning scheme and sign all land allocation papers. The existence of such a committee usually coincides with the transfer of a fixed portion of the money to the community for development. However, popular attempts to set up such committees have mostly been frustrated by the chiefs (cf. Edusah and Simon 2001), and in some villages such as Besease even by the villagers at large, who saw possibilities to sell their own land and were not inclined to hand a portion of the revenue over for community development. Angered by land sales by the chief or frustrated with a lack of progress in negotiations, people occasionally also took the law into their own hands. Several villages witnessed occasions of outright violence against the chief, sometimes by one family, as in the case of Besease, and sometimes by a big mob of villagers, as in the case of Pekyi No. 2 where the chief was chased out of the village with stones.

When direct interaction between chief and community did not have the desired effect, communities sometimes tried to bring in influential persons to reason with their chief. Often this person would be another chief, for instance the chief from the place of origin, the paramount chief or the *Asantehene*. Other encountered strategies were to bring in certain agencies, such as the Environmental Protection Agency[21] or the Commission for Human Rights and Administrative Justice, or to seek publicity through local radio stations. When more or less friendly negotiations proved unsuccessful, some communities threatened with or actually tried to press for a destoolment of their chief by the paramount chief, but this is a cumbersome and long process that is seen as a last resort and not often carried through.

A third cluster of resistance techniques could be classified as strategies to 'get around' the chief. Confronted with a lack of success in negotiations with the chief and therefore with the risk of losing their land, farmers and families started to sell their own land before the chief would do it. 'If you are very persistent the chief cannot take your land away. You can sell it and give part (of the money) to the chief. But if you are unlucky the chief will take the land, and if you don't fight it you won't get anything'.[22] This was done either without informing the chief at all, or by informing him only after the sale, when he was offered a moderate fee for the signing of the allocation note. Another way to deal with the problem without entering into direct struggle with the chief was by aiming the anger at the buyer instead. In many instances farmers have physically prevented buyers from entering on their new land, or destroyed the foundations of new-built structures, as soon as the buyer had left the land (cf. Kasanga and Kotey 2001).

The actions of resistance against the maladministration of stool land by the chief were often not successful. Before turning to the reasons for this lack of success, let me warn for the ostensible contradiction between chief and community that might have been created by the brevity of the description of actions of resistance as sketched above. Obviously chiefs are in no way unrelated to or separate from the community they live in. They form part of and have various linkages within the community. A chief's position within the community and his ability to build a coalition with his elders and other powerful people within the community are crucial for creating room for manoeuvre with regard to land administration.[23]

Traditional controls on chiefly administration

A number of the chiefs categorically rejected the suggestions and claims of the people to adjust stool land administration and continued to rule as they pleased. This poses the question as to how it is possible that these chiefs cannot be steered clear from their devastating track. Are there no checks and balances on their administration? A literature survey of some of Ghana's 'grand old men' in the field of customary land tenure yields the following quotes: '(T)he occupant of the stool can only bind the stool, i.e. the town or community, if he acts with the consent and concurrence of the whole town or community represented by the sub-chiefs, and the principal councillors from the various sections' (Ollennu 1962:130).

> Hereditary councillors,[24] or elders as they are called in the lower councils, and chiefs or sub-chiefs in the higher ones, are the heads of houses, families, or towns who have been elected by members of a house, family, or town to be their respective head, patriarch, or chief. (...) They hold their offices in the pleasure not of the Chief or head Chief, but by the sufferance of the people who have elected them to the Council. (...) It is of utmost importance, in view of our form of government, for the Chief, who is always the President of his Council, to give due weight and make full allowance of the expressed opinion of these councillors (Danquah 1928b:57).

'The chief was bound by his oath to consult the elders on all matters, and to obey their advice' (Busia 1951:14). To supplement these authoritative but not too recent writers[25] with a contemporary influential voice,

I turn to Kasanga who, less specific but equally romantic, states that 'there are reasonable checks at the local level on almost everybody' (Kasanga 2002:36).[26]

According to these writers traditional responsibility for village chiefs thus rests on two pillars. The first pillar is made up of a council of elders, selected by and representing all major factions of the community, without whose consent the chief cannot make any decision. The second pillar consists of the possibility to destool seriously malfunctioning chiefs. Leaving aside whether traditional rule was ever as equitable and well-balanced as these authors claim – which has been convincingly refuted in the extensive oeuvre of McCaskie[27] – current performance of chiefs in peri-urban Kumasi disabuses us of the idea that the two pillars function effectively in present-day village practice and suggests an erosion compared to their earlier functioning. To begin with, in a number of case study villages, the council is fully or to a large extent composed of elders from the royal family only, as is the case in Kotwi. The Kotwi Stool was originally carved out of the Asampong Stool, and the *Kotwihene* was like a sub-chief to the *Asamponghene* and thus did not have his own sub-chiefs. Later the *Kotwihene* was upgraded and he now swears his oath directly to the *Asantehene*. Although he could now have sub-chiefs, he has not installed any. He has continued to discuss village affairs with the elders from his family, and when there is a public ceremony the *Asamponghene* will join them with all his sub-chiefs. The absence of a council representing the whole community was encountered in a number of the other case study villages as well. Furthermore, the rule that elders hold their offices not in the pleasure of the chief but to serve the family that has elected them, also seems to be under strain. For instance in Nkoransa, where the secretary of the chief explains that 'it is not the rule that a certain family always brings a sub-chief. It is the chief who picks them. When one dies, he can choose a new one.'[28] This is underpinned by the abundance of conflicts between elders and their own family, who can no longer dismiss them when unsatisfied.[29] Regardless of the composition of the council, the chief often co-opts his elders by sharing the benefits from land administration with them, removing their incentives to effectively check the use of power and if necessary stand up against the chief (cf. Abudulai 2002:83). 'The sub-chiefs support the chief', says a UC-member of Tikrom, 'because they get a share of the money. When they argue with him, they won't get anything'.[30] Even at the *Asantehene*'s Land Secretariat it is acknowledged that 'in many villages the elders connive with the chief'.[31] And those elders that are not co-opted are often simply ignored by the chief, as is aptly illustrated by the following statement: 'Beseasehene is a new chief. He doesn't mind the rules', says his Kontrehene sub-chief, 'I tried to talk to him, but he didn't take my advice. If I wasn't educated, he would try to cheat me as well'.[32]

When a community wants to press destoolment charges against its chief for maladministration of land, they have to bring a case to the Traditional Council, made up of the paramount chief and his sub-chiefs.[33] A first hurdle is that destoolment charges cannot be voiced by mere commoners, but only by the 'kingmakers', i.e. those sub-chiefs and members of the royal family who can also make or enstool a chief (Hayford 1970:36). As discussed above, these sub-chiefs are often co-opted and therefore not likely to take the lead in actions against the chief. And if they do dare take action against their chief, this is usually only 'after many years of wrongdoing. The chief will first be given the benefit of the doubt', says one of the sub-chiefs of the *Ejisuhene* and, to explain why they have waited so long to start a destoolment case against the latter, he adds: 'The kingmakers have deposed the previous *Ejisuhene* and installed this one, of whom they had high expectations. They will now lose part of their legitimacy if they want to destool the one they selected'.[34] When the long duration of the destoolment process is added to the period it takes for kingmakers to undertake action, one can imagine that a chief can alienate a considerable amount of stool land in those years and spend the proceeds as well. A second obstacle lies in the fact that the paramount chief, who chairs the Traditional Council, is usually not disinterested in village land affairs, since he often receives a share of the villages' land revenues. The paramount chief of Ejisu for instance favoured exactly those chiefs who alienated large amounts of stool land. Furthermore, to mention a third hindrance, the members of the Traditional Council consist of direct colleagues of the chief-on-trial. Often the charges, such as selling farmland and not using enough stool land revenue for community development, are also items of contestation in the villages of the judging chiefs. Obviously, their personal interest in such cases could stand in the way of objective and impartial judgments.

The main customary checks and balances on chiefs – ruling in council with the sub-chiefs and the possibility of destoolment – are thus not very effective. One can add to this the fact that chiefly accountability is extremely low. Through a lack of registration most land administration is concealed. A good chief may account for his administration on his own accord, but this is an exception rather than the rule. To ask a chief to account is often considered a vote of no confidence and most people will not dare to do that unless there are more than clear indications of serious misrule by the chief. And even then, who is to bell the cat? The chief is still a powerful figure in most villages and you are sure to bring his wrath upon you by agitating against him. Moreover, most people consider it the task of the royal family to take action against a chief. And if the royal family does not discharge itself of this task, how can commoners be expected to take it upon themselves?[35]

The fact that the current customary system lacks effective checks and balances and accountability is not surprising when the historical development of the position of chiefs is taken into account. Without sketching a pristine view of egalitarian, consensual pre-colonial societies, it is clear that the colonial regime removed many of the traditional limitations to chiefs' authority (Toulmin and Quan 2000b:10; Van Rouveroy van Nieuwaal 1987:11). For instance, the British government overrode the traditional rules of investiture and reserved for itself the right to appoint and dismiss chiefs (Annor 1985; Busia 1951:105-106; Van Rouveroy van Nieuwaal 1987:11). Where commoners tried to reassert local checks and balances, a chief who was on friendly terms with the British administrator could easily neutralise these commoners by branding them malcontents and troublemakers (Kumado 1990-1992:203). Thus whilst losing his sovereignty, the chief held increasing powers over his subjects, because the local checks and balances were removed or at least watered down by the colonial authorities. The British gave the chiefs strong rights in land, by accepting their claims that according to customary law all land belonged to a customary community with the chief as the administrator. However, they did not give the chiefs free reign in all aspects. They regularly held them to account, monitored the bye-laws they made, and intervened in local conflicts, thereby to some extent compensating the lack of local checks and balances, at least in the field of land administration. After independence, the pre-colonial local checks and balances and accountability structures have not been furbished or rebuilt. A crucial question therefore is whether the current government also effectuates some state constraints on the administration of chiefs to compensate the lack of local checks and balances.

Before turning towards the level of the government, it is worth considering briefly whether any regulation or change towards more equity and community influence can be expected to come from *within* the traditional system. Some chiefs distribute land and land revenue fairly over the community members and display serious commitment to developing their villages. Could these chiefs serve as a role model and can they be expected to advise or correct their fellow chiefs? As we have seen, at all levels of traditional leadership – from village level to the *Asantehene* – both discourse and practice moves away from individual rights of community members in stool land to almost unrestricted rights of the chief to administer this land. It is important to realise that there is no one-to-one relationship between development-oriented leadership and willingness to abide by certain principles of good governance, such as accounting for administration and co-operating with a re-

presentative Plot Allocation Committee. For instance the *Jachiehene*, a
chief who was vigorously developing his village, not only abolished the
local Plot Allocation Committee, but outright stated that 'land in Jachie
belongs solely to the royal family' and 'a chief does not need to account, only if things go wrong'.[36] Development projects may also be
used by chiefs to enhance their power. Some chiefs have started development foundations to solicit funding for local projects, which can also
establish greater control over people and natural resources. E.g. the
Okyenhene uses his environmental foundation to attract funding, control forest-related livelihoods of youth and gain greater control over natural resources. The *Asantehene* attracts large funds, among others from
the World Bank, with his Education Fund. And the *Juabenhene* has established an agribusiness oil palm project through which he attempts
to extend his claims on land. Most chiefs, including the development-
oriented ones, supported a rather extreme level of chiefly discretionary
powers. This usually made them unwilling to condemn the maladministration of chiefs in other villages, let alone call such chiefs to account.
Furthermore, chiefs are in general unwilling to interfere in other
chiefs' businesses, with an appeal to the sacrosanct 'internal village affairs'.

Government's policy of non-interference

In the media, government officials regularly and vehemently proclaim
that they will not 'meddle in chieftaincy affairs'.[37] Land administration
is the main area about which such 'non-interference-statements' are
made. These statements not only claim that the government should
not interfere in chieftaincy affairs, but also allege that it is unnecessary:
since chiefs do not rule alone but in council with their elders, and
since they can be destooled when they seriously malfunction, the local
arena can deal with its own problems. Despite frequent indications that
these local checks and balances are not very effective, the government
takes refuge behind them, denying the people an opportunity to complain. Obviously, such state discourse provides chiefs with additional legitimacy in the field of land administration, and communicates little
fear for stately control and ample room for manoeuvre.

The discourse described above is an example of what I call the government's 'policy of non-interference'. Another salient example can be
found in the wording, drafting process, and content of the National
Land Policy – the first comprehensive land policy ever formulated by
the Ghanaian government – and its implementing Land Administration Program (Ministry of Lands and Forestry 1999; World Bank
2003a). Although program and policy aim to tackle the current problems in land administration, both the role of chiefs in the administra-

tion of stool land and the possible checks and balances the state can put in place with regard to stool land administration, are not critically examined. On the contrary, the role of chiefs as caretakers of stool land is taken as a fixed point of departure for all changes with regard to customary land administration. One might say that the policy of non-interference is currently so pervasive, that some problems and possible solutions are not even open for public discussion. The present government, unlike the colonial government, therefore does not keep 'chiefly landlordism' in check.[38]

The government's lack of enthusiasm to get involved in stool land administration can largely be explained by two factors: the first factor is the political power of chiefs, who are still regarded as strongly influential, and 'who are still voter-brokers, especially in the rural areas';[39] the second factor is the current tendency to fill chieftaincy positions with highly educated professionals, which fades the traditional distinction between state elite and chiefs, and creates new alliances between these two groups.[40] Nevertheless, there is an internal debate between modernisers and neo-traditionalists within the government, which is quite intense and highly sensitive. The modernisers, particularly in the land agencies and the Land Administration Program staff, try to break the silence around the maladministration of chiefs, but their efforts are thwarted by their superiors. Altogether, it seems that there is currently no political party willing to enter into any real battle, such as any land reform would cause, with the chiefs.[41]

In Part 1 of this chapter we have seen that, despite fierce resistance by the citizens, chiefs are the main beneficiaries of land conversions in peri-urban Kumasi. Three explanatory factors emerge from the analysis: 1) the position of chiefs as guardians of stool land and authorities in the field of customary law offers strong opportunities to point to custom to acquire and legitimate power over land; 2) the erosion of customary checks and balances hinders the control of chiefly functioning; and 3) the government's policy of non-interference gives additional legitimacy to the chiefs, provides them with ample leeway to administer land, and places the power to define customary law squarely in their hands. Without clinging to a pristine view of traditional rule in preceding periods, it seems safe to state that the democratic and participatory level of traditional rule are currently minimal. The fragile balance between chiefs and people has been seriously disrupted. This has given chiefs the power to abuse their prominent position as experts of customary law and guardians of stool land and to overstretch the somewhat dynamic nature of customary law by manipulating it to suit their needs and legitimise their claims.

Popular perceptions of chiefs and chieftaincy

The often negative role of chiefs in the conversion of farmland poses the questions to what extent and how chiefs' dealings with land affect people's views on the other tasks and activities of chiefs, as well as people's attitude towards chiefs and chieftaincy in general. According to the assemblyman of Esereso 'now that the chief does not supply the families with land they can speak disrespectfully of him in the village'.[42] Along the same lines, the *Kontrehene* sub-chief of the *Beseasehene* states that because of the maladministration of land by the *Beseasehene* 'No one recognises him as the chief. No one goes to him for dispute settlement'.[43] This same issue has been raised in other countries. Claassens, analysing local land administration in South Africa, states that '(s)elling land undermines the legitimacy and support base of traditional leaders among community members' (Claassens 2006:26). And Fisiy says of Cameroon: 'The rampant alienation of land by sale, especially to strangers (Fulani graziers), is seen as egoistic and potentially ruinous to the institution' (Fisiy 1992).

To study this issue in peri-urban Kumasi this chapter first analyses how people feel about the land conversions by the chiefs. Then it turns to other functions and activities of the chief and asks a number of questions: What roles and tasks do the people want chiefs to perform, and what are the limits to their powers? How do the activities of chiefs relate to the tasks and functions of local government? How do people assess the performance of chiefs, local government and chieftaincy? The chapter then concludes with some observations on the effects of the performance of chiefs on people's perceptions of the institution of chieftaincy.

Land administration

How do people in the villages regard the land conversions by the chief? It has been put forward that people in the villages generally accept that the development of residential plots is primarily the chief's concern (NRI and UST 1997:23). Others claim the opposite, i.e. that most people in peri-urban Kumasi want to minimalise the role of the chief in land administration (Van Leeuwen and Van Steekelenburg 1995:59). In the current research, the chiefs' claim that they can allocate farmland to strangers for residential purposes was accepted by 56.1 per cent of the respondents (Table 7.1).

Acceptance was high in the villages of Jachie, Tikrom and Ahenema Kokoben. One might expect that this acceptance stems from the fact that in these villages the chiefs are using the land and the revenue accruing from the conversions in the best interest of the community. In-

Table 7.1   *Who can allocate farmland to strangers for residential development?*[44]

Name of village	Village chief (%)	Head of family (%)	Farmer (%)
Jachie	100.0	0.0	0.0
Tikrom	91.3	4.3	4.3
Ahenema Kokoben	72.7	4.5	13.6
Adadeentem	53.8	15.4	26.9
Nkoranza	47.6	28.6	14.3
Kotwi	33.3	13.3	40.0
Boankra	33.3	40.7	22.2
Brofoyeduru	20.0	15.0	50.0
Total	56.1	13.5	24.0

deed, the *Jachiehene* for instance allowed members of the community to buy residential land at a very low price. And the revenue generated by leasing the remaining residential plots to outsiders was used for community development. In the first four years of his reign, the *Jachiehene* had built a library, a school, and a palace, and had allocated part of his land to a Technical School in exchange for scholarships. However, the same cannot be said for the chiefs of Tikrom and Ahenema Kokoben. In these villages chiefs reallocated large amounts of farmland without proper compensation and hardly any revenue was utilised for community development.

The high percentage of people accepting the power of the chief to re-allocate their farmland in the three villages can perhaps be understood rather as an acceptance of the reality of daily life. For in all three villages the chiefs not only claimed the right to allocate their farmland to strangers, but have also effectuated this right. In the other villages studied, either not so much land was converted yet, or the people were themselves highly involved in land allocations. For instance in Boankra the stool has been vacant for many years due to a chieftaincy dispute and families have been selling their land independent of the royal family. In Brofoyeduru local farmers are converting and selling their own land, after which they direct the buyer to the chief who will sign the allocation papers for a moderate signing fee. Although most people in the first three villages accepted that the chief converted farmland, in both Tikrom and Ahenema Kokoben the chief's right to spend the revenues at will was challenged. There was a lot of individual and communal resistance against the way chiefs used the revenues and against non-compliance of chiefs with planning schemes and environmental rules.

Table 7.2 *What are the main functions of the chief?*

Main functions of chief	%
Dispute settlement	78.1
Ensuring community participation in development	59.1
Ensuring peace in the community	53.0
Looking after the physical development of the town	50.0
Land management	43.8
Organising communal labour	27.7
Celebrating traditional festivals	8.3

Local development projects

Table 7.2 displays what the respondents considered the main functions of the chief. This table includes three tasks within the realm of local government, i.e. ensuring community participation in development (59.1 per cent), looking after the physical development of the town (50 per cent), and organising communal labour (27.7 per cent). Such activities often involve both the village chief and local government. The case-study villages in peri-urban Kumasi each have their own Unit Committee (UC)[45] and every one to three villages elect a representative for the District Assembly (DA). DAs exercise deliberative, legislative and executive functions and supervise all other administrative authorities in the district.[46]

The involvement of chiefs and local government in the same tasks leads us to ask who the people in peri-urban Kumasi regard as the most appropriate actor for various administrative tasks, including the three tasks mentioned above. Table 7.3 shows whom the respondents consider the most appropriate actors to perform certain tasks. For all five tasks in Table 7.3 the chief is only considered the third or fourth most appropriate actor. It is striking that for three of the main tasks of the chief mentioned in Table 7.2 – ensuring community participation, physical development of the town, and organisation of communal labour – both the UC and the local assembly member are considered more appropriate actors than the chief. 'Communal labour in Besease used to be arranged by the chief,' says the queenmother of Besease, 'but because of the dissatisfaction with the chief's land administration, nowadays when the gong is beaten, they use the names of the UC and the assemblyman, not the chief'.[47]

In the survey, people were also asked to score the performance of their chief, assembly member and UC on a 5-point scale (1 is very bad, 5 is very good), see Table 7.4. In total the assembly members score significantly lower (2.85) than both the chiefs (3.52) and UCs (3.57). This reflects the difficulty of their jobs. Despite the lack of remuneration as-

Table 7.3 *Which actor(s) should perform certain tasks?*

Tasks	Unit Committee	Assembly member	District Assembly	Chief	Central govt
Ensuring community participation	59.1 (1)	36.0 (2)	1.2 (4)	15.7 (3)	0.4 (5)
Physical development of the town	24.8 (2)	58.3 (1)	5.0 (5)	16.9 (3)	16.9 (3)
Organisation of communal labour	87.6 (1)	18.6 (2)	0.4 (5)	7.0 (3)	0.8 (4)
Check concurrence with building regulations and planning schemes	33.9 (1)	25.2 (3)	31.4 (2)	7.0 (4)	1.7 (5)
Promotion of economic development	27.3 (2)	43.0 (1)	12.4 (4)	20.7 (3)	9.9 (5)

Table 7.4 *Performance assessments of chief, Unit Committee and District Assembly member*

Village	Chief	UC	DA member
Jachie	4.72	4.07***	3.65***
Nkoranza	4.17	3.54*	3.93
Kotwi	4.04	3.58	3.09*
Brofoyeduru	3.54	4.12*	1.96***
Adadeentem	2.97	4.00**	2.15
Tikrom	2.62	2.92	2.00*
Ahenema Kokoben	2.59	2.83	2.50
Boankra	No chief	3.56	3.50
All villages	3.52	3.57	2.85*

* Difference with assessment performance chief is significant at the 0.05 level.
** Difference with assessment performance chief is significant at the 0.01 level.
*** Difference with assessment performance chief is significant at the 0.001 level.

sembly members are expected to serve not only in their own village but in one or two other villages as well. In these villages people often complain that the assembly member never visits them, or even that they don't know him/her, and that these members only care about their own villages. In the four survey villages (N=120) where the assembly member lived in the village, 98.35 per cent of the people knew their assembly member, compared to 72.93 per cent in the four villages where the assembly member did not live (N=122). In the first villages the performance of the assembly members is assessed with an average of 3.37, whereas in the last villages they score only 2.27. Furthermore the assembly members are mainly judged on their success in obtaining development projects from the DA, which itself is low on funds.

The average score for chiefs is 3.52, which signifies something in between average and good. In three villages the chiefs score under average, in four villages above. There is a strong correlation between their
score and their 'style' of land management and its effects in the locality. In Ahenema Kokoben (2.59) and Tikrom (2.62) the chief has sold
much land, with little revenue for the community. In Adadeentmen
(2.97) the former chief sold a large tract of land very much against the
wishes of the people, which sharply contrasts with the new chief who
has not sold any land yet, but has already started building a primary
school from his own money.[48] In Brofoyeduru (3.54) it is mainly the
people who are profiting from the land conversions by selling their
own land, a process which is being condoned by the chief. In Kotwi
(4.04) many farmers had already sold their land to commercial farmers
in the last decade. The current conversion of these lands therefore does
not take away local people's livelihoods. Nkoranza (4.17) still has more
than sufficient agricultural land, as a result of which the people hardly
feel the effect of land sales by the chief. The *Jachiehene* (4.72) has converted much farmland into residential land, but he shared both the
land and the profits with the community.

Despite this strong correlation, when asked about their overall performance chiefs do not receive very bad assessments, even when in interviews people expressed outright criticism about the way they managed the land. Should the relatively favourable assessment of chiefs then
be attributed to their performance in other fields?[49] We have now discussed four of the main tasks of the chief mentioned in Table 7.2. With
regard to land administration, many villagers do not consider the
chiefs to play a very positive role. With regard to physical development
of the town, organising communal labour, and ensuring community
participation, we have seen that for these tasks local government is
now preferred over chiefly rule. The next sections will therefore discuss
the last three tasks mentioned: dispute settlement, ensuring peace in
the community and celebrating traditional festivals.

Law and order: Dispute settlement and ensuring peace

'Dispute settlement' ranks first as the main task of the chief (78.1 per
cent), and is closely connected to the third ranking 'ensuring peace in
the community' (53 per cent) (Table 7.2). When asked the hypothetical
question, whether they would go to the chief if they had a land problem, 76.4 per cent of the respondents answered in the affirmative. In-
depth interviews, however, showed that in cases where the chief is one
of the parties to the conflict – as is often the case when farmland is
converted to residential land – people do not consider the chief's courts
an acceptable forum for settlement of the dispute.

Of the people surveyed 10.4 per cent had at some date taken a dispute to the chief,[50] 25.6 per cent had been witnesses in such a case.
These figures are difficult to read without knowledge of how many people were involved in disputes, and how many went to other dispute settlers. Crook et al. seem to be the only researchers providing empirical
data on such questions regarding the use of various dispute settlement
systems in Ghana (Crook et al. 2005). In a survey, they asked 677 people whom they would most trust to settle any problem they might have
concerning their land. The people most frequently mentioned as
'trusted a lot' were, firstly village chiefs, second family heads and third
court judges, with UC Chairmen coming a close fourth (see Crook in
this volume, Table 6.3 on page 145). In peri-urban Kumasi, the UC
Chairmen ranked third, paramount chiefs fourth and court judges
fifth. The general trust rankings showed very little difference in levels
of trust between men and women, between various age groups, or between people with different levels of education. Only the origin of respondents produced some interesting differences; migrants from a different district or region showed much less propensity to trust a paramount chief and were more likely to trust a judge (Crook et al.
2005:73-77).

A widely shared belief is put into words by Boafo-Arthur when he
states that 'there are many instances, at the rural level, where societal
conflicts are referred, first and foremost, to the traditional ruler for arbitration. In most cases, it is where the parties are not satisfied by the
judgment of the traditional arbitration system that the case is taken to
court' (Boafo-Arthur 2001:10, cf. Schott 1980:125-6). Crook et al., however, come to a different conclusion. They show that from 153 respondents that said they had personally experienced a land dispute, only
26.1 per cent had turned in the first instance to the chief, while 73.9
per cent had initially taken other roads to settle the issue: they turned
to their family or to the court, used arbitration by respected persons, or
had the issue sorted out through negotiation with the other party
(Crook et al. 2005:72). A division of respondents according to origin
demonstrated that non-locals were only half as likely as locals to have
used a chief's court (16.3 per cent and 31.1 per cent respectively,
ibid.:78). Additionally, they demonstrate that out of 168 land case litigants in Kumasi High Court, 52.2 per cent went straight to court, without first employing any other dispute settlement mechanism (*id.:* 30).

It is clear from the data from Crook et al. that chiefs remain an important source of dispute settlement at the local level and enjoy high
levels of trust in that area. The position of Ashanti chiefs in dispute
settlement has even been somewhat enhanced by – and the role of
state courts has equally suffered from – an appeal by the *Asantehene* at
his inaugural meeting with the Kumasi Traditional Council in 1999 to

the chiefs to withdraw cases pending in the state courts and in the Houses of Chiefs and bring them to his court for settlement.[51] Since this appeal – which was followed by quite a number of people, although numerous cases were also not withdrawn from state courts – over 500 land, chieftaincy, criminal and civil cases have been settled in the *Asantehene's* traditional court (Boafo-Arthur 2003:147; Otumfuo Osei Tutu II 2004). Crook et al., however, also demonstrate an ambiguity. Whereas village chiefs are still cited by the general population as most trusted persons for resolving a dispute, actual personal experiences of dealings with a dispute showed a rather more varied picture. Chiefs accounted for only a minority of dispute settlement institutions resorted to, others being family heads, respected persons and opinion leaders including elected local government representatives (Crook et al. 2005:89). Furthermore – and especially relevant for the popular perception of chiefs' functions as a result of their style of land management – Crook et al. confirm the findings from our qualitative research that the continuing conflict in peri-urban areas over the role which chiefs play in the appropriation of village lands for sale as urban plots, is an important difficulty surrounding the chiefs' role. In such circumstances the chief may be regarded as having too much personal interest to be trusted as an impartial judge of a local land case (*id.:* 74-75).

Traditional religion

In the literature, the person and function of chief are very much connected to traditional religion (Busia 1951; Hagan 2003; Rattray 1969, first published 1929; Ray 2003). According to Ray 'the basis of the respect accorded to the chief is not only that the chief derives his power from the people, but also that the stools, skins and other symbols of office have a spiritual significance – the chief deriving his power from the ancestors and mediating between the people and the ancestors' (Ray 2003:7). Busia wrote in 1951 that ancestor-worship is the basis of the chief's authority as well as the sanction for morality in the community. The belief that the ancestors were the custodians of the laws and customs and that they punished those who infringed them with sickness or misfortune acted as a check on commoners and chiefs alike (Busia 1951:24; Fortes 1962:78).

Of the respondents only 0.8 per cent claimed traditional religion as their faith, with 45.6 per cent orthodox Christians, 37.8 per cent charismatic Christians, and 6.6 per cent Muslims. Despite the variety of 'new' religions, some researchers claim that the chief's role is 'well-defined and is embedded in local cosmological views, norms and values *which are respected by everyone in the particular society*' (emphasis added, Ray and Van Rouveroy van Nieuwaal 1996:25). Others assume that in a society in which political and religious office are combined in the chief, new religions are regarded as a challenge to traditional leadership. These researchers look more critically at the effects of the changing religions and worldviews on chiefly rule. Asiama for instance thinks that 'the effect of education and European acculturation, coupled with the departure of a majority of the people from the traditional African religion built on ancestral worship, have made people believe less in the divinity of the chiefs and the strength of their connections with the departed ancestors' (Asiama 2003:13). According to Hagan divergent faiths and world views not consonant with traditional beliefs will lead either to the secularization of the institution or to the narrowing of faith allegiance to the stool (Hagan 2003:7). Historical evidence shows that in many places and for many years people have been using conversion to free themselves of service to their chiefs, justifying their behaviour by claiming that they do not want to take part in 'fetish observances' (Busia 1951:134; Hagan 2003:7).

Only 8.3 per cent of the respondents mentioned the celebration of traditional festivals such as *Akwasidae* as a main task of the chief (Table 7.2). Some Christian charismatic churches agitate against such traditional religious practices. The pastor of the 'Assemblies of God' in Besease explains his church's stance towards chieftaincy and traditional religion thus:

> We teach that pouring libation and praying to dead people is against the law of God. We preach against it in church. You must separate from it to see God. We should tell Him all our problems. Chiefs and heads of families who are born again refuse to pour libation. They let one of their elders do it for them. That is accepted by the church. The church does not agree with the celebration of *Akwasidae*. But we can't say they should abolish it, everyone has its freedom of worship. We just don't want anything to do with that, but we don't fight against it. We teach our members not to get involved. But some of the members are not properly committed, these might still pour libation. Chieftaincy is still important for the people. Even in the bible there are kings. They are very important to the nation, if there is no chief, people will behave unruly. If there is a chief, people will fear for punishment. We therefore do not preach against chieftaincy as a function. Although the chief has a role to play in dispute settlement, we teach the people not to go to non-Christians. We will settle all issues in the church amicably. In that sense, the church takes over part of the role of the chief.[52]

The orthodox Christian churches, on the other hand, see no harm in traditional practices such as pouring libation and celebrating *Akwasidae*. Many Christians condone or partake in them.[53] According to one elder, 'almost anybody will pour libation, to remember the ancestors. To know they are remembered, you mention their names'.[54] Celebration of the traditional festival of *Akwasidae* has changed a lot over the last decades. '*Akwasidae* used to be celebrated by the whole town in the open, first in Ejisu and then in Besease', a chief narrates. 'Libation would be poured, a sheep or goat killed, and no one would go to the farm that day. Now it is a closed ceremony, with only the chief and the linguist present. This year one *Akwasidae* was not celebrated because it fell on Easter Sunday.'[55] The fetish priest used to dance and drum on festive days. But since the priest died, they have been unable to find a new one. 'Christianity has made the shrine so low', explained one of the villagers.[56]

At the same time, when asked whether they would mind if the celebration of the traditional festival of *Akwasidae* were to be cancelled 54.5 per cent of the people – and 60.6 per cent of the people that originated from the survey villages – said yes.[57] Two villagers' views on traditional religion are worth quoting: 'If it were a public ceremony I would not go because it is not the calling of the supreme God. It is fetish,' says a female charismatic Christian from Besease, 'but it should not be cancelled. We met our parents and grandparents doing that'.[58] A woman from a different charismatic church in Besease says: '*Akwasidae* should not be taken out. It is custom (*amanne*). It should be there for the ones who want it.'[59] Some people thus refuse to actively partake in traditional religious practices. A chief recollects: 'When my father and mother opted to be Catholics, they cherished the church so much that anything relating to custom was taboo for them.'[60] This has also led certain people to decline an offer to become chief, because of the inherent necessity to pour libation and 'feed the stools'.[61] Some years back, a chief declared in a radio interview that he no longer believed in the sacred rituals of the stool room. He refused to pour libation to the ancestors, which he considered to be demonic. Because of these statements, the chief was destooled before the *Asantehene*, the late Opoku Ware II (Hagan 2003:7).

These data again present an ambiguous picture. Only 0.8 per cent of the respondents claimed traditional religion as their faith. We may conclude, in line with Hagan, that this trend most likely leads to the narrowing of faith allegiance to the stool (Hagan 2003:7). It might also have its effect on other functions of the chief, such as dispute settlement. It cannot be interpreted, however, as a rejection of all aspects of traditional religion. Many Christians and Muslims still condone or adhere to facets of traditional religion and ancestor worship. And while

only a small minority of the people mention the celebration of traditional festivals as a main task of the chief, a majority attaches importance to their continuation.

Popular assessments of chiefs and chieftaincy

We have seen that the assessment of village chiefs is correlated to their
'style' of land management. But despite very negative judgments on
chiefly performance in that area, chiefs' overall performance assessments are not overly negative; they range from a bit under average to
good. We have posed the question whether this could be attributed to
the performance of chiefs in other fields. If that were so, however, variation in chiefly performance in these other fields would influence
their assessment, which does not square with the clear correlation between style of land management and performance assessment that we
found for peri-urban Kumasi. For an answer to this question of relative
positive assessments of chiefly functioning we should therefore look in
another direction, for which we need to make a distinction between the
institution of chieftaincy and the person of the chief.

In Table 7.5 the assessment of village chiefs is compared to the assessment of the *Asantehene* and of the institution of chieftaincy. These
data display firstly that the assessment of chieftaincy shows a low correlation[62] to the assessment of the village chief and, secondly, that the
assessment of chieftaincy does not differ significantly per village. This
clearly shows that people's opinions about chieftaincy hardly depend
on the performance of current village chiefs or, to put it differently, that
the way a chief governs barely reflects on the institution. A distinction
between the institution of chieftaincy and its incumbent has also been
described in political oratory among the Barolong boo Ratshidi on the
South Africa-Botswana borderland (Comaroff 1975)[63] and for Sesotho
culture in South Africa (Oomen 2002:205). Unlike the data presented
here, Oomen's data led to the conclusion that this 'delinking' of chief-

Table 7.5 *Performance assessments of village chief, Asantehene and chieftaincy*

Village	Chief	Asantehene	Chieftaincy
Jachie	4.72	4.81	3.72
Nkoranza	4.17	4.82	3.33
Kotwi	4.04	4.93	3.80
Brofoyeduru	3.54	4.88	3.45
Adadeentem	2.97	4.93	3.57
Tikrom	2.62	4.66	3.30
Ahenema Kokoben	2.59	4.69	3.22
Boankra	No chief	4.93	3.56
All villages	**3.52**	**4.81**	**3.49**

taincy from individual chiefs in local political debate did not take place in people's assessments of chiefs and chieftaincy. Quite the reverse, she shows a clear causal relationship between the way people feel about their chief and their opinions on chieftaincy. As said earlier, in peri-urban Kumasi this causal relationship is missing: the way people feel about their chief seems not to influence their opinion on the institution of chieftaincy. Perhaps we could even turn the argument around and suggest that respect for the institution of chieftaincy carries weight in and contributes to the assessment of individual chiefs, which could explain the fact that individual chiefs are assessed rather better than was to be expected on the basis of their land practices. Respect for the institution of chieftaincy, however, should not be confused with respect for the person on the stool. As we have seen from the villagers in Besease swearing and shouting at the chief during the village meeting to install a Plot Allocation Committee, the latter does not always prevail. In general, it was quite common during the fieldwork to hear villagers talk in derogatory terms of their chiefs.

This dissimilarity between the Ashantis and the Sotho matches with the fact that the institution of chieftaincy is highly debated in contemporary South Africa, whereas it is almost a fact of nature in Ashanti. In peri-urban Kumasi dissatisfaction with local land administration and anger towards a particular chief hardly seem to lead to discussions of the desirability of the institution of chieftaincy. For the majority, chieftaincy is a fact. According to a youngster: 'The youth don't respect the chief as they used to. When they have a dispute they would sooner go to the police or to court than to the chief. But chieftaincy has to be there. It is not old fashioned.'[64] It is almost unthinkable for a village not to have a chief. Without a chief there is no village, for who will represent the community at traditional and cultural festivals and ceremonies? 'Chieftaincy is the culture of the people,' explains the District Chief Executive. 'They feel an emptiness if there is no chief. They think leadership is lacking, authority is no longer there. Especially on festive occasions, people want to belong to a chief.'[65] These utterances see to the realms of culture and identity, to which Oomen (2002:223) also points to explain people's support for chieftaincy.[66]

Table 7.5 also shows a significant difference between the assessment of the village chiefs and of the *Asantehene*.[67] The assessment of the *Asantehene* is strikingly high in all villages. This is understandable, since it is felt that the prestige of the *Asantehene* reflects on the status of Asante and the Ashantis. This has its bearing on the same issue of representation. For you need a village chief to communicate with higher chiefs and with the *Asantehene*, who is highly revered and whose position is unquestionable.

Conclusion

In this chapter we have looked at the effects of commoditisation of land. In the first part, we have seen that the increasing value of land leads many chiefs to convert agricultural land in use by their people to residential land. This land is mainly allocated to outsiders and a considerable part of the revenues generated does not flow back to the farmers and communities. People are highly critical of the chiefs' allocations of land and seek various ways to resist them or share in the proceeds. Due to the chiefs' position as guardians of stool land and authorities in the field of customary law, combined with the erosion of customary checks and balances and a non-interfering government, these attempts to resist are often not very successful. Many people in peri-urban Kumasi have thus lost their land and witnessed severe effects on their livelihoods.

In the second part of this chapter we have discussed the seven main functions of the chief as listed by the people (Table 7.2). We started with a description of dealings with land in peri-urban Kumasi and saw that many people are dissatisfied with this aspect of chiefly rule. For three other functions mentioned as main tasks – physical development of the town, communal labour and ensuring community participation – the chief was regarded as only the third or fourth most appropriate actor, behind the UC and the local assembly member. The last three tasks, connected to law and order and traditional religion, showed a stronger but also not unambiguous role for chiefs. Whereas village chiefs are considered the most trusted persons for resolving a dispute, chiefs accounted for only a minority of dispute settlement institutions resorted to, and in peri-urban areas the continuing conflict over the role that chiefs play in the appropriation of village lands for sale as urban plots seriously affects their ability to judge land cases. Most respondents were Christians and Muslims, but this did not imply a total rejection of all aspects of traditional religion or the role of chiefs in its performance. Despite people's aversion to the chiefs' land practices, the overall assessments of chiefs were not overly negative. It was explained that this cannot be attributed to their performance in other fields. The cases in peri-urban Kumasi lead to the conclusion that the performance of chiefs barely reflects on the institution of chieftaincy. Rather, the respect for the institution seems to carry weight in the assessment of the individual chiefs.

The cases in peri-urban Kumasi show that the support for chieftaincy is not based on high satisfaction with the way chiefs perform their tasks. Reasons are rather found in the realms of culture and identity. This is an important lesson for African governments and international policymakers, since it demonstrates that people's support for the institution of chieftaincy does not necessarily go hand-in-hand with satisfaction regarding chiefly performance. People can simultaneously support the institution of chieftaincy and be highly critical of the performance of certain chiefs or certain tasks. Policymakers should critically assess chiefly rule – and popular perceptions of it – in various fields, taking into account the performance of other actors in these fields, including local government representatives. Based on such assessments, governments should determine the desirability to recognise, formalise, or enhance, in a ceremonial or more material form, the various functions of the chiefs. And if necessary they should place checks and balances on the functioning of chiefs in general and regulate or control certain fields in particular.

Notes

1   These nine villages housed a total of twelve landowning chiefs. My main village of study was Besease, situated approximately twenty-three kilometres from Kumasi on the road to Accra. Furthermore, I have studied four other villages on or near this road – Jachie, Tikrom, Adadeentem, and Boankra – and four villages on the road to Obuasi – Ahenema Kokoben, Kotwi, Brofoyeduru, and Nkoransa. All villages are at a range of ten to forty kilometres from Kumasi.
2   To protect the identity of local informants, names of interviewees are not given. They are identified as villager, Unit Committee member, elder etc.
3   The customary community is called 'stool' in reference to the carved wooden stool which is believed to contain the souls of the ancestors, and is a traditional symbol of chieftainship.
4   See articles 36(8) and 267(1) of the 1992 Constitution.
5   Under Ashanti customary law individual property is inherited by the matrilineal family. The usufructuary title thus becomes family property after the death of the usufructuary.
6   Forfeiture results from denial of the landlord's title.
7   For a description of case law see Ubink 2002-2004.
8   Interview, 11 May 2003.
9   Interview, 27 May 2003.
10 Although stool land is rather leased than sold – the Constitution prohibits the sale of customary land – nearly everyone speaks of the 'selling' of land and many people, 'sellers' as well as 'buyers', seem to regard it as a definitive transfer.
11 Interview, 1 July 2003.
12 Interview former *Akyeamehene* sub-chief of *Tikromhene*, 7 January 2004; Cf. Rathbone 1996: 511.
13 Although the claim that the allodial title to stool land lies with the royal family has been pushed by royal families in Ashanti since the dynastic civil wars of the 1880s, the argument that the indigenous farmers therefore have no rights in the land is not supported by history. For instance, when cocoa became a valuable cash crop in Ghana, many chiefs started to levy immigrant cocoa growers with taxes, but refrained from or were unsuccessful in imposing such a tax on indigenous farmers, because these were considered to have an inherent right to farm the land. See for literature

on Ghanaian history e.g. Firmin-Sellers 1995; Hill 1963; McCaskie 1995; 2000a; b; Rathbone 1996; Wilks 1966; 1975; 1993.

14 See for literature on the conversion and its consequences in peri-urban Kumasi Berry 2002; Edusah and Simon 2001; Hammond 2005; Kasanga and Kotey 2001; Kasanga and Woodman 2004; Kenton 1999. For other peri-urban areas of Ghana, see for instance Abudulai 2002; DFID 2001; Gough and Yankson 2000; Kasanga et al. 1996; Maxwell et al. 1998; NRI and UST 1997; Alden Wily and Hammond 2001.

15 The number of people still depending wholly or partly on farming varied widely between the villages, depending mainly on the distance to Kumasi. For instance in the village closest to Kumasi, Ahenema Kokoben, the population has increased from 302 in 1984 to 3400 in 2000 (GSS 2002) and farming has lost its importance.

16 First, the influx of strangers into the villages – often civil servants, people with other formal jobs or rich business people – has significantly changed the social stratification of peri-urban communities. Second, more villagers leave early in the morning to work in the city, returning late in the evening. This new lifestyle allows less social interaction among the people and therefore the strong traditional bonds associated with rural settlements are gradually breaking down (Edusah and Simon 2001).

17 Interview villager Besease, 19 May 2005.

18 Interview villager Besease, 16 May 2003.

19 In the nine case study villages none of these cases had been taken to court in the recent past.

20 The case-study villages in peri-urban Kumasi each have their own UC. UCs are meant to function as the base structure of Ghana's local government system. They perform roles such as public education, organisation of communal labour, revenue generation, and registration of marriages, births and deaths. The first UC elections were held in 1998. UCs consist of not more than fifteen persons, of whom ten are elected in non-partisan elections and five are government appointees. These appointments are made after consultation with traditional authorities and other interest groups. The UCs viability has been questioned on the basis of lack of financial and administrative backup (Ayee 1999; Crook 1991a; IBIS 1998; NCCE 1998; USAID 2003:30-31).

21 This happened when the chief was mining sand and thereby degrading farmland close to streams. The Environmental Protection Agency, however, lacks the power to prosecute. That power lies with the District Assembly that hardly ever acts upon it.

22 Interview villager Besease, 27 August 2003.

23 See for a more elaborate description of customary land administration in peri-urban Kumasi, Ubink 2008, in press.

24 The position of both chiefs and councillors is hereditary in the sense that it has to be filled by a person from a certain, in the Ashanti Region matrilinear, family. Within such a family, there are usually a number of people eligible to fill the position, of which the family will choose the most suitable candidate. Besides hereditary councillors, a chief can also appoint a number of 'non-hereditary' councillors, on the basis of their personal merit. When such a councillor dies, the position disappears and the family will thus not be permitted to select a successor. See for a more elaborate discussion of election of chiefs and sub-chiefs amongst others Busia 1951; Danquah 1928b; Hayford 1970; Kofi-Sackey 1983; Kumado 1990-1992; Obeng 1988; Sarbah 1968.

25 See also Hayford 1970 ; Pogucki 1962: 66, 87.

26 See also Kasanga and Kotey 2001:31.

27 Including McCaskie 1992; 1995; 2000a.

28 Interview, 28 October 2003.

29 Interview UC member Tikrom, 26 June 2003. See also Abudulai 1996; Kasanga 1996.

30 Interview, 26 June 2003.

31 Interview *Asantehene's* Land Secretariat, 2 July 2003.

32 Interview *Kontrehene* sub-chief Besease, 1 July 2003.

33 Section 15 of the Chieftaincy Act, 1971 (Act 370), confers exclusive jurisdiction in any 'cause or matter affecting chieftaincy' – as defined at section 117 of the Courts Act, 1993 (Act 459), i.e. an action concerned with the nomination, appointment, election of a chief or destoolment – to the Traditional Council or, if a paramount chief is involved, to the Regional House of Chiefs. From such a case an appeal lies to the Regional House of Chiefs, then to the National House of Chiefs and finally even to the Supreme Court. This means that one cannot take such cases to the regular state courts, only to the Supreme Court in last instance. It must however be noted that the courts have not allowed for such a broad interpretation of the words 'cause or matter affecting chieftaincy' that the entire functioning of Traditional Councils falls outside their scope. For instance, land cases that are not concerned with the nomination, appointment, election or destoolment of a chief can be taken to the state courts.

34 Interview *Kontrehene* sub-chief of *Ejisuhene*, 27 May 2003.

35 The only kind of functioning accountability is what I call 'end-term-accountability'. During destoolment procedures, a chief will have to account for all stool revenue. However, by then most of the money is usually spent and very hard to recover.

36 Interview, 29 June 2003.

37 See a.o. *Daily Graphic* 25 August 2003:3; *Ghanaian Times* 5 August, 2003:1 and 25 August, 2003:3. These statements are sometimes made in reaction to chieftaincy disputes, for which the law explicitly declares the government has no jurisdiction (section 15, Chieftaincy Act, 1971 (Act 370)), but also more in general, expressing that the government will not interfere in chiefly administration.

38 Another example is found in the unwillingness of the political establishment to bring before the court the question whether 'drink money' is stool land revenue in the sense of the OASL Act. In line with the historical practice to bring a bottle of schnapps when requesting a chief for land, chiefs claim that 'drink money' constitutes a mere symbolic gift to show allegiance to the chief. Since this 'drink money' currently equals the marker price for land, many officials suggest it amounts to stool land revenue in the sense of the OASL Act. When the District Chief Executive of Ejisu-Juaben district wanted to go to court over a case of approximately 300,000 Euro of 'drink-money', he was stopped by the government. See Ubink and Quan 2008.

39 Interview Ejisu-Juaben District Assembly, 12 January 2004. Chiefs are said to be especially influential in the Ashanti Region with its hierarchical chiefly structure with the *Asantehene* at the top.

40 Additionally, it could be argued that the rampant irregularities and mismanagement by state institutions in procedures of compulsory acquisition of land do not give the state a strong moral position from which to judge the quality of chiefly land administration, see Daily Graphic 22 August 2002:17; Kotey 1996. Furthermore, when the state wants to acquire land itself, a good relationship with chiefs is useful, and the payment will be lower when only the chief has to be redeemed, instead of the whole community.

41 The current mildly favourable climate for chieftaincy has even rekindled discussions on the creation of a second chamber of parliament made up of chiefs, and on whether chiefs should again have their own representatives on District Assemblies.

42 Interview, 10 April 2003.

43 Interview, 1 July 2003.

44 Only the three most quoted categories are represented in this table.

45 See note 20. UCs have no official role with regard to land management.

46 The legislative instruments setting up each DA provide a very specific list of up to eighty-six particular duties. Of its members 70 percent are elected, on non-partisan basis, but the District Chief Executive – the single most powerful local government position that dominates district level government – and the other 30 per cent of the DA members are appointed by the President in consultation with traditional authorities and other interest groups. With regard to land management, the making of bye-laws with respect to building, sanitation and the environment, the preparation and approval of planning schemes, the granting of building permits, and the enforcement of regulations and sanctions for non-compliance all rest with the DA (Kasanga and Kotey 2001:9).

47 Interview, 29 May 2003.

48 Although the people of Adadeentem have elected this chief, the *Ejisuhene*, the paramount chief of the area, has refused to enstool him, favouring a different chief-elect with whom he had already been cooperating under the former chief.

49 It has also been suggested that the traditional respect for chieftaincy makes it difficult to grade chiefs with an unsatisfactory mark. This argument seems to be brought down, however, by the fact that during interviews and participant observations severe criticism of the chief was freely and frequently voiced.

50 Of the 25 disputes, 13 (52 per cent) concerned land.

51 Although this is an understandable and sensible appeal considering the enormous backlogs in state courts, this move is also a highly political one in which the *Asantehene* reclaims the traditional *trias politica* of legislator, administrator and judge.

52 Interview, 12 September 2003.

53 With religion being such an important sphere of life in the villages, some of the religious leaders take an active role in the personal affairs of their followers. This was mainly confined to counseling and dispute settling in the field of family matters and witchcraft. What was not encountered in the case study villages was that religious leaders took an active role in opposing the chief when his rule brought hardship to the people. Even in Besease, where the assembly member was also minister in one of the twenty three local churches, this merely resulted in regular get-togethers of all religious leaders to pray for the welfare of the village.

54 Interview elder of the *Kontrehene* of *Ejisuhene*, Besease, 7 May 2003.

55 Interview *Kontrehene* of *Ejisuhene*, Besease, 27 May 2003.

56 Personal communication villager Besease, 12 May 2003.

57 In answer to this question 57.3 per cent of the charismatic Christians said yes, 51.6 per cent of the orthodox Christians, 31.3 of the Muslims and 66.7 per cent of people with 'no religion'.

58 Interview villager Besease, 27 August 2003.

59 Interview villager Besease, 26 August 2003.

60 Interview *Kontrehene* of *Ejisuhene*, Besease, 27 May 2003.

61 Personal communication researcher Institute for Land Management and Development, Kumasi, 15 April 2003.

62 The correlation is 0.357, significant at the 0.01 level.

63 Comaroff describes that the people use a formal code to praise the qualities of the institution of chieftaincy in contrast with an evaluative code – which can be highly critical – when they speak about a particular chief.

64 Interview youth Besease, 15 June 2003.

65 Interview District Chief Executive Ejisu-Juaben, 9 September 2003.

66 Oomen in her research (at 219-222) also points to the role of chiefs as 'portals of the government' and to the lack of alternatives for chiefly rule, but both these reasons were hardly mentioned in peri-urban Kumasi.

67 Significant at the 0.001 level.

8   Risks and opportunities of state intervention in customary land management: Emergent findings from the Land Administration Project Ghana

Julian Quan, Janine Ubink and Adarkwah Antwi*

Introduction

A key element in the new policy consensus on land tenure reform in sub-Saharan Africa is that in order to provide tenure security to ordinary land users, land law and formal land administration arrangements need to give recognition to the range of customary rights and arrangements under which people access and manage land. In order to do this, land administration – the process of recording and validating land rights and land transactions – needs to become more decentralised so as to be more accessible to the people, and to facilitate the gradual documentation of customary rights and management arrangements at a variety of levels (Deininger 2003; Quan and Toulmin 2005; Toulmin and Quan 2000b; World Bank 2003b). Increasingly, development agencies believe that these decentralised approaches should recognise and enable the registration of customary land rights and engage directly or indirectly with customary institutions and authorities, where they play a significant role in the control and regulation of land affairs.

Ghana is characterised by a very high incidence of disputes surrounding customary land. These disputes are on the one hand caused by the increasing monetisation of customary transactions, resulting in contestations and renegotiations of customary tenure and a concentration of control of economic benefits flowing from land in the hands of traditional authorities. On the other hand, the way is paved for these disputes by the failure of formal land law and land administration and tenure systems to regulate the diversity and dynamics of customary land rights and transactions. This has now been clearly recognised by the government (Ministry of Lands and Forestry 1999) and its development partners. This is despite a colonial legacy of an extensive land administration infrastructure and the substantial interpenetration of formal land law and customary principles and practice that developed during the colonial period – both relatively unusual for sub-Saharan Africa.

In view of the deficiencies of existing formal institutions in managing customary land rights, and with the aim of facilitating access to land for agricultural, business, and urban development, Ghana has embarked upon a Land Administration Project (LAP). This long-term project with multi-donor support is intended to reform land institutions and develop land policy so as to provide greater certainty of land rights for ordinary land users and enable greater discipline and efficiency in the land market. The project includes a specific component to pilot the establishment of Customary Land Secretariats (CLSs) under the aegis of traditional authorities. This component is supported by DFID and managed by the Ministry of Lands, Forestry and Mines (MLFM).[1]

In this paper we first set out the background to customary land management in Ghana today, along with the problems involved. We then summarise the main features of the Ghana LAP and the on-going DFID project to support the pilot introduction of CLSs. Next we consider critiques of the policy of supporting management of land by customary institutions in Ghana, and the evidence and risks emerging from implementation of the CLS pilot programme in a political-economic context. We conclude by offering some pointers as to a way forward to mitigate the risks.

The nature of landholding in Ghana

In Ghana the customary sector holds around 80 per cent of the land (Antwi and Adams 2003, Kasanga and Kotey 2001). This sector thus provides land for the residential and other economic activities of most of Ghana's citizens. Historically, customary authorities, essentially chiefs, sub-chiefs, family heads, and councils of elders responsible for decision-making have been understood to manage land and make land allocation decisions on behalf of their communities. In some regions, colonial indirect rule through chieftaincy institutions provided opportunities for powerful chiefs to centralise political control, including control over land through the institutions of the paramount 'stool' or 'skin' which came to predominate across the territories in which those particular chiefs were regarded as the highest customary authority. In Kumasi (Ashanti Region) and Akyem Abuakua (Eastern Region), the colonial government supported paramount chiefs to establish secretariats to facilitate formalised land allocations. The colonial government, however, also removed control of large areas of land from the chiefs, notably in urban areas, by vesting rights in the President. This has never been reversed – the land remains administered directly by the state – and although the 1999 National Land Policy provides for compensation to be paid or land to be de-vested, these lands are still the subject of considerable tensions between the state and traditional authorities (Kasanga and Kotey 2001).

Post-independence governments under Nkrumah and subsequent presidents have introduced legislative measures that have eroded the established legislative and judicial functions of chiefs, as well as their powers to manage the development of land and to collect land revenues. One of the first measures after independence was the introduction of a stool land account. Aware that land transactions in the form of land rentals to outsiders, together with forest and mineral resources, represent considerable sources of revenue to customary authorities, the state established an infrastructure for revenue collection. This revenue collection is currently being done by the institution of the Office of the Administrator of Stool Lands (OASL), which redistributes revenues collected from any given stool amongst District Assemblies, the customary authority who issued the lease, the stool, and the OASL itself.[2] This control of customary land revenues by the state has fuelled resentment amongst traditional leaders who resist disclosure of the greater proportion of revenues accruing from sales of customary land. In areas where market demand for land has led to rising land values, even though ground rents remain relatively low, chiefs have converted traditional ritual obligations of the lessee once paid in kind and now in money ('drinks money') into a fee which is in effect a free market purchase price of the land lease (Edusah and Simon 2001; Firmin-Sellers 1996; Kasanga and Kotey 2001; Ubink 2007 and 2008b). Especially in urban areas the myth of 'drinks money' obscures the disposal of land for private gain which can involve dispossession of subjects' land rights (see Brobby 1991 for other strategies for dispossessing subjects of their rights). This fee is generally not disclosed and continues to be represented by chiefs as a ritual obligation rather than a capital gain from disposal of land. Declaration of the purchase price would require that OASL collects and redistributes it, in effect leading to the chief losing a large percentage of the money.[3] To date the revenues which are collected and distributed by OASL itself have also never been publicly disclosed, and so the use of land revenues received by all parties is not transparent, although at least they are now reported to parliament. Although there are indications that chiefs may be grateful for the receipt of some revenues which they themselves would be unable to collect, there is also resentment and suspicion regarding the use of land revenues by District Assemblies, which chiefs tend to regard as rival political authorities.

In some regions of Ghana, land is still under the control of extended families or lineages, where family heads and councils of elders, as opposed to the stools themselves have asserted their rights to allocate land and collect land revenues. In these cases, the Constitution does not require the collection and management of revenues by the OASL, and ground rents can be collected directly by the landholding family. Prior to the centralisation of stools under paramount chiefs encouraged by colonial government a similar system existed in other regions: although families might hold political allegiance to a higher chief, that chief would not have control over land allocation. Today this can lead to situations of disputed and ambiguous authority over land allocation and the right to control land revenues. Where land allocation is controlled by stools, and land is scarce or of high value, there are likely to be struggles between chiefs, sub-chiefs, family heads and farmers for the rights to dispose of land, to convert it to non-agricultural use and to control land revenues. On the other hand there may also be cases in which chiefs may allow family heads to allocate land and collect land rents (circumventing the requirement for land revenues to be collected and distributed by OASL, which applies only to land allocations managed centrally by the stool itself rather than land owning families) and also retain shares of 'drinks money', enabling a greater proportion of land revenues to remain within the community. Nevertheless the rights and entitlements of ordinary land users to remain on the land or to gain compensation or shares of land revenues remain opaque and subject to widely varying locally negotiated formulae.

In rural areas, labour migration (broadly from North to South and from East to West) into more productive forest belt areas suitable for cocoa and high value horticultural production has led to the established practices of sharecropping and land rentals by migrants from indigenous landholders as a means to access land. In some of these areas such as Wassa, Kyebi, Sandema, and Dormaa, contractual agreements between landholding community members and settlers seem to have occurred primarily without any involvement of the stool. In many cases landholders appear to have transacted quasi-freehold rights via, for instance, sharecropping arrangements leading to what have been understood to be very secure tenure arrangements for the tenants, equivalent to tenancies or leases held in perpetuity and subject to payment of agreed production shares and/or provision of labour. The stool's involvement was only invoked when documentary evidence of the arrangement was required. In other areas, traditional authorities themselves have transacted vast amounts of the land to migrant farmers. As supplies of land have become exhausted, and indigenous populations have grown, the customary contracts and the nature of the secondary rights so created are subject to negotiation and interpretation. The rights of migrants have become re-interpreted and subject to contestation and some political tension between 'stranger' farmers and indigenous landholders or customary chiefs, as each claim the equivalent of freehold rights, and land owning groups seek to rescind oral contracts, which may have been entered into generations ago, or convert them into formal leaseholds. In this context, land relations and land access have become increasingly monetised, and land scarcity has been a source of tension, both between indigenous landholding groups and migrants and between generations (see Amanor 2006; Boni 2006).

The above introduces the major contestations and struggles over rights and prerogatives within customary land tenure in contemporary Ghana. This context helps explain the overlapping and conflicting allocations of land by different authorities and individuals, tensions over access to land between landholding groups and long established tenants, and sales by customary authorities of land occupied and used by members of landholding communities. In addition to overt disputes and litigations, these problems have created widespread tenure insecurity and difficulties in establishing uncontested access to land, especially in peri-urban areas, creating problems for investment in landed property and thus for economic development in Ghana.

Underlying this state of affairs is a general absence of effective practical administrative links between rights established through customary rules and informal transactions, and the formal governmental land administration system. Ghana operates a dual land rights regime, but the link between administration of interests in land created through customary practice and formal titles to landed property is tenuous to nonexistent. This problem is recognised by the government, which aims to create such a link with the LAP. In recent decades leading chiefs have consistently campaigned to reverse any measures that eroded their functions and power. Since the present NPP government under President Kufuor is politically committed to the introduction of CLSs and is broadly pro-chieftaincy in its orientation, powerful chiefs have seen in LAP an opportunity to restore and extend their political and economic control over land.

The aims of LAP-CLS

The goal of the LAP is to lay the foundation for an accountable, harmonious and transparent customary land administration system from the bottom up which will then form the bedrock for an enhanced formal land administration in Ghana (World Bank 2003a). LAP is conceived of as a long term project (government documents refer to a 25-year planning horizon, and the World Bank has adopted a three phase, 15-year funding framework). Under the LAP the medium to long-term plan is that the government should divest itself of direct responsibility for the management of stool lands. This should proceed incrementally, on the basis of the satisfaction of certain criteria, including the setting up of Customary Land Secretariats (CLSs) with appropriate governance structures to assure institutionalised community-level participation and accountability in the use of stool land and the revenue it generates. Despite this intention, the government's clear political choice at the inception of LAP was that CLSs should fall under the aegis of traditional authorities, rather than seeking to develop more community based approaches to the management of customary land. Placing CLSs directly under the chiefs ignores a reality in which the notion of the 'customary' powers and rights of chiefs is loaded with political inventions and is used to endorse the roles that chiefs were accorded in land administration in the colonial period, as if this were a timeless principle of customary tenure (Amanor 2005: 110-111). In its first phase (2004-2008) LAP has, however, adopted a pilot approach to the implementation of technical and institutional innovations, including CLSs, through which major blunders that might have lasting negative impacts on land administration in Ghana could be avoided.

The DFID CLS project document sets out four principal outputs sought for this component of LAP (DFID/Toulmin et al. 2004):

- CLSs established and/or strengthened in pilot areas, in partnership with government land sector agencies;

- Improved quality of records and accessibility of information at CLS level on land use and holdings, land transactions and availability, and associated financial and cadastral records;

- Improved CLS accountability, in line with the Constitutional provisions, in a way that protects the rights of all landholders within their communities, recognises the community interest in land management, and provides an effective interface with democratic local and national government;

- Better informed policy development. The implementation of the National Land Policy by way of the LAP will involve further policy development in order to realise its key goals. The information that this component generates, in relation to CLSs, will be actively managed in order to ensure that the process can be developed in the light of the best possible knowledge.

Early results of pilot CLSs

At the time of writing, pilot CLSs have been established in all ten administrative regions of Ghana, and a further ten pilots have been identified. Following discussions with Regional Houses of Chiefs proposals for CLSs, and interest and willingness to support their establishment and to meet their recurrent costs have been expressed by other chieftaincies, in particular within the Ashanti Region.

Of the first ten pilot CLSs, Gbawe (Greater Accra) and Kumasi (*Asantehene's* land secretariat in Ashanti Region) were pre-existing, and intended to benefit from support under LAP. An additional four pilots were inaugurated in 2005: in Wassa Emenfi (Western Region); Kyebi (Eastern Region);[4] Tabiase (Upper East Region); and Tamale (Northern Region). In early 2006 a further four CLSs were inaugurated: Odupong Kpehe (Kasoa in Central Region); Dormaa Ahenkro (Brong Ahafo Region); Sandema (Upper East Region); and Kete Krachie (Volta Region). The first group of CLSs were established according to political criteria, including provision of support to powerful, politically influential chiefs, and achievement of an overall regional balance, so as to avoid concentrating CLS resources in the hands of particular groups.

Based on past history of government interventions, chiefs were initially suspicious of government's proposals to introduce CLSs. The World Bank's natural resource management specialist for Ghana noted that 'at first, chiefs were afraid that the government would take away their land'. However, these fears were soon dispelled. 'We reacted quickly and got their support. Now they like the project because we do not prescribe anything'.[5] At the inception of LAP, and prior to recruitment of dedicated CLS development personnel, the government presented CLSs to traditional leaders as packages of equipment and technical support to help resource and improve the efficiency of their existing land management practices and has been reluctant to impose requirements of equity and accountability, or to otherwise interfere with how chiefs manage and dispose of land. According to a former DFID Ghana rural livelihoods advisor, in conveying this message, 'LAPU (the LAP Unit at the MLFM) has done more wrong than right in its first year of the CLS project. Chiefs are now asking for their money and package'. The approach taken has led to expectations that government and donors will assume responsibility for meeting CLS salary costs and other recurrent expenditures.[6]

Gbawe in Greater Accra is generally regarded as the paradigm of CLS good practice (Kasanga and Kotey 2001). It is a fully functioning CLS *avant la lettre* which was installed by the Gbawe elders prior to LAP, and provided a source of inspiration for the design of the CLS component of LAP. In Gbawe, LAP is working to help consolidate better rent collection systems, improved land and financial records, including published accounts, the provision of secure, registered rights to settlers, and the use of land revenues to support community facilities. The existence of an organised land allocation system, which facilitates settlers' access to documented land rights, alongside investments in local infrastructure undertaken by the land owners, are reflected in a high level of demand for residential plots. In 2005 the family elders explained compensation arrangements for farmers who lose agricultural land, including the provision of a residential plot, new farm land where available, and entitlement to the proceeds of sale of an additional residential plot.[7] The elders noted that a number of displaced farmers were able to use compensation money to invest in more intensive snail, mushroom, and poultry production ventures. Within a year, however, the family head pointed out that no more agricultural land was available, having been lost to residential development including encroachment by neighbouring groups, and that Gbawe was 'engulfed by Accra.' The development of the CLS was cited by the elders as an important factor stimulating the demand for residential land in Gbawe, leading to increased income for the family, as well as resources for investment in community infrastructure. Examples of new community investment underway since the previous year include the construction of a police station, a youth employment project, plans to improve sanitation, street lighting, and the provision of public toilet facilities.[8] The CLS does not, however, record or disclose payments of 'drinks money' to the family head, which, as noted earlier, constitutes the greater part of all land revenues. Despite this sizeable limitation, the Gbawe CLS provides an example of progressive practice in land management as a spontaneous innovation by customary authorities.

In contrast, in other pilot CLSs linked to large and powerful stools, the orientation of traditional authorities has been to use the CLS to consolidate the centralised control of the stool over leasehold transactions. In Kyebi the paramount chief is concerned with reining in local chiefs who transact in land without authorisation and without accounting fully to the paramount stool. The *Okyenhene*, or Kyebi paramount chief, has adopted a system whereby 'caretaker chiefs' are responsible to the paramount chief for documenting and authorising land transactions. In this manner, he seeks to control any local land transactions involving commercial investment such as development of plantation crops and residential land, including the conversion to new uses of cocoa plantations established by tenant farmers under long standing sharecropping arrangements with local families. The 'drinks money' is then divided between the local chiefs and the *Okyenhene*. 5 per cent is intended to go to the land user who has sought to dispose of the land or has been required to give it up, but the use to which the money is put by the chiefs is not disclosed.[9] In Kumasi the *Asantehene's* Land Secretariat has operated since colonial times a system for administering and registering land transactions in the Kumasi traditional council area – also involving 'caretaker chiefs' – which has facilitated the stool's centralised collection and management of 'drinks money'.[10] In both Kumasi and Kyebi, the LAP has been perceived as an opportunity for the traditional authorities to regain the official support and authority over land they formerly enjoyed under British control. In both of these cases the expectations expressed by CLS staff appointed by the chiefs and members of their traditional councils were that government would provide financial, technical, and material support to facilitate sales of residential plots to outsiders and improve centralised control of land revenues on behalf of the stool. In Kyebi, the response of the LAP-CLS facilitator team was to organise systematic inventories of existing land occupation so as to document the land claims of indigenous land users, tenant farmers, and urban settlers. This exercise may in turn provide a basis for eventual formal registration of land rights and more orderly processes of land use change in which the tenure rights of all are respected. In Kumasi, LAP has not yet reached an agreement with the traditional authorities about how to work with the *Asantehene's* CLS, and no concrete actions have been taken, apart from the initial supply of computer equipment and furniture.

In Wassa Emenfi in Western Region, government's proposal to establish a CLS was welcomed by the chief. This is a predominantly rural area with a high incidence of migrant sharecropping principally for cocoa, where access to land is now becoming more competitive, resulting in tension and disputes between indigenous and migrant groups. At first the Stool's objectives in developing a CLS were not clear, but it soon became evident that the CLS was seen by senior members of the landholding community as a way of seeking to maximise land availability for profitable leasehold disposals to outsiders and, by changing existing tenure arrangements, to strengthen the claims of stool members on lands held by outsiders. A first proposal of the local CLS coordinator, appointed by the chief, was to use the CLS to convert the secure tenure arrangements of migrants created through long-established oral and sometimes written sharecropping contracts with landholding families, arguably equivalent to land purchases (Alden Wily and Hammond 2001; Amanor and Diderutuah 2001), into fixed term leaseholds subject to rent collection and eventual discretionary renewal by the CLS.[11] LAP project staff disabused the CLS of the legitimacy and legality of such a move. The principles under which LAP operated, with the support of the donors, were to encourage CLSs to document, without discrimination, the full range of land claims on the ground, including the established customary rights of both indigenes, which become vulnerable when chiefs sell their land, and tenants, who are vulnerable where indigenous groups try to repossess their land. Following dialogue with the Wassa chief and sub-chiefs, and a public 'durbar', it was agreed that the CLS should seek to document land rights and support the management of land transactions in the interests of all land users, and the CLS is now registering indigenes' land rights, which should be followed by the registration of migrants. However, as the inventory of land occupation proceeded (a process coordinated by LAP project staff as a pilot CLS activity), in at least one case LAP enumerators and visiting evaluators were directed firmly away from migrant cocoa farmer settlements by local sub-chiefs, apparently because of sensitivities surrounding the competing land claims of indigenous and migrant groups.

Elsewhere, pilot CLSs have been inaugurated in areas where customary political and land management systems are less centralised. In Kate Krache in Volta Region a number of land-owning families have come together to establish a CLS. In parts of Upper East, including in peri-urban areas of Bolgatanga, the regional capital, where the customary jurisdiction of traditional land priests (*Tindana* or *Tendamba*) over land allocation is frequently now disputed by chiefs (Hammond 2003), the establishment of CLSs has been regarded as a non-starter by the ministry. However at a recent LAP implementation support mission held by government and donors, it was recognised that the pilot CLS process may in fact provide opportunities to address these issues.

In response to lessons learned in the establishment of the first CLSs, the CLS pilot programme has now moved from a supply-led approach, with pilot sites selected by government to receive packages of equipment and technical support to a demand-led approach, whereby the potential benefits of CLSs are explained to traditional authorities, which are encouraged to make proposals and indicate how they will assist CLSs. Three key principles have been established as criteria for deciding whether or not the LAP can provide support:

- CLSs should undertake fully inclusive documentation of land occupation and forms of tenure in traditional areas not confined to leasehold transactions – usually traditional authorities' and often government's main concern because these generate revenue for the stool and for the chiefs themselves and supply land for investment, residential and commercial use, and for urban development. This measure encourages CLSs to address the needs of all types of land users and provides them with a minimum level of security for existing land users;

- CLSs should link with existing customary institutions such as land allocation committees and dispute resolution by councils of elders. Traditional authorities should be willing to expand these to make them more effective and representative, for instance by inclusion of land professionals, women, and of District Assembly and land users' representatives;

- Traditional authorities should be willing to provide premises for the CLS to operate and to meet its recurrent costs (including maintenance of equipment and payment of staff); this ensures a sense of ownership of CLSs by chiefs and landholding groups and a minimum degree of sustainability.

The programme remains at too early a stage to provide systematic evidence of the effectiveness of establishing CLSs as a policy intervention. Nevertheless, following the three years since the first pilot CLS was established, indications of outcomes, challenges, and risks can be observed. Rather than simply making casual observations about the performance, potential, and risks of CLS establishment, we discuss these in Section 3 from a political-economic perspective. First, however, we consider critiques of approaches to land reform based on customary practice and authority.

Critiques of customary land administration reform

Customary land rights are not the products of immutable customary 'law' but rather the outcomes of negotiations and implicit agreements embedded in social relations of family, kinship, and community (Berry 1993). The renewed policy emphasis on the importance of recognising and supporting customary tenure systems is subject to critique because these social relations are inherently unequal, involving power relations between ordinary land users and customary authorities. Chiefs' powers and opportunities to redefine customary 'law' in their own interests may be increased by seeking to formalise or promote the customary tenure systems over which they exert significant influence and control. Under growing demographic pressure, market development, and land scarcity, the phenomenon of local elites using their power to privatise, enclose, and dispose of land previously held in reserve for community use has been identified in a variety of African countries (see for instance Alden Wily 2003; Woodhouse 2003).

    In the case of Ghana specifically, the approach adopted to CLS development by LAP, which places a strengthened customary land management institution under the control and authority of the traditional chief, is criticised on the grounds that customary authorities in many cases do not manage lands in the interests of their 'subjects' or of other customary rights holders, because of the opportunities to generate revenues from sales and transactions in land. These critiques (for instance Amanor 2001:32-40 and 2005, Lentz 2006b, Maxwell et al. 1998; Ubink 2008a) draw on anthropological and historical analysis of the nature of customary rights which has questioned the long standing assumption that within customary tenure systems, an individual's rights

are clearly defined by the individual's place and status within the kinship group. Investigation has revealed that in practice, land rights are
negotiable, kinship relations can be manipulated by the actors concerned, and customary institutional rules can be ambiguous, so that individuals' rights to resources pertaining to the group are not given,
once and for all (Berry 1993, Chauveau et al. 2006). In addition there
is empirical evidence of contestation of land interests and transactions
between customary authorities and land users (see for instance Amanor 2006, Ubink 2007 and 2008b). Customary land management can
also discriminate against female landholders (Tsikata 2003), and some
analysts directly criticise the attempts by LAP to reach an accommodation with the chiefs and argue for the replacement of customary land
management by more democratic land administration systems under
the control of district authorities (Whitehead and Tsikata 2003). Moreover the CLS approach can also be perceived as in direct alignment
with a neo-liberal economic agenda which actively promotes privatisa-
tion of land rights and the emergence of free land markets (Amanor
2005). Some writers counsel that the conflict and contestation inherent
in the re-interpretation and re-articulation of customary land in order
to support the interest of competing land claimants is essentially insol-
uble by administrative means (Lentz 2006b); and that attempts to institute an equitable framework for customary land administration via
state and/or donor intervention are likely to be futile. Although these
critiques may suggest that it is better to do nothing than to do something, which risks strengthening the hand of traditional authorities,
they are otherwise silent on how policy ought to address customary
land tenure problems, even where existing policies and practices contribute to problems of insecurity, conflict, loss of land rights, and poverty.

Political economy of customary land administration

There is considerable diversity in customary tenure practices and land
management arrangements in Ghana, and the choice of pilot CLSs so
far reflects this. CLSs operate in a context in which the traditional political regimes governing customary territories interact with the formal
economy and polity, as well as with society at large. The same forces
that impinge on the economics and politics of agents and organisations
in the broader economy therefore also interact with the traditional regimes and have a bearing on the success or otherwise of CLS operations. Of particular interest is any potential re-alignment (real or perceived) of power relations among chiefs, their subjects (the possessory
land rights owners within the landholding group, traditionally subject
to the moral and political authority of the stool) and the government

bureaucracy, together with the changing pattern of economic incentives these realignments may present. It is therefore pertinent to discuss the emerging evidence from the CLS pilots within a theoretical framework of the changing political economic relations and incentives between state, chiefs, and citizenry, as well as the political interests driving patterns and styles of CLS establishment. In this section we discuss in turn: how the design of CLSs could enhance the tenure security of smallholder farmers and tenants; the interests of traditional authorities in a customary land management system that lacks transparency; the interests within government bureaucracy in resisting the transfer of responsibility to customary authorities; the impact of donor strategies for aid delivery on LAP; and moral hazards inherent in the CLS experiment. We go on in Section 4 to summarise the risks and challenges for CLSs and consider possible ways forward.

CLSs, land markets and tenure security

With the establishment of CLSs the LAP aims to enhance certainty of land rights for ordinary land users and enable greater discipline and efficiency in the land market. It is frequently argued that allowing markets to develop in peasant land rights creates landlessness and, rather than reducing poverty, may entrench it. This view is contrary to the conventional wisdom of neo-classical economics that enabling trade (including trading in land rights) extends opportunities, creates growth and, in the end, reduces poverty. Both lines of arguments appear to have some empirical support from experiences in various parts of the developing world. We argue that establishing CLSs to support land rights transactions amongst land users themselves makes sense for two reasons. First, land rights transactions are a reality in the land sector in Ghana. There is no way of stopping them with policy. In fact they provide the principle means of land delivery in expanding urban areas and for rural migrants seeking farming opportunities, and increasingly, for the younger generation in general. Greater transparency and efficiency will therefore be beneficial to all land users. Second, CLSs provide an opportunity to combine the registration of newly transacted rights (the initial priority of the chiefs, in order to facilitate leasehold allocations and the generation of land revenues) with the registration of existing rights. Considering the current insecure position of many smallholders in Ghana facing risks of losing land and livelihoods as a result of land disposals by chiefs, this can considerably enhance their tenure security.

For CLSs to develop along the lines originally envisaged – to provide greater equity, fairness, and transparency – they must provide better security of tenure for small land owners against the actions of powerful chiefs and elders. In order to do so they would need to evolve simple and cost-effective land rights documentation practices suitably attuned to the interests held by ordinary members of landholding communities and by tenants who have acquired rights from those communities. If this can be done effectively it would obviate the excessively high cost and complex system of title documentation processes which the CLS Project Memorandum (DFID/Toulmin et al. 2004) views as a barrier preventing many customary land users from obtaining documented land rights. Given secure documentation of land rights, land markets could indeed perform more efficiently and operate in the interests of the diversity of land users themselves and promote broader development.

The implication here is therefore simple: when chiefs get involved in transactions of land rights, they should do so in a fiduciary capacity (see also Ollennu 1962) as recognised in the Constitution and in a historical understanding of customary principles. The relevant issue which policy should address is therefore the extent to which the CLSs, or any alternative solutions for that matter, would align the interests of chiefs with those of their subjects and the broader range of land users concerning land transactions. Efficiency gains that emanate from trading land rights predicted by neo-classical economics will occur only if the CLS as an institution is designed to ensure that members of landholding communities are principal rather than subordinate beneficiaries of land transactions.

Suggestions for the replacement of customary land management by more democratic land administration systems under the control of district authorities (e.g. Whitehead and Tsikata 2003) implicitly assume that the interests of the key personnel at the district authorities would coincide with those of land users, whereas the interests of the chiefs would not. The cavalier attitude with which District Chief Executives (DCEs) are reported to handle finances of the District Assemblies suggests that such a solution is likely to end up only replacing a vampire stool occupier (who happens to be a royal from the land owning community) with corrupt bureaucrats or politicians who might not even be members of the land owning community. Although it has not been a priority in practice, a central issue for LAP to deal with is how the CLSs are to be organised institutionally so as to promote the land rights of subjects (smallholder farmers and urban residents) against the stool and ensure that the opposite does not happen. The precise institutional arrangements for the management of CLSs are particularly important given government's choice that they should fall under the aegis of traditional authorities.

Chiefs, family heads and rights in land

As CLSs fall under the aegis of traditional authorities, we should consider the incentive structure of the representatives of the customary es-
tablishments – chiefs, family heads, and their councils of elders. In various cases, the chiefs and elders of certain communities have coalesced
into an interest group that is vehemently defending and sometimes re-
interpreting customary land law to support the current opaque, sometimes inequitable, and somewhat convoluted system of customary land
administration. The chiefs' administrative role in land rights transactions enables them to appropriate subjects' interests in land for purely
economic motives in ways that customary rules and principles, otherwise interpreted, would not make possible. The LAP-CLS objectives of
delivering accountable and equitable land administration run counter
to those of these established interest groups, whose resistance to the
development of more accountable and representative CLSs as envisaged by LAP is therefore predictable. Ubink's (2007 and 2008a) findings of contestation of land interests and transactions between customary authorities and land users and between different levels of traditional hierarchies for command of proceeds from land rights
transactions provides evidence of this power-game being played out in
practice (see also Abudulai 2002; Alden Wily and Hammond 2001).
These circumstances are a consequence of the hierarchical power relations within customary land administration structures.

The establishment of CLSs, and the opportunities this provides for
centralising the management of land transactions and the recording
and formal documentation of land rights this entails can be observed
to create a number of risks, as these processes become subject to the
interests of chiefs and land owning families in a number of ways.
Firstly, they may seek to use the CLS to convert secure long standing
tenancy arrangements to short term leases, eroding the rights of the
tenants and raising the spectre of repossession by the landholding
group. Alternatively by concentrating on facilitating and documenting
new land transactions, and failing to document the rights of indigenous landholders in a context of growing land scarcity, the CLS may become an instrument for land disposals by the local elite, fuelling resentment between traditional authorities and farmers as well as between the landholding group and newcomers acquiring land through
the CLS.

Land users, chiefs, and the bureaucracy

The opacity and complexity of customary land transactions results at
least in part from the opportunities for chiefs and family heads to

make substantial untaxed profits from land disposals, but this takes place in a context without effective links between formal land and customary land administration arrangements. In fact the behaviour of government land sector agencies (LSAs) in relation to the management of customary land is in line with that predicted by economic analysis of bureaucracies' disposition to centralise decision-making. The current system creates incentives for key staff to build empires to maximise income and power and to operate administrative systems represented as indispensable which enable officials to extract rents from processes such as deeds registration (Niskanen 1975 and 1994). These rents arise both officially, in the form of stipulated fees, and unofficially, in the form of bribes to ensure that applications and transactions are actually processed, while in fact adding no value to the services provided. We find evidence of this in the need for the Lands Commission's consent and/or concurrence of certain customary land transactions and the obvious lack of effective links between actual customary land transactions and formal administrative requirements.

In this context it is no accident that government bureaucracies – despite expert legal views to the contrary[12] – have insisted on an interpretation of article 267(5) of the 1992 Constitution in a manner that requires them to process all stool land transactions as leaseholds, when in fact freehold or quasi-freehold transactions tend to predominate. The treatment of all customary transactions as equivalent to leasehold transactions plays into the hands of centralising chiefs who assert their rights to dispose of land while also creating sources of revenue for the Office of the Administrator of Stool Lands (OASL) and for District Assemblies, who receive the greatest share of the money collected by the OASL. At the same time, government's failure to allow registration of customary freeholds denies members of landholding groups the opportunities to document and secure their rights, and downgrades long established land sharing arrangements between landholding groups and outsiders, effectively making large numbers of land users tenants on their own lands. Although there are those in government and within LSAs who seek to modernise the agencies' roles, there is as yet no forthright attempt to do so as a result of vested interests which have developed on all sides.

One can therefore expect the bureaucracy to attempt to employ all sorts of tactics to ensure that the LAP-CLS intervention does not upset this power game. Indeed with landholding community subjects – the possessory land rights owners – and land users so dispersed and lacking a combined force to counterbalance chiefly interest groups on the one hand, and the bureaucrats on the other, it is tempting to accept arguments about the futility of the CLS idea. Given time, the LAP-CLS project should however, be able to provide fuller evidence regarding this.

LAP and the harmonisation of development aid

An important contextual feature of the LAP is the move within development aid towards the harmonisation of donor strategies and interventions.[13] As a result of this move, the contemporary development architecture emphasises direct budget support linked to the objectives of Poverty Reduction Strategy Programs. In countries which are considered not to qualify for medium term budget support, or as in Ghana – which does qualify, but where specific sectors such as land are not priorities for support through the national budget though they stand in need of substantial support and reform – sector wide support can be provided through pooled donor contributions for common programmes of action. LAP is the channel for multi-donor support to the land sector, to effect a complex programme of implementation and institutional change. This, however, is problematic because the process is managed directly by MLFM as the beneficiary institution, and the various Land Sector Agencies are expected to utilise the resources to reform themselves, build their capacity for new ways of doing business, and moreover, the ministry is to pilot and develop the policy and institutional framework for CLSs as new institutions intended to relieve government of direct responsibility for the management of customary land.

Under the approach agreed by government and donors, donor support is provided directly to government structures to implement agreed programme objectives. This approach – generally referred to as 'mainstreaming' – is, quite properly, intended to ensure knowledge transfer and prevent the tendency of project outcomes to gradually dissipate when the project is over and the project staff have left. However government bureaucracy is inherently resistant to change, and mainstreaming is regarded by MLFM and land sector agency staff as a mechanism to bring additional resources into MLFM and land sector agencies to conduct business as usual. This reduces the incentives of staff to implement change, since they are expected to incorporate the project in their 'mainstream' activities at existing salary levels. This is something which they are extremely stretched in doing, particularly in view of the innovative character of many of LAP activities. To complicate matters further, mainstreaming subjects LAP activities to the motives of politicians, whose goals can be expected to include the use of project resources to legitimate their authority and to maximise votes, without necessarily having regard for objectives of equity and/or efficiency (see Tullock 1976).

In sum, the practice of mainstreaming, at least in regard to the establishment of CLSs, enhances the ability of the land sector agencies to preserve the status quo and encourages a reluctance to bring about in-

stitutional change which could lead to job losses or override vested interests by removing rent-seeking opportunities. Institutional change, in
other words can jeopardise populist political agendas to maximise votes
if it undermines vested interests of traditional authorities, public sector
trade unions, or professional associations in the existing institutional
arrangements. For example, the initial top-down selection of the first
CLS pilot locations was motivated by political considerations to appease
powerful chiefs while being seen to be even handed by distributing
support for CLSs across the ten regions. This 'supply driven' approach
has proved inimical to the establishment of pilot CLSs as laboratories
for lesson learning on how to improve equity, transparency, and accountability in the management of customary land. During the early
years of LAP, this has held back the development of CLS models that
are more demand driven, community based, or problem-centred, focussed on resolving land management problems, reducing disputes, facilitating market transactions amongst land rights holders, and generating revenues for community use.

The cumbersome system of procurement of goods and services practiced in MLFM presents another problem deriving from mainstreaming and frustrating the piloting of a series of technical and institutional
innovations including CLSs as a basis for lesson learning to guide future strategy in the land sector. This has delayed progress and frustrated efficient decision-making required for the implementation of
an innovative project. Although the problems are frequently blamed on
the Procurement Act itself, as well as government procurement systems, it functions to the benefit of key managers, as it allows them to
maintain direct control of procurement and enables political influence
over the award of contracts and the selection of staff.

Moral hazards and CLS sustainability

There is also the potential problem, which economists often describe as
'moral hazard', of raising expectations that the state will provide on-
going support to CLSs, leading to a dependency culture amongst traditional leaders. The moral hazard is the possibility that traditional authorities, after being supported with equipment and necessary training for
efficient operation of CLSs, employ the supplied resources with less
care, diligence, and efficiency than they would have done if they had
spent their own monies to acquire the resources. For example, there
have been expectations that the government would organise repair of
photocopiers supplied to Wassa and Tamale CLSs. This implies a perception of CLSs as a state or donor initiative, rather than something
owned by the customary authority or by the community. There may
also, however, be general problems of affordability or access to technical

support services, in which case the appropriateness of a pre-conceived package of CLS equipment must be questioned. There are many examples of chiefs and village land committees investing in simple ledgers and manual filing systems as a means of keeping land records, and some CLSs, notably Gbawe, have established their own offices and bought computer equipment and hired staff without outside support.

The willingness of customary authorities to pay CLS staff salaries provides a key indicator of CLS ownership and sustainability. Although all of the pilot CLSs have identified at least part-time staff, these are often friends or family members of chiefs, whose limited basic skills education makes them unsuitable for further training and professional roles. Inability or unwillingness of customary authorities to pay to retain staff is emerging as a common constraint to CLS development. In cases where land market activity and land revenues are low the establishment of a full-blown CLS may not be justified or affordable; on the other hand in cases where the land market is more active, it is clear that chiefs are not yet sufficiently convinced of the value of a CLS to commit additional resources (even though their incomes may derive in large part from 'drinks money'), for which the 'upkeep of the stool' and their personal income are always competing priorities. One option here may be to develop greater cooperation with the OASL and use part of the share of land revenues it retains to support salaries of CLS staff.[14]

Another main question regarding sustainability is whether CLSs will be able to self-finance comprehensive exercises to document existing landholding and established customary rights, both of indigenes and of 'strangers' or tenants. This is being done in two of the pilots – Wassa and Kyebi –, though initiated by the CLS component of LAP and organised with project resources rather than by the customary land owners themselves. The CLS programme has learnt lessons from the approach it has adopted and is now seeking to extend and replicate these initiatives using simpler, manual systems; however, the compilation of such inventories is nevertheless likely to prove time consuming and to require LAP or MLFM to meet the costs involved (transport, management, trained personnel, and incentives for local traditional authorities and key informants to collaborate).

Without clear incentives for ownership of CLSs, not only by traditional authorities but by landholding communities as a whole, there are risks that equipment and resources continue to be inefficiently employed, with the result that CLSs never grow beyond their embryonic stage and continuously need funding from the Ghana government and/or donors. Concentrating project resources on a limited number of CLSs may allow them to do a more comprehensive job, but this approach would prove impossible to replicate and would prevent the development of any real ownership of CLSs by traditional authorities and local communities. The situation points to the need for state-traditional authority and civil society partnerships to develop CLSs as institutions which can bring benefits all round: to land users in simplifying land access and improving security, to traditional authorities in exercising legitimate fiduciary roles, and to the state as a means of improving land management generally. This would also provide a firmer basis for CLS accountability and eventual development of a reformed regulatory and institutional framework for customary land management within which CLSs have a clear role to play.

Challenges and ways forward

In this paper, we have discussed the involvement of traditional authorities in customary land management and their attempts to appropriate the interests of smallholder farmers. An important contextual feature of this behaviour is the absence of adequate checks and balances on the behaviour of the chiefs in managing and disposing of land (see Abudulai 2002:83; Ubink 2007). Existing checks and balances within the customary system are confined to the roles of traditional councils, with whom chiefs are supposed to consult, or to the threat of destoolment of the chief. In either case challenges to chiefly authority require the collaboration of the hierarchy of chiefs, elders, queenmothers and other notables, yet the indications are that in those areas where the land market is most active and land users are most vulnerable to dispossession, these groups have common incentives – the maximisation of private gain accruing to chiefly and land owning families – and tend to act together. The issue is an absence of remedies for individuals and communities aggrieved by the actions of traditional elites.

The risks that the CLSs may be used by the occupiers of stools/skins to further tendencies of dispossessing their subjects of lands are real and have the potential of capturing and exploiting the good intentions of the LAP CLS component. However there is at present no alternative model backed by official Land Sector Agencies for establishing CLSs under District Assemblies. In view of frequent tensions between chiefs and District Assemblies such an approach may prove difficult politically, and there are no guarantees that it would offer a better alternative for ordinary land users than the present approach to CLSs. There is a significant risk that the government may not commit fully to building equity and accountability in customary land management arrangements. If the state were to press ahead with creation of CLSs as unregulated estate agencies run by chiefs and landholding families, the CLS experiment in improving governance and equity in land matters would be a failure. Empowerment of chiefs through resourcing CLSs without progressing appropriate checks and balances could acquire a longer term political momentum of its own. In response to this problem LAP began in 2008 to encourage pilot CLSs to develop better accountability by including independent community members and representatives of District Assemblies on land committees which supervise CLS operations.

Another possible course of action in seeking to improve accountability in customary land management would be to change the formal arrangements and the balance of power and incentives between the state and customary authorities in control of land and land revenues by changing the mandate and redesigning the operations of the OASL. However in the short to medium term, government is unlikely to risk antagonising the chiefs by requiring public disclosure of land revenues and accountability in their use, in order to secure the votes that the chiefs command. Yet there is also an opportunity for the state to lead by example in seeking to strengthen accountability: since lack of transparency in the use of land revenues by the state is a significant complaint of the chiefs, a first step would be the public disclosure by the government of the land revenues collected and distributed by OASL from each customary authority and of the uses made of these monies by District Assemblies and by OASL itself. Disclosure of this information be likely to strengthen public demands for accountability in the use of land revenues by both chiefs and state. It would also give an idea of the level of resources generated from land sales and rentals in specific areas, and in which traditional authorities the operation of a CLS should ultimately be sustainable – through funding by the stools themselves, by OASL (who might for instance provide training or second part time staff), by District Assemblies, or some combination of these in a partnership arrangement.

The possibility that NGOs and civil society groups might play a more active role in CLS development and advocacy in challenging land management by both state and customary chiefs is often invoked by both government and donors. The state of development of civil society as a whole in Ghana remains weak, in part because of historical tendencies for emergent community and youth organisations to be co-opted, either by the chiefs themselves or by the state (Amanor 2001: 112-113), and because the predominantly centralist orientation of post-independence governments has restricted the emergence of a strong civil society. In 2007 LAP created a small grants fund intended to support engagement of civil society with LAP activities at local level, including the development of pilot CLSs, although at the time of writing, little progress had been made.

In sum, analysis undertaken for donor agencies has concluded that a variety of models of customary land management are possible and merit experimentation, which do not involve the direct control of land administration by powerful chiefs, and that an enabling and regulatory framework for the development of customary land administration will eventually be required. This however would call for a more diversified approach to CLSs than has been adopted so far, in order to identify what CLS models are feasible, equitable, and sustainable. This in turn is likely to involve a closer linkage in LAP between the reform of the LSAs and the development of CLSs to overcome the present situation in which these are parallel streams of activity supported by different donors within the loosely coordinated but poorly integrated framework that LAP presently provides.

If LAP can in fact maintain flexibility to develop alternative approaches to CLS development and to redirect efforts to address the wider policy and governance issues in customary land management both within government and more widely, there may be grounds for a longer term donor engagement with the CLS process. A decision to promulgate the Attorney General's ruling on the validity of customary freeholds and an active programme to adjudicate and register customary freehold or quasi freehold interests in land could potentially have a major impact in improving tenure security and certainty in land access for both smallholders and investors. This is something in which CLSs would need to play a major role.

To summarise the challenges, they include:

- Balancing quantity and quality in CLS establishment: the need to ensure an in-depth understanding of the implications of different approaches to CLSs in different contexts, as opposed to a focus on numbers of CLSs established through the model of equipment supplied to cooperative chiefs;

- Strengthening collaboration with chiefs while maintaining a focus on transparency, accountability, and equity in land access. Although action can be taken at local level, this is likely to involve efforts to achieve a wider political settlement between chiefs and the state, involving the return of vested lands, greater collaboration between CLSs and the LSAs (in particular the OASL), better democratic accountability on all sides in return for greater control of land revenues by the CLSs, and potentially a professional training and staffing scheme for CLSs supported by government;

- Developing civil society and professional engagement in the establishment of CLSs locally and nationally;

- Fostering greater collaboration between customary authorities, CLSs, local communities, and local government, through joint engagement in land use planning schemes for urban land delivery, investing land revenues in community services and providing land for local economic development through, for instance, high value horticultural projects and other investment schemes. Once again this will require specific initiatives by LAP to bring together separate actions supported by different donors (a land use planning component supported by the Nordic Development Fund (NDF) and CLSs supported by DFID) and with other actors such as the US based Millennium Challenge Corporation (MCC) / Millennium Development Account (MiDA) which is seeking to link securing land rights with agricultural development;

- Building up knowledge of existing customary land management practices to inform CLS piloting, along with the associated policy and subsequent legislative development. This is also likely to require better integration of parallel streams of activity within the LAP framework. One priority would be to link more closely the CLS development process with the 'ascertainment' of customary law and negotiations with Regional and National Houses of Chiefs supported by GTZ. This will also involve fuller empirical documentation of tenure dynamics and land management practices and issues in CLS catchment areas to ensure that the Houses of Chiefs are not able to represent and re-articulate custom and advocate the oversimplification and premature codification of customary 'law' to suit their own political and economic interests. These processes should also be linked to area and region specific public debate about acceptable principles and interpretations of customary law efforts, and to efforts to develop a proper legislative framework for customary land and for CLSs. This should include recognition of the validity of customary freehold, clarification of its modalities and the roles of different land authorities and decision-makers in different parts of Ghana within different customary traditions, and arrangements for adjudicating the nature and strength of the rights held by different land users, including both members of stools and landholding families, as well as their lessees and tenants.

Meeting these challenges, however, requires a relatively sophisticated strategic approach by government, and the full cooperation of the different development partners. There are already significant problems with the delivery of the LAP through the existing 'mainstreamed' implementation mechanisms, which may compromise the emergence of

an effective policy, legal, and institutional framework in which decentralised land management systems can develop. Despite government's
commitment to working with customary chiefs, and the commitment
of key officials to the programme, the MLFM presently lacks the capacity to implement a complex programme, and to procure and manage
the wide range of technical input required. The MLFM is a difficult institutional context in which to implement a multi donor programme
aiming to deliver assistance through sector budgetary support, and in
which to undertake institutional reform of the land sector agencies it
oversees. This applies to LAP as a whole and specifically to the pilot
programme for CLSs. At the outset of LAP, a number of observers expressed reservations about 'bolting-on' a sub-component for support for
CLS piloting to the original framework of LAP which concentrated on
reforms to land administration in the formal sector. In fact the way in
which LAP has been implemented in practice demonstrates that despite overall agreement on objectives and the need to cooperate, donors
to LAP do not share a common understanding and diagnosis of problems and proposed solutions, particularly in relation to customary
land management, having been instead primarily concerned with rea-
lising the specific objectives and priorities of their own projects which
ensure disbursement of allocated funds.

A continuing programme of land administration reform and capacity
building must engage directly with major land policy and institutional
change issues determining the governance of land resources, in which
arrangements for the management of customary land are central. CLS
development needs to become a core part of LAP business, something
which is now being recognised. LAP should also become central to
MLFM business, rather than the present situation in which mainstreaming is interpreted as incorporation of project resources into
MLFM and LSA business as usual, which involves preservation of the
institutional status quo, of political allocation of resources, and of rent-
seeking opportunities for officials.

Arguably, this might be tackled by greater rather than lesser mainstreaming of donor resources for LAP in a subsequent phase – so as to
encourage government to articulate a clear vision for reforming its relationship with the chiefs in relation to land management and to permit
the joint definition of key targets and milestones by government and
donors. Although full coordination of the different components of LAP
within a common programme framework is required, in order to obtain the necessary flexibility – for instance to commission appropriate
research into tenure dynamics, organise public debates at local and national levels, and experiment with different models of CLS development – the MLFM should be prepared to relinquish direct control over
some components of the LAP budget and the necessary procurement,

by appointing appropriate managing agents, while building capacity of a new, reformed LSA to operate in more business-like, efficient ways.

Conclusion

Unresolved tensions in relations amongst state, customary authority, and citizens are a major cause of Ghana's land problems. LAP presents some opportunities to address this, but for this project to be effective broad political will and clarity of overall vision are required.

The extent of local struggles and disputes over land in Ghana point to the need to resolve two major issues:

- Clarification of the land rights of smallholder farmers – whether 'subjects' of stools and members of landholding families or immigrant farmers – vis à vis the powers of chiefs and family heads to dispose of land;

- An equitable settlement between the chiefs and the state regarding the control of land revenues involving formal recognition of traditional authorities' and land owning families' land management responsibilities in relation to those of the state.

The attempt under the LAP to establish and strengthen CLSs takes place in this context. However, the requirements for reform of revenue collection and distribution arrangements and for transforming the role of the OASL were not properly considered during project design. Moreover the interests of the traditional authorities go beyond formalising their responsibilities and building capacities for land administration, and a more far reaching settlement between chiefs and state would most likely include the widespread return of vested lands, collaborative programmes to improve relations between traditional authorities and District Assemblies and to develop a workable division of rights and responsibilities.

To achieve more equitable and efficient arrangements for the management of customary land in the longer term a clearer legal, regulatory, and policy framework is likely to be required. This in turn is likely to require amendment of the constitutional framework governing the roles of traditional authorities and the OASL, in addition to the legislative and institutional reforms presently contemplated under LAP and the practical implementation of existing provisions for the registration of customary freehold land interests. In order to prepare the ground in practice, and if the pilot CLS experiment under LAP is to prove a success, not only will this take a longer period to bear fruit, it will likely require a new approach. This includes a critical role for action research in gathering evidence and assessing the impact of pilots and experimental approaches, as well as in engaging policymakers in debate. The fostering of public engagement in land debates is also required at a variety of levels, for land users, land administrators, customary leaders, government officials, and politicians.

Notes

*   Julian Quan has from 2002 provided policy and technical advice on the development and from 2005 until the present on the implementation of the Land Administration Programme (LAP) Ghana on behalf of DFID. Janine Ubink has written her PhD-thesis on customary land management in Ghana, which included an analysis of the LAP. Adarkwah Antwi worked from 2005-2007 as the National Facilitator for the Customary Land Secretariat component of the LAP.

1   In addition the Attorney General's Department, with support from GTZ, is working to develop detailed knowledge of customary land management practice and debate the scope for formalisation and harmonisation of customary land 'law' with Regional and National Houses of Chiefs.

2   Article 267(6), Constitution of the Republic of Ghana, 1992 and sections 3 and 8, OASL Act, 1994 (Act 481).

3   For a quantitative analysis of rent-seeking behaviour generated by this arrangement, see Antwi and Adams 2003.

4   The CLS in Kyebi is intended to improve the management of the lands of the Akim Abuakua Stool, under the *Okyenhene*, one of the most powerful paramount chiefs in Ghana. A land secretariat at the *Okyenhene's* palace was originally established during the colonial period but following independence this was closed as the Nkrumah regime sought to take control of land administration and limit the powers accumulated by chiefs. Under the pro-chieftaincy Kufuor regime, re-establishing the *Okyenhene's* land secretariat was a priority at the beginning of LAP.

5   Interview with World Bank natural resource management specialist, 19 January 2004.

6   Interview with DFID Ghana rural livelihoods adviser, 27 January 2004.

7   Interview with Gbawe Kwatey family elders, 11 August 2005.

8   Interview with Gbawe Kwatey family head Nii Adom Kwatey and elders, 9 June 2006.

9   Interview with Kyebi CLS registrar, Kyebi, 15 August 2005.

10 Interview with staff of the Asantehene's Land Secretariat, Kumasi, 16 August 2005.

11 Interview with coordinator of Wassa Emenfi CLS, Wassa Akropong, 18 August 2005.

12 See the position paper of Gyan 2005, which was accepted by the Attorney General's office.

13 See the *Paris Declaration on Aid Effectiveness: Ownership, harmonisation, alignment results and mutual accountability*. OECD Paris 2005   Available at www1.worldbank.org/harmonisation/Paris/FINALPARISDECLARATION.pdf

14 Although chiefs often express the view that all land revenues should be paid to and controlled by the stools, government treats the question of CLSs as a potential means to improve efficiency and equity in land management quite separately from the control of land revenues. Under the Constitution, stool land revenues are collected and distributed by the OASL, and a change to this system would involve constitutional change.

References

Abudulai, S. (1996). Perceptions of Land Rights, Rural-urban Land Use Dynamics and Policy Development. Managing Land Tenure and Resource Access in West Africa: Proceedings of a Regional Workshop held at Gorée, Sénégal, November 18-22, 1996. Ministère de la Coopération, Overseas Development Administration, L'Université de Saint Louis, GRET and IIED. London, IIED: 107-127.
— (2002). Land Rights, Land-Use Dynamics & Policy in Peri-urban Tamale, Ghana. *The Dynamics of Resource Tenure in West Africa.* C. Toulmin, P. Lavigne Delville and S. Traoré. London, IIED: 72-85.
Addo-Fening, R. (1987). Customary land-tenure system in Akyem-Abuakwa. *Universitas* 9: 95-107.
— (1997). *Akyem Abuakwa 1700-1943: From Ofori Panin to Sir Ofori Atta.* Trondheim, Department of History, Norwegian University of Science and Technology.
Adomako-Sarfoh, J. (1974). Migrant Asante Cocoa Farmers and their Families. *Domestic Rights and Duties in Southern Ghana.* C. Oppong. Legon Institute of African Studies, University of Ghana 1: 129-144.
Agbosu, L.K. (1978). Statutory Foundations of Land Administration in the Northern and Upper Regions of Ghana. *Land Ownership and Registration in Ghana.* A.K. Mensah-Brown, Kumasi, Land Administration Research Centre, University of Science and Technology: 122-139.
— (1990). Land registration in Ghana: Past, present and the future. *Journal of African Law* 34(2): 104-127.
Aidoo, J.B. (1996). Tenancy and the Land Reform Debate in Ghana. Paper produced as part of the 'Our Common Estate' Programme of the Royal Institution of Chartered Surveyors, London. London, The Royal Institution of Chartered Surveyors.
Akindès, F.A. (2004). *The Roots of the Military-Political Crises in Côte d'Ivoire.* Uppsala, Nordic Africa Institute.
Akwabi-Ameyaw, K. (1974). The Development of the Cocoa Industry in Eastern Ashanti. *The Economics of Cocoa Production and Marketing: Proceedings of Cocoa Economics Research Conference Legon, April 1973.* R.A. Kotey, C. Okali and B.E. Rourke. Legon, University of Ghana, Institute of Statistical, Social and Economic Research: 183-195.
Alden Wily, L. (2003). Governance and Land Relations: A Review of Decentralisation of Land Administration and Management in Africa. London, International Institute for Environment and Development.
Alden Wily, L. and D.N.A. Hammond (2001). *Land Security and the Poor in Ghana. Is There a Way Forward?* DFID Ghana Rural livelihoods Program.
Allman, J.M. (1993). *The Quills of the Porcupine: Asante Nationalism in an Emergent Ghana, 1954-57.* Madison, University of Wisconsin Press.
Allman, J.M. and J. Parker (2005). *Tongnaab: The History of a West African God.* Bloomington, Indiana University Press.
Allman, J.M. and V.B. Tashjian (2000). *'I Will Not Eat Stone': A Women's History of Colonial Asante.* Oxford, James Currey.

Allott, A.N. (1994). Judicial Ascertainment of Customary Law in British Africa. *Folk Law: Essays in the Theory and Practice of Lex Non Scripta*. Dundes Renteln, A and A. Dundes, New York, Garland Publishing: 295-318.

Amamoo, J.G. (1958). *The New Ghana: The Birth of a New Nation*. London, Pan Books.

Amanor, K.S. (1994). *The New Frontier: Farmers' Responses to Land Degradation*. London, Zed Press.

— (1999). *Global Restructuring and Land Rights in Ghana: Forest Food Chains, Timber and Rural Livelihoods*. Uppsala, Nordiska Afrikainstitutet.

— (2001). Land, Labour and the Family in Southern Ghana: A Critique of Land Policy under Neo-Liberalisation. Uppsala, Nordiska Afrikainstitutet: 127.

— (2002). Shifting Tradition: Forest Resource Tenure in Ghana. *The Dynamics of Resource Tenure in West Africa* C. Toulmin, P. Lavigne Delville and S. Traoré. Portsmouth, Heinemann: 48-60.

— (2005). Global and Local Land Markets: The Role of the Customary. *Land in Africa: Market Asset or Secure Livelihood? Proceedings and Summary of Conclusions from the Land in Africa Conference held in London, November 8-9, 2004*. J. Quan, S.F. Tan and C. Toulmin. London, IIED, NRI, Royal African Society: 103-114.

— (2006). Family Values, Land Sales and Agricultural Commodification in Ghana. Paper presented at the colloquium: *At the Frontier of Land Issues: Social Embeddedness of Rights and Public Policy*. Montpellier, France.

Amanor, K.S. and M.K. Diderutuah (2001). *Share Contracts in the Oil Palm and Citrus Belt of Ghana*. London, International Institute for Environment and Development.

Annor, K.P. (1985). Cultural and social identities in Africa: Chieftaincy and political change in Ghana. *Verfassung und Recht in Ubersee* 18: 153-159.

Antwi, A.Y. and J. Adams (2003). Rent-seeking behaviour and its economic costs in urban land transactions in Accra, Ghana. *Urban Studies* 40(10): 2083-2098.

Arhin, B. (2001). *Transformations in Traditional Rule in Ghana (1951-1996)* Accra, Sedco.

Arhin, K. (1974). Some Asante views of colonial rule: As seen in the controversy relating to death duties. *Transactions of the Historical Society of Ghana* 15: 63-84.

— (1986). *The Expansion of Cocoa Production in Ghana: The Working Conditions of Migrant Cocoa Farmers in the Central and Western Regions*. Legon, Institute of Statistical, Social and Economic Research, University of Ghana.

— (1993). *The Life and Work of Kwame Nkrumah*. Trenton, NJ, Africa World Press.

Aryee, J. (1992). Decentralisation and effective government: The case of Ghana's District Assemblies. *Africa Insight* 25(3): 186-194.

Aryeetey, E., J. Harrigan, et al., Eds. (2000). *Economic Reforms in Ghana: The Miracle and the Mirage*. Oxford, James Currey.

Asante, S.K.B. (1969). Interests in land in the customary law of Ghana – a new appraisal. *University of Ghana Law Journal* 6(2): 99-139.

Asiama, S.O. (2003). Current changes in customary/traditional delivery systems in Sub-Saharan African cities - Ghana. *Africa*. 2.

Asiamah, A.E.A. (2000). *The Mass Factor in Rural Politics: The Case of the Asafo Revolution in Kwahu Political History*. Accra, Ghana Universities Press.

Atwood, D.A. (1990). Land registration in Africa: The impact on agricultural production. *World Development* 18(5): 659-671.

Austin, G. (1987). The emergence of capitalist relations in South Asante cocoa-farming, C. 1916-1933. *The Journal of African History* 28(2): 259-279.

— *Labour, Land and Capital in Ghana: From Slavery to Free Labour in Asante, 1807-1956*. Rochester, NY, University of Rochester Press.

Ayee, J.R.A. (1999). Ghana. *Public Administration in Africa. Main Issues and Selected Country Studies*. L. Adamolekun. Boulder, Oxford, Westview Press: 250-274.

Bassett, T.J. (1993). Introduction: The Land Question and Agricultural Transformation in Sub-Saharan Africa. *Land in African Agrarian Systems*. T.J. Bassett and D.E. Crummey. Madison, University of Wisconsin Press: 3-34.

Becher, C. (1996). *'Das Land Gehört zu den Männer': Landzugang von Frauen im Norden Ghanas im Rahmen Dynamischer Transformationsprozesse*. Bielefeld, University of Bielefeld, Faculty of Sociology.

Beckett, W.H. (1944). *Akokoaso: A Survey of a Gold Coast Village*. London P. Lund, Humphries.

— (1945). Korasang: A Gold Coast Cocoa Farm. *Korasang Cocoa Farm: 1904-1970*. W.H. Beckett. Legon, Institute of Statistical, Social and Economic Research. Technical Publication No. 31 [1972].

Benjaminsen, T.A. and C. Lund (2003). Formalisation and Informalisation of Land and Water Rights in Africa: An Introduction. *Securing Land Rights in Africa*. T.A. Benjaminsen and C. Lund. London, Frank Cass: 1-10.

Benneh, G. (1970). The impact of cocoa cultivation on the traditional land tenure system of the Akan of Ghana. *Ghana Journal of Sociology* 6(1): 43-61.

— The Land Tenure and Agrarian System in the New Cocoa Frontier of Ghana: Wassa Akropong Case Study. Agricultural Expansion and Pioneer Settlements in the Humid Tropics: Selected papers presented at a workshop *'Resource Use of Frontiers and Pioneer Settlements in the Humid Tropics'* held in Kuala Lumpur, 17-21 September 1985. W. Manshard and W. B. Morgan. Tokyo: The United Nations University 88.III.A.4.

Bentsi-Enchill, K. (1964). *Ghana Land Law: An Exposition, Analysis and Critique*. London, Sweet & Maxwell.

Berry, S. (1993). *No Condition is Permanent: The Social Dynamics of Agrarian Change in Sub-Saharan Africa*. Madison, The University of Wisconsin Press.

— (1997). Tomatoes, land and hearsay: Property and history in Asante in the time of structural adjustment. *World Development* 25(8): 1225-1241.

— (2001). *Chiefs Know Their Boundaries: Essays on Property, Power, and the Past in Asante, 1896-1996*. Portsmouth, Heinemann.

— (2002). The Everyday Politics of Rent-seeking: Land Allocation on the Outskirts of Kumase, Ghana. *Negotiating Property in Africa*. K. Juul and C. Lund. Portsmouth, Heinemann: 107-134.

— (2006). Privatization and the Politics of Belonging in West Africa. *Land and the Politics of Belonging in West Africa*. R. Kuba and C. Lentz. Leiden, Brill: 241-263.

Binswanger, H.P. and K. Deininger (1993). South African land policy: The legacy of history and current options. *World Development* 21(9): 1451-1475.

Blion, R. and S. Bredeloup (1997). La Côte d'Ivoire dans les Stratégies Migratoires des Burkinabè et des Sénégalais. *Le Modèle Ivoirien en Question: Crises, Ajustements et Recompositions*. B. Contamin and H.H. Memel-Foté. Paris, Karthala.

Boafo-Arthur, K. (2001). 'Tradition' against the State? Confronting Chiefs and State Authority in Ghana. *African Studies Centre Seminar*. Leiden.

— (2003). Chieftaincy in Ghana: Challenges and prospects in the 21st century. *African and Asian Studies* 2(2): 125-154.

Boni, S. (1999). La Struttura Politica 'Tradizionale' Sefwi (Ghana) tra Invenzione e Ordinamento. *Africa: Rivista Trimestrale di Studi e Documentazione* 54(4): 535-556.

— (2000). Contents and contexts: The rhetoric of oral traditions in the oman of Sefwi Wiawso, Ghana. *Africa: Journal of the International African Institute* 70(4): 568-594.

— (2001). Twentieth-century transformations in notions of gender, parenthood, and marriage in southern Ghana: A critique of the hypothesis of 'retrograde steps' for Akan women. *History in Africa: A Journal of Method* 28(15-41).

— (2003). *Le Strutture della Disuguaglianza: Capi, Appartenenze e Gerarchie nel Mondo Akan dell'Africa Occidentale*. Milano, Franco Angeli.

— (2004). Dipendenza, Violenza, Integrazione: L'utilizzo Liminare della Forza e il suo Superamento tra i Sefwi (Ghana). *Guerra e Violenza in Africa Occidentale*. F. Viti. Milano, Franco Angeli: 252-285.

— (2005). *Clearing the Ghanaian Forest: Theories and Practices of Acquisition, Transfer and Utilisation of Farming Titles in the Sefwi-Akan Area*. Legon, Institute of African Studies.

— (2006). Indigenous Blood and Foreign Labor: The Ancestralization of Land Rights in Sefwi (Ghana). *Land and the Politics of Belonging in West Africa*. R. Kuba and C. Lentz. Leiden, Boston, Brill: 161-186.

Boone, C. (2003). *Political Topographies of the African State: Territorial Authority and Institutional Choice* Cambridge, Cambridge University Press.

Brobby, K.W. (1991). Customary tenure and locus standi in compensation claims in Ghana. *Journal of Property Valuation & Investment* 9(4): 313-322.

Brown, H.J. and A.L. Marriott (1999). *ADR Principles and Practice*. London, Sweet & Maxwell.

Bruce, J.W. (1988). A perspective on indigenous land tenure systems and land concentration. *Land and Society in Contemporary Africa*. R.E. Downs and S.P. Reyna. Hannover, London, University Press of New England: 23-52.

Bruce, J.W. and S. E. Migot-Adholla, eds. (1994). *Searching for Land Tenure Security in Africa*. Dubuque, Kendall/Hunt Publishing Company.

Bruce, J.W., S.E. Migot-Adholla, et al. (1994). The findings and their policy implications: Institutional adaptation or replacement? *Searching for Land Tenure Security in Africa*. J.W. Bruce and S.E. Migot-Adholla. Dubuque, Kendall/Hunt Publishing Company: 251-266.

Busia, K.A. (1951). *The Position of the Chief in the Modern Political System of Ashanti: A Study of the Influence of Contemporary Social Changes on Ashanti Political Institutions*. Oxford, Oxford University Press.

Chanock, M. (1991). Paradigms, policies and property: A review of the customary law of land tenure. *Law in Colonial Africa*. K. Mann and Richard Roberts. Portsmouth, Heinemann: 61-84.

Chauveau, J.-P. (1982). Le statut du foncier dans l'analyse de l'économie de plantation au Ghana. *Enjeux fonciers en Afrique Noire*. E. Le Bris, E. Le Roy and F. Leimdorfer. Paris, Karthala: 45-56.

— (2000). *The Land Question in Côte d'Ivoire: A Lesson in History*. London, IIED.

— (2002). *Une lecture sociologique de la loi ivoirienne de 1998 sur le domaine foncier*. Montpellier, IRD-Unité de Recherche Regulations Foncieres.

— (2005). How does an institution evolve? Land, politics, intergenerational relations and the institution of the tutorat amongst autochthones and immigrants. *Land Rights and the Politics of Belonging in West Africa*. R. Kuba and C. Lentz. Leiden, E.J. Brill.

Chauveau, J.-P. and K.S. Bobo (2003). La situation de guerre dans l'arène villageoise: Un exemple dans le centre-ouest ivoirien *Politique africaine* 89: 12-32.

Chauveau, J.-P. and J.-P. Dozon (1987). Au coeur des ethnies ivoiriennes. *L'état contemporain en Afrique*. E. Terray. Paris, L'Harmattan.

Chauveau, J.-P. and E. Léonard (1996). Côte d'Ivoire's pioneer fronts: Historical and political determinants of the spread of cocoa cultivation. *Cocoa Pioneer Fronts Since 1800*. W.G. Clarence-Smith. London & NY, Macmillan & St. Martin's.

Chauveau, J.-P. and J. Richard (1977). Une périphérie recentrée: à propos d'un système d'économie de plantation et 'nouveaux milieux sociaux. *Cahiers d'Etudes Africaines* XVII (4): 485-524.

Chauveau, J.-P., J.P. Colin, et al. (2006). Changes in land access and governance in West Africa: Markets, social mediations and public policies. Results of the CLAIMS research project. London, IIED.

Claassens, A. (2006). Land rights, power and traditional leaders. The Communal Land Rights Act of 2004. *Acta Juridica*. 2005.

Clark, G. (1999). Negotiating Asante Family Survival in Kumasi, Ghana. *Africa* 69(1): 66-86.

Cleveland, D. (1991). Migration in West Africa: A savanna village perspective. *Africa* 61(2): 222-245.

Colin, J. (2005). Le développement d'un marché foncier? Une perspective ivoirienne. *Afrique contemporaine* 213: 89-106.

Comaroff, J. (1975). Talking politics: Oratory and authority in a Tswana chiefdom. *Political Language and Oratory in Traditional Society*. M. Bloch. London, New York, San Francisco, Academic Press: 141-161.

Cousins, B. (2002). Legislating negotiability: Tenure reform in post-apartheid South Africa. *Negotiating Property in Africa*. K. Juul and C. Lund. Portsmouth, Heinemann: 67-106.

Cowen, M. and R.W. Shenton (1994). British neo-Hegelian idealism and official colonial practice in Africa: The Oluwa land case of 1921. *Journal of Imperial and Commonwealth History* 22:(2): 217-250.

Crook, R. (1973). Colonial rule and political culture in modern Ashanti. *Journal of Commonwealth political studies* 11(1): 3-27.

— (1986). Decolonization, the colonial state, and chieftaincy in the Gold Coast. *African Affairs* 85(338): 75-105.

— (1990). Politics, the cocoa crisis, and administration in Côte d'Ivoire. *Journal of Modern African Studies* 28(4): 649-669.

— (1991a). Decentralisation and participation in Ghana and Côte d'Ivoire. *Government and Participation: Institutional Development, Decentralisation and Democracy in the Third World*. R.C. Crook and A.M. Jerve. Bergen, Chr. Michelsen Institute: Ch. 6.

— (1991b). State, society and political institutions in Ghana and Côte d'Ivoire. *Rethinking Third World politics*. J. Manor. London & New York, Longman.

— (1997). Winning coalitions and ethno-regional politics: The failure of the opposition in the 1990 and 1995 elections in Côte d'Ivoire. African Affairs 96(383): 215-242.

— (1999). No-party politics and local democracy in Africa: Rawlings' Ghana and the Ugandan model in the 1990s. *Democratization* 6(4): 114-138.

Crook, R.C., S. Affou, et al. (2005). *The Law, Legal Institutions and the Protection of Land Rights in Ghana and Côte d'Ivoire: Developing a More Effective and Equitable System*. Final Report SSRU Project R 7993.

— (2007). *The Law, Legal Institutions and the Protection of Land Rights in Ghana and Côte d'Ivoire: Developing a More Effective and Equitable System*. IDS Research Report 58. Falmer, Sussex, IDS.

Crook, R. and J. Manor (1998). *Democracy and Decentralisation in South Asia and West Africa: Participation, accountability and performance*. Cambridge, Cambridge University Press.

Cutolo, A. (1999). Avvicinarsi agli antenati: tradizione orale e autorità nel paese Anno. *Africa: rivista trimestrale di studi e documentazione* 54(4): 514-534.

Daley, E. and M. Hobley (2005). Land: Changing contexts, changing relationships, changing rights. Paper for the Urban-Rural Change Team, DFID.

Danquah, J.B. (1928a). *The Akim Abuakwa Handbook*. London, Forster Groom & Co.

— *Gold Coast: Akan Laws and Customs and the Akim Abuakwa Constitution*. London, Routledge.

DaRocha, B.J. and C.H.K. Lodoh (1995). *Ghana Land Law and Conveyancing*. Accra, Anaseem Publications.

Deininger, K. (2003). *Land Policies for Growth and Poverty Reduction*. A World Bank policy research report. Washington, Oxford, World Bank, Oxford University Press.

Deininger, K. and H. Binswanger (1999). The evolution of the World Bank's land policy: Principles, experience, and future challenges. *The World Bank Research Observer* 14(2): 247-76.

Dembélé, O. (2003). Côte d'Ivoire: la fracture communautaire. *Politique africaine* (89): 34-48.

Der, G.B. (2000). The traditional political systems of Northern Ghana reconsidered. *Regionalism and Public Policy in Northern Ghana*. Y. Saaka. New York, Peter Lang. 10: 35-65.

Derrick, J. (1984). West Africa's worst year of famine. *African affairs* 83 (332): 281-299.

DFID (2001). *Further Knowledge of Livelihoods Affected by Urban Transition, Kumasi, Ghana. Natural Resources Systems Programme*. Final Technical Report, DFID.

DFID/Toulmin, C., D. Brown, et al. (2004). *Project Memorandum: Ghana Land Administration Project Institutional Reform & Development: Strengthening Customary Land Administration*.

Diomande, K. (1997). Finances publiques et interventions de l'état. *Le modèle ivoirien en question*. B. Contamin and H. Memel-Foté. Paris: Karthala & ORSTOM.

Dozon, J.-P. (1985). *La société Bété, Côte d'Ivoire*. Paris, Karthala.

— (2000). La Côte d'Ivoire au péril de l'ivoirité. *Afrique contemporaine* 193: 13-24.

Dunn, J. and A.F. Robertson (1973). *Dependence and Opportunity: Political Change in Ahafo*. Cambridge, Cambridge University Press.

Edusah, S.E. and D. Simon (2001). Land use and land allocation in Kumasi peri-urban villages. CEDAR/IRNR Kumasi paper 9, DFID Project R7330, Royal Holloway, University of London and University of Science and Technology, Kumasi. 2006.

Feder, G. and R. Noronha (1987). Land rights systems and agricultural development in sub-Saharan Africa. *Research Observer* 2(2): 143-169.

Feeny, D. (1988). The Development of Property Rights in Land: A comparative study. *Towards a Political Economy of Development*. R. Bates. Berkeley, University of California Press: 272-299.

Field, M.J. (1948). *Akim – Kotoku: An Oman of the Gold Coast*. London Crown Afents for the Colonies.

Firmin-Sellers, K. (1995). The politics of property rights. *The American Political Science Review* 89(4): 867-881.

— (1996). *The Transformation of Property Rights in the Gold Coast*. Cambridge, Cambridge University Press.

Fisiy, C.F. (1992). *Power and Privilege in the Administration of Law: Land Law Reforms and Social Differentiation in Cameroon*. Leiden, African Studies Centre.

Fortes, M. (1948). Ashanti Survey, 1945-46: An experiment in social research. *Geographical Journal* 110(4-6): 149-79.

— (1962). Ritual and office in tribal society. *Essays on the Ritual of Social Relations*. M. Gluckman. Manchester, Manchester University Press: 53-88.

Fox Bourne, H.R. (1901). *Blacks and Whites in West Africa*. London, P.S. King and Son.

Fukuyama, F. (1992). *The end of history and the last man*. New York, Free Press.

Garceau, J.-D. (1982). L'économie du cacao dans une chefferie Akan (Ghana): appropiation des terres et exploitation d'une main-d'oevre étrangère. Une approche diachronique. *Culture* II(2): 99-112.

Genn, H. (1999). *Paths to Justice: What People Think and Do About Going to Law*. Oxford, Hart Publishing.

Gocking, R. (1993). British justice and the native tribunals of the southern Gold Coast Colony. *The Journal of African History* 34(1): 93-113.

Goody, J. (1980). Rice-burning and the Green Revolution in Northern Ghana. *Journal of Development Studies* 16(2): 136-155.

Gough, K.V. and P.W.K. Yankson (2000). Land markets in African cities: The case of peri-urban Accra, Ghana. *Urban Studies* 37(13): 1485-1500.

Grande, E. (1999). Alternative Dispute Resolution, Africa and the structure of law and power: The horn in context. *Journal of African Law* 43(1): 63-70.

Grier, B. (1987). Contradiction, crisis and class conflict: The state and capitalist development in Ghana Prior to 1948. *Studies in Power and Class in Africa*. I.L. Markovitz Oxford, Oxford University Press: 27-49.

GSS (2002). Population and Housing Census Report 2000. Accra, GSS.

GTZ (2002). *Land Disputes Settlement in Ghana: the Role of Traditional Authorities. Workshop for National House of Chiefs.* Accra, German Technical Co-operation (GTZ), Legal Pluralism and Gender Project, Nkum Associates.

Gutschmidt, S. (1996). *Bäuerliche Strategien des Wirtschaftens im Norden Ghanas und deren soziale Einbettung.* Bielefeld, Universität, Fakultät Soziologie.

Gyan, K. (2005). Article 267(5) of the 1992 Constitution and the Death of the Freehold Interest in Stool Land in Ghana. Unpublished position paper for the Ministry of Lands, Forestry and Mines, accepted by the Attorney General's office.

Hagan, G.P. (2003). Chieftaincy the way forward – new wines and broken bottles. *Chieftaincy in Africa: Culture, Governance and Development.* Accra. 113: 193-208.

Hailey, L. (1951). *Native Administration in the British African Territories: Part III: West Africa: Nigeria, Gold Coast, Sierra Leone, Gambia.* London, HMSO.

Hammond, D.N.A. (2003). *Land Rights and Legal Institutions in Ghana (Nadowli Case Study).* Accra Roundtable on 'Land Rights and Legal Institutions in Ghana and La Côte d'Ivoire', Accra.

— (2005). *Protection of land rights and relations between state and customary authorities in Kumasi and Wa.* Workshop on Adjudication of Land Disputes, Legal Pluralism and the Protection of Land Rights in Ghana and Côte d'Ivoire, London.

Hansen, E. (1989). The state and food agriculture. *The State Development and Politics in Ghana.* E. Hansen and K.A. Ninson. London, Codesria: 184-221.

Hayford, J.E.C. (1970). *Gold Coast Native Institutions: With Thoughts upon a Healthy Imperial Policy for the Gold Coast and Ashanti.* London, Frank Cass & Co. Ltd.

Hecht, R. (1985). The Ivory Coast 'miracle': What benefit for African farmers. *Journal of Modern African Studies* 21(1): 25-53.

Hill, P. (1956). *The Gold Coast Cocoa Farmer.* London, Oxford University Press.

— (1959). *The Cocoa Farmers of Asafo and Maase with Special Reference to the Position of Women.* Accra, Economic Research Division, University College of Ghana.

— (1963). *The Migrant Cocoa-Farmers of Southern Ghana. A study in Rural Capitalism.* Cambridge, Cambridge University Press.

Hill, P. and C. McGlade (1957). *An Economic Survey of Cocoa Farmers in Sefwi-Wiawso.* Legon, University College of Ghana, Economics Research Division.

Howard, R. (1978). *Colonialism and Underdevelopment in Ghana.* London, Croom Helm.

IBIS (1998). Education for Development. Accra. 1998.

ICOUR *Tono Irrigation Project: A Brief Description.* Navrongo, Irrigation Company Of Upper Region Ltd. (ICOUR).

IFAD (1989). *Upper East Region Land Conservation and Smallholder Rehabilitation Project / Unpublished Working Papers.* Accra, International Fund for Agricultural Development (IFAD).

IMF, S. Lizondo, et al., Eds. (2005). *Ghana: 2005 Article IV Consultation, Third Review Under the Poverty Reduction and Growth Facility, and Request for Waiver of Non observance of Performance Criteria and Extension of the Arrangement (Prepared by the African Department).* IMF Country Report. Washington, D.C., International Monetary Fund.

Juul, K. and C. Lund (2002). *Negotiating Property in Africa.* Portsmouth, Heinemann.

Kasanga, K. (1992). *Agricultural Land Administration and Social Differentiation: A Case Study of the Tano, Vea and Fumbisi Belts of Northeastern Ghana.* New York, Social Science Research Council, Joint Committee on African Studies.

— (1996). Land tenure, resource access and decentralisation: The political economy of land tenure in Ghana. *Managing Land Tenure and Resource Access in West Africa: Proceedings of a Regional Workshop held at Gorée, Sénégal, November 18-22, 1996.* Ministère de la Coopération, Overseas Development Administration, L'Université de Saint Louis, GRET and IIED. London, IIED: 84-106.

— (2002). Land tenure, resource access & decentralisation in Ghana. *The Dynamics of Resource Tenure in West Africa*. C. Toulmin, P. Lavigne Delville and S. Traoré. London, IIED: 25-36.

Kasanga, K., J. Cochrane, et al. (1996). Land Markets and Legal Contradictions in the Peri-Urban Area of Accra Ghana: Informant Interviews and Secondary Data Investigations. LTC Research Paper 127. Madison, Kumasi, Land Tenure Center.

Kasanga, K. and N.A. Kotey (2001). *Land Management in Ghana: Building on Tradition and Modernity*. London, IIED.

Kasanga, K. and G.R. Woodman (2004). Ghana: Local law making and land conversion in Kumasi, Ashanti. *Local Land Law and Globalization: A Comparative Study of Peri-Urban Areas in Benin, Ghana and Tanzania*. G.R. Woodman, U. Wanitzek and H. Sippel. Münster, Lit Verlag: 153-332.

Kasanga, R.K. (1988). *Land Tenure and the Development Dialogue: The Myth concerning Communal Landholding in Ghana*. Cambridge, University of Cambridge, Dept. of Land Economy.

Kenton, N. (1999). *Land Tenure and Resource Access in West Africa: Issues and Opportunities for the Next Twenty Five Years*. London, IIED.

Khadiagala, L.S. (2001). The failure of popular justice in Uganda: Local councils and women's property rights. *Development and Change* 32: 55-76.

Kimble, D. (1963). *A Political History of Ghana: The Rise of Gold Coast Nationalism, 1850-1928*. Oxford, Clarendon Press.

Kofi-Sackey, H.W. (1983). Chieftaincy, law and custom in Asante, Ghana. *Jahrbuch für Afrikanisches Recht* 4: 65-79.

Koné, M. (2002). *Gaining Rights of Access to Land in West-Central Côte d'Ivoire*. London, International Institute for Environment and Development.

Konings, P. (1986). *The State and Rural Class Formation in Ghana: A Comparative Analysis*. London, Routledge & Kegan Paul.

Kotey, N.A. (1996). The 1992 Constitution and compulsory acquisition of land in Ghana: Opening new vistas? *Managing Land Tenure and Resource Access in West Africa: Proceedings of a Regional Workshop held at Gorée, Sénégal, November 18-22, 1996*. Ministère de la Coopération, Overseas Development Administration, L'Université de Saint Louis, GRET and IIED. London, IIED: 244-261.

— (2002). Compulsory acquisition of land in Ghana: Does the 1992 Constitution open new vistas? *Dynamics of resource tenure in West Africa*. C. Toulmin. London, Oxford & Portsmouth, IIED, James Currey & Heinemann.

— (2004). *Ghana LAP Legislative and Judicial Review: Draft Report submitted to the Coordinator, Ghana LAP', Ministry of Lands and Forestry, Accra*.

Kotey, N.A. and M.O. Yeboah (2003). GTZ Legal Pluralism and Gender Project (Land Law Focal Area). Report of a Study on Peri-Urbanism, Land Relations and Women in Ghana, GTZ.

Kumado, C.E.K. (1990-1992). Chieftaincy and the law in modern Ghana. *University of Ghana Law Journal* XVIII: 194-216.

Kunbuor, B. (2003). Multiple layers of land rights and 'multiple owners': The case of land disputes in the upper west region of Ghana. *Ghana's North. Research on Culture, Religion and Politics of Societies in Transition*. F. Kröger and B. Meier. Frankfurt am Main, Peter Lang: 101-128.

Kyerematen, A.A.Y. (1971). *Inter-State Boundary Litigation in Ashanti*. Leiden, African Studies Centre.

Lachenmann, G. (1995). *Transformationsprozesse in Westafrika*. Bielefeld, Universität Bielefeld, Forschungsschwerpunkt Entwicklungssoziologie.

Laube, W. (2005). *Changing Natural Resource Regimes in Northern Ghana: Actors, Structures and Institutions: Dissertation*. Cologne, University of Cologne, Faculty of Philosophy.

Lavigne Delville, P. (2000). Harmonising formal law and customary land rights in French-speaking West Africa. *Evolving Land rights, Policy and Tenure in Africa*. C. Toulmin and J. Quan. London, DFID/IIED/NRI: 97-122.

— (2003). When farmers use 'pieces of paper' to record their land transactions in Francophone rural Africa: Insights into the dynamics of institutional innovation. *Securing Land Rights in Africa*. T.A. Benjaminsen and C. Lund. London, Frank Cass: 89-108.

Lavigne Delville, P., C. Toulmin, et al. (2002). *Negotiating Access to land in West Africa: A Synthesis of Findings from Research on Derived Rights to Land*. London, International Institute for Environment and Development.

Lentz, C. (2006a). First-comers and late-comers: Indigenous theories of land ownership in the West African Savanna. *Land and the Politics of Belonging in West Africa*. R. Kuba and C. Lentz. Leiden, Brill 9: 35-56.

— (2006b). Is land inalienable? Historical and current debates on land transfers in Northern Ghana. Paper presented at the colloquium: *At the Frontier of Land Issues: Social Embeddedness of Rights and Public Policy*. Montpellier, France.

— (2006c). Land rights and the politics of belonging in Africa: An introduction. *Land and the Politics of Belonging in West Africa*. R. Kuba and C. Lentz. Leiden, Boston, Brill: 1-34.

Léonard, É. and J.G. Ibo (1994). Appropriation et gestion de la rente forestière en Côte-d'Ivoire. *Politique africaine* (53): 25-36.

Leonard, E. and M. Oswald (1995). Cocoa smallholders facing a double structural adjustment in Côte d'Ivoire: Responses to a predicted crisis. *Cocoa Cycles: The Economics of Cocoa Supply*. F. Ruf and P.S. Siswoputranto. Cambridge, Woodhead.

Lipton, M. (1993). Land Reform as Commenced Business: The evidence against stopping. *World Development* 21(4): 641-657.

Losch, B. (2000). La Côte d'Ivoire en quête d'un nouveau projet national. *Politique Africaine* 78(5): 5-25.

Lund, C. (2000). *African Land Tenure: Questioning Basic Assumptions*. London, IIED.

— (2002). Negotiating property institutions: On the symbiosis of property and authority in Africa. *Negotiating Property in Africa*. K. Juul and C. Lund. Portsmouth, Heinemann: 11-44.

— (2006). Who owns Bolgatanga? A story of inconclusive encounters. *Land and the Politics of Belonging in West Africa*. R. Kuba and C. Lentz. Leiden, Boston, Brill: 77-98.

— (2008). *Local Politics and the Dynamics of Property in Africa*. Cambridge, Cambridge University Press.

Macmillan, W.M. (1946). African Development. *Europe and West Africa*. C.K. Meek, W.M. Macmillan and E.R.J. Hussey. London, Macmillan. Part 2: 41-115.

Maxwell, D., W.O. Larbi, et al. (1998). *Farming in the Shadow of the City: Changes in Land Rights and Livelihoods in Peri-Urban Accra*. Ottawa, The International Development Research Centre: 34.

McCaskie, T.C. (1992). Review article. Empire state: Asante and the historians. *Journal of African History* 33: 467-476.

— (1995). *State and Society in Pre-colonial Asante*. Cambridge, Cambridge University Press.

— (2000a). *Asante Identities: History and Modernity in an African Village 1850-1950*. Edinburgh, Edinburgh University Press.

— (2000b). The consuming passions of Kwame Boakye: An essay on agency and identity in Asante history. *Journal of African Cultural Studies* 13(1): 43-62.

Memel-Foté, H. (1997). De la stabilité au changement. Les représentations de la crise politique et la réalité des changements. *Le modèle ivoirien en questions: crises, ajustements, recompositions*. B. Contamin and H. Memel-Foté. Paris, Karthala: Orstom.

— (1999). Une mythe politique des Akans en Côte d'Ivoire: Le sens de l'état. *Mondes akan: Identité et pouvoir en Afrique occidentale (Akan worlds: Identity and power in West Africa)*. P. Valsecchi and F. Viti. Paris, L'Harmattan.

Mensah-Brown, K. (1968). Marriage in Sefwi-Akan customary law: A comparative study in ethno-jurisprudence. *Présence africaine: revue culturelle du monde noir* (68): 61-87.

Mensah, B.K.F. (1996). *Changes, Ambiguities and Conflicts: Negotiating Land Rights in Buem-Kator, Ghana*. Johns Hopkins University.

Mensah Sarbah, J. (1897). *Fanti Customary Laws: A Brief Introduction to the Principles of the Native Laws and Customs of the Fanti and Akan Sections of the Gold Coast with a Selection of Cases thereon Decided in the Law Courts*. London, Clowes.

Mikell, G. (1984). Filiation, economic crisis and the status of women in rural Ghana. *Canadian Journal of African Studies* 18(1): 195-218.

— (1985). Expansion and contraction in economic access for rural women in Ghana. *Rural Africana: Current Research in the Social Sciences* (21): 13-30.

— (1989). *Cocoa and Chaos in Ghana*. Washington, D.C., Howard University Press.

Ministry of Lands and Forestry (1999). National Land Policy. Accra, Ministry of Lands and Forestry.

Nader, L. (2001). Thinking about Law and Development – The Underside of Conflict Management – In Africa and Elsewhere. *IDS bulletin* 32(1): 19-27.

NCCE (1998). Unit Committees, National Commission for Civic Education, Accra.

Ninsin, K.A. (1989). The land question since the 1950s. *The State Development and Politics in Ghana*. E. Hansen and K.A. Ninsin. London, Codesria: 165-183.

Niskanen, W.A. (1975). Bureaucrats and politicians. *Journal of Law and Economics* XVIII(3): 617-43.

— (1994). *Bureaucracy and Public Economics*. Aldershot, Edward Elgar.

NRI and UST (1997). Kumasi Natural Resource Management Research Project, Inception Report. Chatham, NRI (Natural Resources Institute), UST (University of Science and Technology), .

Nugent, P. (2002). *Smugglers, Secessionists & Loyal Citizens on the Ghana-Togo Frontier: The Lie of the Borderlands Since 1914*. Athens, Ohio: Oxford, University Press, James Currey.

Nyanteng, V. and A.W. Seini (2000). Agricultural policy and the impact on growth and productivity 1970-95. *Economic Reforms in Ghana: The Miracle and The Mirage*. E. Aryeetey, J. Harrigan and M. Nissanke. Oxford, James Currey and Woeli Publishers: 267-283.

Obeng, E.E. (1988). *Ancient Ashanti Chieftaincy*. Tema, Ghana Publishing Corporation.

Oduro, A. (2000). Performance of the external trade sector since 1970. *Economic Reforms in Ghana: The Miracle and the Mirage*. E. Aryeetey. Oxford, James Currey; Woeli Publishing Services; Africa World Press.

Okali, C. (1983). *Cocoa and Kinship in Ghana: The Matrilineal Akan of Ghana*. London; Boston, Kegan Paul International.

Ollennu, N.A. (1962). *Principles of Customary Land Law in Ghana*. London, Sweet & Maxwell.

Ollennu, N.A. (1967). Aspects of land tenure. *A Study of Contemporary Ghana. Volume two: Some Aspects of Social Structure*. Birmingham, Neustadt and Omaboe. London, George Allen & Unwin Ltd.: 251-266.

Oomen, B. (2002). Chiefs! Law, Power and Culture in Contemporary South Africa, Leiden University.

Opoku, A.A. (1963). Across the Prah. *Migrant Cocoa-Farmers of Southern Ghana: A Study in Rural Capitalism*. P. Hill. Cambridge, Cambridge University Press: 30-37.

Otumfuo Osei Tutu II, A. (2004). Traditional systems of governance and the modern state, Keynote address. *Fourth African Development Forum*. Addis Ababa.

Palumbo, B. (1991). *Le noci della discordia. Terra, eredità e parentela in una comunità Nzema (Ghana)*. Roma, Università degli studi 'La Sapienza.

Peters, P.E. (2002). The limits of negotiability: Security, equity and class formation in Africa's legal systems. *Negotiating Property in Africa*. K. Juul and C. Lund. Portsmouth, Heinemann: 45-66.

— (2004). Inequality and social conflict over land in Africa. *Journal of Agrarian Change* 4 (3): 269-314.

Phillips, A. (1989). *The Enigma of Colonialism: British Policy in West Africa.* Oxford and Bloomington, Indiana University Press.

Platteau, J.P. (1996). The evolutionary theory of land rights as applied to Sub-Saharan Africa: A critical assessment. *Development and Change* 27: 29-86.

Pogucki, R.J.H. (1955). *Report on Land Tenure in Native Customary Law of the Protectorate of the Northern Territories of the Gold Coast.* Accra, Ghana, Lands Department.

Pogucki, R.J.H. (1962). The main principles of rural land tenure. *Agriculture and Land Use in Ghana.* B. Wills. London, Accra, New York, Oxford University Press: 179-191.

PRI (2001). *Access to Justice in Sub-Saharan Africa: The Role of Traditional and Informal Justice Systems.* London, Penal Reform International.

Quan, J. and C. Toulmin (2005). Formalising and securing land rights in Africa: overview. *Land in Africa: Market Asset or Secure Livelihood? Proceedings and Summary of Conclusions from the Land in Africa Conference held in London November 8-9, 2004.* J. Quan, C. Toulmin and S.F. Tan. London, IIED/NRI/RAS: 75-88.

Rabbe, J. (2004). Aspekte des Viehhandels im Norden Ghanas unter Berücksichtigung der Beziehungen zwischen Frafra-Kleinhändlern und Fulbe-Viehzüchtern. *Ethnizität und Markt: Zur ethnischen Struktur von Viehmärkten in Westafrika.* G. Schlee. Cologne, Rüdiger Köppe Verlag. 4: 95-129.

Ranger, T. (1983). The invention of tradition in colonial Africa. *The Invention of Tradition.* E. Hobsbaum and T. Ranger. Cambridge, Cambridge University Press: 211-262.

Rathbone, R. (1993). *Murder and Politics in Colonial Ghana.* New Haven: Yale University Press.

— (1996). Defining Akyemfo: The construction of citizenship in Akyem Abuakwa, Ghana, 1700-1939. *Africa* 66(4): 506-525.

— (2000). *Nkrumah & the Chiefs. The Politics of Chieftaincy in Ghana 1951-60.* Oxford, James Currey.

Rattray, R.S. (1969, first published 1929). *Ashanti Law and Constitution.* Oxford, Clarendon Press.

Ray, D.I. (2003). Rural local governance and traditional leadership in Africa and the Afro-Caribbean: Policy and research implications from Africa to the Americas and Australasia. *Grassroots Governance? Chiefs in Africa and the Afro-Caribbean.* D.I. Ray and P.S. Reddy. Calgary, University of Calgary Press: 1-30.

Ray, D.I. and E.A.B. van Rouveroy van Nieuwaal (1996). The new relevance of traditional authorities in Africa. The conference; major themes; reflections on chieftaincy in Africa; future directions. *Journal of Legal Pluralism* 37/38: 1-37.

Roberts, P.A. (1987). The state and the regulation of marriage: Sefwi Wiawso (Ghana), 1900-1940. *Women, State and Ideology.* H. Afshar. London, MacMillan Press: 48-69.

Ruf, F. (1991). Les crises cacaoyères: la malédiction des âges d'or? *Cahiers d'études africaines* 31(121/122): 83-134.

— (1995). From 'forest rent' to 'tree capital': Basic 'laws' of cocoa supply. *Cocoa Cycles: The Economics of Cocoa Supply.* F. Ruf and P.S. Siswoputranto. Cambridge, Woodhead.

Ryan, E. (2000). ADR, the judiciary and justice: Coming to terms with the alternatives. *Harvard Law Review* 113(7): 1851-1875.

Sarbah, J.M. (1968). *Fanti Customary Laws. A brief Introduction to the Principles of the Native Laws and Customs of the Fanti and Akan Districts of the Gold Coast with a Report of some Cases thereon Decided in the Law Courts.* London, Frank Cass.

Schott, R. (1980). Justice versus the law: Traditional and modern jurisdiction among the Bulsa of Northern Ghana. *Law and State: A Biannual Collection of Recent German Contributions to these Fields* 21: 123-133.

Scott, J.C. (1985). *Weapons of the Weak: Everyday Forms of Peasant Resistance*. New Haven, London, Yale University Press.

Shepherd, A.W. (1981). Agrarian change in Northern Ghana: Public investment, capitalist farming and famine. *Rural Development in Tropical Africa*. J. Heyer, P. Roberts and G. Williams. London, MacMillan: 168-192.

Shipton, P. (2002). Foreword. *Negotiating Property in Africa*. K. Juul and C. Lund. Portsmouth, Heinemann: ix-xiii.

Silbey, S.S. and A. Sarat (1989). Dispute processing in law and legal scholarship: From institutional critique to the reconstitution of the juridical subject. *University of Denver Law Review* 66(3): 437-498.

Simensen, J. (1975a). *Commoners, Chiefs and Colonial Government: British Policy and Local Politics in Akim Abuakwa, Ghana, under Colonial Rule*. Trondheim, University of Trondheim, Department of history.

— (1975b). Nationalism from below: The Akyem Abuakwa example. *Akyem Abuakwa and the Politics of the Inter-War Period in Ghana*. R. Addo-Fening. Basel, Basler Afrika-Bibliographien. 12: 31-60.

Sogodogo, A. (1997). Dévaluation, croissance et équilibres macroéconomiques: Le cas de Côte d'Ivoire. *Le modèle ivoirien en question*. B. Contamin and H. Memel-Foté. Paris, Karthala & ORSTOM.

Stryker, R. (1970). *Center and Locality: Linkage and Political Change in Côte d'Ivoire*. Washington, D.C., Smithsonian.

Tabatabai, H. (1988). Agricultural decline and access to food in Ghana. *International labour review* 127(6): 703-734.

Takane, T. (2002). *The Cocoa Farmers of Southern Ghana: Incentives, Institutions, and Change in Rural West Africa*. Chiba, Institute of Developing Economies; Japan External Trade Organization.

Tashjian, V.B. (1995). *It's Mine and It's Ours Are Not the Same Thing: A History of Marriage in Rural Asante, 1900-1957*: PhD Thesis, Northwestern University, Evanston, Illinois, Northwestern University.

— (1996). 'It's mine' and 'It's ours' are not the same thing: Changing Economic Relations between Spouses in Asante. *The Cloth of Many Colored Silks*. J. Hunwick and N. Lawler Evanston, Northwestern University Press: 205-222.

Tonah, S. (1993). *The development of agropastoral households in Northern Ghana: policy analysis, project appraisal and future perspectives*. Saarbrücken [etc.], Breitenbach.

— (1994). Agricultural extension services and smallholder farmers' indebtedness in northeastern Ghana. *Journal of Asian and African studies* 29(1-2): 119/128.

— (2002). Fulani pastoralists, indigenous farmers and the contest for land in Northern Ghana. *Afrika Spectrum* 37(1): 43-60.

— (2006). Migration and farmer-herder conflicts in Ghana's Volta basin. *Canadian Journal of African Studies* 40(1): 152-178.

Toulmin, C., P. Lavigne Delville, et al., Eds. (2002). *The Dynamics of Resource Tenure in West Africa*. London, IIED.

Toulmin, C. and J. Quan, eds. (2000a). *Evolving Land Rights, Policy and Tenure in Africa*. London, DFID/IIED/NRI.

Toulmin, C. and J. Quan (2000b). Evolving land rights, tenure and policy in sub-Saharan Africa. *Evolving Land Rights, Policy and Tenure in Africa*. C. Toulmin and J. Quan. London, DFID/IIED/NRI: 1-30.

Tsikata, D. (1996). Gender, kinship and the control of resources in colonial Southern Ghana. *Contextualising Gender and Kinship in South Asia and Sub-Saharan Africa*. R. Palriwale and C. Risseeuw London, Sage: 110-132.

— (2003). Securing women's interests within land tenure reforms: Recent debates in Tanzania. *Journal of Agrarian Change* 3(1-2): 149-183.

Tullock, G. (1976). *The Vote Motive. An Essay in the Economics of Politics, with Applications to the British Economy*. London, Institute of Economic Affairs.

Ubink, J.M. (2006). Land, chiefs and custom in peri-urban Ghana. *International Conference on Land, Poverty, Social Practice and Development*. The Hague, ISS and ICCO.

— (2002-2004). Courts and peri-urban practice: Customary land law in Ghana. *University of Ghana Law Journal* XXII: 25-77.

— (2007). Customary tenure security: Wishful policy thinking or reality? A case from peri-urban Ghana. *Journal of African Law* 51(2): 215-248.

— (2008a). *In the Land of the Chiefs: Customary Law, Land Conflicts, and the Role of the State in Peri-urban Ghana*. Leiden, Leiden University Press.

— (2008b). Negotiated or negated? The rhetoric and reality of customary tenure in an Ashanti village in Ghana. *Africa* 78(2): 264-287.

— (2008, in press). Land, chiefs and custom in peri-urban Ghana: Traditional governance in an environment of legal and institutional pluralism. *The Governance of Legal Pluralism*. W. Zips and M. Weilenmann. Münster, Lit Verlag.

Ubink, J.M. and J.F. Quan (2008). How to combine tradition and modernity? Regulating customary land management in Ghana. *Land Use Policy* 25: 198-213.

USAID (2003). Country Strategic Plan 2004-2010. Empowering Ghanaians through Partnership to Build a Prosperous Nation. Accra, USAID/Ghana.

Van Donge, J.K. (1999). Law and order as a development issue: Land conflicts and the creation of social order in southern Malawi. *Journal of Development Studies* 36(2): 48-70.

Van Hear, N. (1998). *New Diasporas: The Mass Exodus, Dispersal and Regrouping of Migrant Communities*. Seattle, WA, University of Washington Press.

Van Leeuwen, F.K.C. and E.M. van Steekelenburg (1995). *The Process of Land Acquisition: A Case Study of Kumasi*. Amsterdam, Institute of Planning and Demography.

Van Rouveroy van Nieuwaal, E.A.B. (1987). Chiefs and African states: Some introductory notes and an extensive bibliography on African chieftaincy. *Journal of Legal Pluralism* 25/26: 1-46.

Vellenga, D.D. (1977). Differentiation among women farmers in two rural areas in Ghana. *Labour and Society* 2(2): 197-208.

— (1986). Matriliny, patriliny, and class formation among women cocoa farmers in two rural areas of Ghana. *Women and class in Africa*. C. Robertson and I. Berger. New York, Africana: 62-77.

Whitehead, A. and D. Tsikata (2003). Policy discourses on women's land rights in sub-Saharan Africa: The implications of the re-turn to the customary. *Journal of Agrarian Change* 3 (1 and 2): 67-112.

Wilks, I. (1966). Aspects of bureaucratization in Ashanti in the nineteenth century. *Journal of African History* VII(2): 215-232.

— (1975). *Asante in the Nineteenth Century - The Structure and Evolution of a Political Order*. Cambridge, Cambridge University Press.

— (1993). *Forests of Gold: Essays on the Akan and the Kingdom of Asante*. Athens, Ohio University Press.

— (1958). *Akwamu 1640-1750: Study of the Rise and Fall of a West African Empire*. Bangor, University of Wales. MA thesis.

Wood, J.G. (2002). The courts and land dispute resolution in Ghana. *Land Disputes Settlement in Ghana Seminar*. Labadi Beach Hotel, Accra, GTZ Ghana, Legal Pluralism and Gender Project.

Woodhouse, P. (2003). African enclosures: A default mode of development. *World Development* 31(10): 1705-1720.

Woodman, G.R. (1987). Land title registration without prejudice: The Ghana Land Title Registration Law, 1986. *Journal of African law* 31(1/2): 119-135.

Woodman, G.R. (1988). How state courts create customary law in Ghana and Nigeria. *Indigenous Law and the State*. B. W. Morse and G. R. Woodman. Dordrecht, Foris Publications: 181-220.

Woodman, G.R. (1996). *Customary Land Law in the Ghanaian Courts*. Accra, Ghana Universities Press.

World Bank (2003a). *Ghana Land Administration Project*. Washington D.C., World Bank.

— (2003b). *Land Policies for Growth and Poverty Reduction*. Washington D.C., World Bank.

World Bank (1986). *Financing Adjustment with Growth in Sub-Saharan Africa, 1986-90*. Washington, D.C. World Bank.

Yeboah, M.O. (2005). The chiefs' customary courts in Ghana: How popular? How just? *International Workshop on Adjudication of Land Disputes, Legal Pluralism and the Protection of Land Rights in Ghana and Côte d'Ivoire*. University of London, Institute of Commonwealth Studies.

Archives

Personal Archives

Pepe Roberts Papers

National Archives of Ghana

NAG- Accra: National Archives of Ghana, Accra.

NAG- Kumasi: National Archives of Ghana, Kumasi.

NAG- Sekondi: National Archives of Ghana, Sekondi.

Archives of Sefwi Wiawso

SWDSW: Sefwi Wiawso Department of Social Welfare, P.O. Box 25, District Administration, Sefwi Wiawso

SWTCA: Sefwi Wiawso Traditional Council Archives, P.O. Box 42, Sefwi Wiawso

SWLCS: Sefwi Wiawso Land Commission Secretariat

List of contributors

Kojo Amanor, Institute of African Studies, University of Ghana

Adarkwah Antwi, currently State Land Advisor, Sudan Customary Land Tenure Project; formerly National Facilitator, Land Administration Project Ghana

Sara Berry, Department of History, Johns Hopkins University

Stefano Boni, Department of Language and Culture Sciences, Università di Modena e Reggio Emilia

Richard Crook, Institute of Commonwealth Studies, University of London

Julian Quan, Natural Resource Institute, University of Greenwich

Steve Tonah, Department of Sociology, University of Ghana

Janine Ubink, Van Vollenhoven Institute for Law, Governance and Development, Leiden University

Index

DATE DUE

African policy displays a growing interest in promoting customary land tenure, based on the idea that the customary represents egalitarian communal arrangements. This approach ignores that customary land relations have been contested throughout history, by various groups that each try to redefine what constitutes custom in a situation of change. In Ghana, land has become increasingly commoditised as a result of the growing value of real estate and the development of new commercial agricultural sectors. This has led to an intensification of attempts by chiefs, earth priests, land users, and governmental actors to redefine land ownership and tenure.

The various contributions to this book critically examine notions about customary land tenure in Ghana. They analyse the relations between the customary and statutory tenure and the institutional interactions between the state and traditional authorities in land administration, addressing issues of power, economic interests, transparency, accountability, conflicts and notions of social justice, equity and negotiation. They examine both past and contemporary policy issues, and present a number of case studies with implications for the integration of customary institutions into the framework of state land administration.

Janine M. Ubink is senior lecturer in law and governance in Africa at the Van Vollenhoven Institute for Law, Governance and Development at Leiden University. *Kojo S. Amanor* is associate professor at the Institute of African Studies at the University of Ghana

ISBN 978 90 8728 047 5

WWW.LUP.NL

Leiden University Press